A Holiness Hermeneutic

A Holiness Hermeneutic

Biblical Interpretation in the American Holiness Movement (1875–1920)

Stephen J. Lennox

Foreword by William J. Abraham

☙PICKWICK *Publications* · Eugene, Oregon

A HOLINESS HERMENEUTIC
Biblical Interpretation in the American Holiness Movement (1875–1920)

Copyright © 2018 Stephen J. Lennox. All rights reserved. Except for brief quotations in critical publications or reviews, no part of this book may be reproduced in any manner without prior written permission from the publisher. Write: Permissions, Wipf and Stock Publishers, 199 W. 8th Ave., Suite 3, Eugene, OR 97401.

Pickwick Publications
An Imprint of Wipf and Stock Publishers
199 W. 8th Ave., Suite 3
Eugene, OR 97401

www.wipfandstock.com

PAPERBACK ISBN: 978-1-5326-3442-0
HARDCOVER ISBN: 978-1-5326-3444-4
EBOOK ISBN: 978-1-5326-3443-7

Cataloguing-in-Publication data:

Names: Lennox, Stephen J., author | Abraham, William J., foreword.

Title: A holiness hermeneutic : biblical interpretation in the American holiness movement (1875–1920) / Stephen J. Lennox ; Foreword by William J. Abraham.

Description: Eugene, OR: Pickwick Publications, 2018 | Includes bibliographical references and index.

Identifiers: ISBN 978-1-5326-3442-0 (paperback). | ISBN 978-1-5326-3444-4 (hardcover). | ISBN 978-1-5326-3443-7 (ebook).

Subjects: LCSH: Bible—Hermeneutics—History—19th century. | Bible—Hermeneutics—History—20th century. | Holiness churches—Hermeneutics.

Classification: BX8495 W5 L46 2018 (print) | BX8495 (ebook).

Manufactured in the U.S.A.   04/06/18

Scripture quotations come from the King James Version, which is in the public domain.

To my wife, Eileen, my greatest encourager
through every phase of this project.

To my late grandmother, Edna Culp Lennox (1892–1993),
who led our family into the holiness movement
and whose life and labors have been a
great source of encouragement to me.

Contents

Foreword by William J. Abraham | ix
Preface | xiii
Acknowledgments | xv

1. Introduction | 1
2. The Populist Hermeneutic in American Biblical Studies | 15
3. The History of the American Holiness Movement | 43
4. The Wesleyan Quadrilateral and Holiness Biblical Interpretation | 61
5. The Populist Hermeneutic in the American Holiness Movement | 82
6. Four Pillars of Holiness Interpretation | 100
7. Summary Observations on Holiness Interpretation | 133
8. Reflections on the Intersection of Critical Biblical Studies with the American Holiness Movement | 139

Bibliography | 161
Index | 175

Foreword

My heart was strangely warmed when I first came across this splendid study of the Holiness Movement as it related to the interpretation of the Bible. My relationship to the Holiness Movement has always been somewhat distant and indirect. In Irish Methodism, it showed up fitfully on the margins of my life, even though the tradition in its own way was steeped in the ethos of holiness. I remember vividly going with a youth group to the Holiness camp-meeting in Killadeas outside Enniskillen, my home town, where holiness and sanctification were the primary focus. The girls in our group were wearing trousers. We were met by a stern but smiling elder statesman who instructed us to look up the verse in Leviticus that stated that 'a man shall not put on that which pertaineth unto a woman and a woman shall not put on that which pertaineth onto a man'. I still retain the King James rendering of the text in my head. It struck me that the good man had no clue what would be involved in girls wearing skirts or dresses riding bicycles on a windy day, and how much this might have been a distraction from holiness for the boys involved. Yet, I admired the deep piety I met in the good folk who were running the Holiness meetings that summer. Later I met a version of the Holiness Movement at Asbury Theological Seminary and came to know its scholars. Once again, I was deeply impressed by the deep piety involved. The scholarship it has produced has never gotten the attention it deserves; the caricatures more broadly of pietism are a scandal of the modern academy. The Holiness Movement is one of the lesser tribes of Israel that is kept out of sight as much as possible. As antidote to this prejudice, this study represents a splendid contribution that deserves the widest possible readership.

To be sure, this may sound like exaggeration. So, let me explain why this work is so important. First, the nineteenth century is a critical period in the history of Western Christianity. The crises were numerous:

philosophical, theological, economic, and cultural. It was a very tough time to be serious about the faith. In reaction we saw the emergence of the Anglo-Catholic tradition, the flowering of Liberal Protestantism, the turn to Revivalism, the invention of the Social Gospel, and so on. It was no easy task to deal with the new developments in science represented by cosmology and evolution. Within this, old doctrines of scripture came under strain because of the growth of historical investigation. Hence, a serious study of the Holiness Movement's handling of the interpretation of scripture is a godsend. We have here a tradition of interpretation outside the mainstream that can at the very least stimulate fresh approaches to a perennial challenge to all Christians.

Second, one of the tragic features of the last generation's work in the history of Methodism has been the demonizing of nineteenth century developments as a lapse into an arid scholasticism. We have now learned to read scholastic texts with a sympathetic and appreciative ear. Yet, the holiness movement, like monastic movements in the thirteenth and fourteenth century, were well aware of the dangers of high-octane forms of inquiry that left out or sidelined the religion of the heart. Thus, a study of the Holiness tradition, such as is provided here, is an invaluable resource both for a fuller picture of the period and for potential corrective for those of us who have discovered the great period of "dogmatic" theology in the history of Methodism.

Third, sorting through the highways and byways of heart religion is a tough assignment. Border Parker Bowne, for example, was steeped in Methodist piety but found the tradition of analysis bequeathed to him did not map the experience of many Methodist preachers whom he taught at Boston University. The Holiness tradition was clearly working in the same arena, sorting through what to do, for example, with baptism of the Spirit. However, this discussion was not done apart from scripture but in conversation with scripture. If we are to understand the grammar of the proposals in this domain, we need to see how scripture was read and interpreted. This study provides exactly what we need to provide critical background music to work on the nature of Christian experience as worked out in the Holiness Movement.

The Bible is an inescapable element in the Christian tradition. It will be read and pondered when we are long gone. So here is a final reason for my enthusiasm for this volume. It is obvious that one crucial goal of scripture is the cultivation of salvation. We read, learn, mark, and inwardly digest the Bible's diverse and often perplexing materials in order to come closer to God. Yet our ontologies of scripture and theories of inspiration do not necessarily reflect this goal. Eavesdropping on the Holiness Movement, as it wrestles with these issues, is surely a mandate for those of us who still take Methodism and its offspring seriously. Perhaps we will be able as a result to either retrieve or invent a vision of Holy Scripture that will be a blessing to our souls and to the whole Church of Jesus Christ.

Stephen Lennox has not sugar-coated his findings. This is a work of mature, even meticulous scholarship. He writes with affection, realizing that every tradition at some point has to bind up the wounds of the Fathers and Mothers who have gone before us. Now a new generation can take up the mantle and carry it into the future. They should not try to do so until they have absorbed the material laid out here with poise and flair.

—William J. Abraham

Preface

"Nothing is too small to know and nothing too big to attempt."
—William C. Van Horne

If Van Horne is right, even the study of a small, socially isolated movement within late nineteenth century American Protestantism is worth undertaking. That was my conviction when I began this investigation of the American holiness movement and remains my assured conviction today.

Much can be learned from studying this movement, not only about the movement itself, but about the culture and, particularly the Christian culture, in which it found itself. To study this small part of this period allows us to better understand the period.

This study sheds light on Pentecostalism, the global phenomenon which traces its roots to the holiness movement. It reveals more about the Fundamentalist/Modernist controversy that gripped the early twentieth century. We also gain a better understanding of Scripture's role in the decline of the church from its role at the pinnacle of culture in the early to mid-nineteenth century to its place today on society's margins.

This look at the American holiness movement also illustrates the inseparability between one's understanding of the Bible and one's social location. It reinforces the important assumption that no person or movement ever reads the Bible in a vacuum.

Whether or not this study constitutes Van Horne's big attempt, this close look at a small movement reveals more than one might expect.

Acknowledgments

THERE ARE SEVERAL PERSONS without whose assistance this project could never have been completed and to whom I owe great appreciation. The topic for this study was first suggested to me by Dr. Clarence Bence, then Academic Dean of Houghton College and after a long-time colleague at Indiana Wesleyan University. I am also grateful to Drs. Kenneth Rowe, Herbert B. Huffmon, and late Robert T. Handy for their scholarly guidance in the early stages of this project. Drs. Ray Seilhamer and Kirby Keller provided wonderful assistance at a crucial juncture in this study.

I am very appreciative to my former colleagues at Indiana Wesleyan University, especially Drs. Keith Drury, Ken Schenck, Chris Bounds, and David Riggs, for helping me sharpen these ideas. My current colleagues at Kingswood University have provided a wonderful environment which has allowed me to bring this project to a happy conclusion.

All of this would have been only an unfulfilled dream had it not been for the support and love of my wife, Eileen. I cannot thank her enough.

My deepest gratitude goes to God who has blessed me with many things, not least my heritage in the American holiness movement.

1

Introduction

America in Crisis

THE 1870S FOUND AMERICAN Christianity in crisis.[1] No marauding Huns were disembarking in New York City to conquer Christianity by force (although some thought the analogy to be close to reality).[2] The threat was not to life and limb but to the heart and soul of the church. This crisis was crucial, not only for the church, but represented one of the most critical periods in American history. The society that entered the final quarter of the nineteenth century was scarcely the same when it emerged less than fifty years later. It had matured, but not gracefully, having been dragged along from an old, traditional America to a new, modern one. Of all the institutions of society, the church was to feel the effects of this transition most keenly.

Clearly the Civil War represented a watershed episode in this transition.[3] Winthrop S. Hudson described it as a war that impacted every family, the nation, and the churches.[4] In addition to the staggering costs in human life and financial resources, there was the dilemma of making sense of such a war. How could it occur in America of all places? After all, this was the

---

1. Marsden, *Fundamentalism*, 11. Although Marsden's specific focus is on Evangelical America, this work and others make clear that the crisis affected all American Christians, as well as other religious groups.
2. See Strong, *Our Country*, 30–46.
3. Hudson, *Religion in America*, 197. See also Handy, *History of the Churches*, 262.
4. Hudson, *Religion in America*, 194.

country chosen by God to demonstrate to the world the power of freedom. Now the same God who had called America to her sacred vocation was being called upon to bring victory to one half of that nation and defeat to the other. Such questions proved most vexing to the church.

Following the devastation of the war came the need to rebuild American society, a Reconstruction that was tragically slow both in society and in the church. The three major denominations that had split over the issue of slavery, the Methodists, Baptists, and Presbyterians, found reunion difficult, and in some cases, undesirable.

While the church was experiencing these tensions and demands, the need for ministry in the West became acute, prompted by the influx of population spurred by new discoveries and national policy. Home mission boards established to meet the needs experienced some success. Bringing organized religion to new settlements in the West was not unlike what the church had been doing since the settling of this country. However, a far greater challenge faced the church in the late nineteenth century, one for which they were essentially unprepared: that of ministry in America's swollen cities.

The urbanization of America had begun prior to the Civil War as people moved from the older rural settlements to the cities. The war and other factors accelerated this process so that from 1860 to 1890, some cities grew by four, six, ten, twenty, even fifty times their size.[5]

America was being revolutionized again, this time, especially, by industrialization. Rapidly advancing technology met workers eager to make their fortune, and met them in the cities. The pace of life increased, as did American productivity, so that the United States became the leading manufacturing nation in the world by 1894.[6]

Many of those coming in search of a better future were coming from other countries. Immigrants arrived in greater and greater numbers, especially beginning in 1840, so that by 1900, one third of America's seventy-five million people were either foreign-born or children of those who were.[7] American homogeneity was turning into a melting pot of color and creed.

Industrialization and the rapid growth of the cities created several problems for American society, and the church in particular. Naturally there were the problems associated with overcrowding and poverty. America had

---

5. Hudson, *Religion in America*, 273.

6. Ibid., 272.

7. Ibid., 197.

INTRODUCTION

also to face the difficult realization that the balance of power, so long settled in the rural areas and small towns, was now shifting to the cities.[8]

With the rapid urbanization it became clear that the Protestant church, whose center of strength lay in the rural areas and small towns,[9] was also losing its influence. W. B. Godbey, a holiness evangelist, portrayed the troubled city in the mid-1890s. "The attractions of Satan are so innumerable and powerful through all sorts of human inventions, that scarcely a tithe of city people ever so much as attend Church. They have enough to do to attend theaters, parties, fandangoes, and other entertainments, which Satan has provided for their damnation."[10]

Somehow, the church would have to adapt to meet the needs of the cities, but adapting was difficult, especially for the church. Buildings could not be erected fast enough in some city neighborhoods, while in others, sanctuaries stood abandoned among factories and slums.[11] Godbey observed, "So fast as our cities grow, the populous interior is actually abandoned by the Churches, and given up to infidelity, heathenism, and the devil. All of our large cities are now missionary ground, like the heathen nations."[12]

Strategies also needed adapting, since the way of reaching the country dweller with the gospel would not work in the city. Noble attempts were made, such as the Salvation Army and the YMCA, and some success reported. Sunday School became an important tool designed to educate the problems out of city-dwellers. Another important effort to reach the city with the gospel was the organized revival campaign, with Dwight L. Moody as the premiere example.[13] However, in spite of all its efforts the church was losing the working-class.

In addition to the trauma and aftermath of the Civil War and the urbanization of America with its accompanying problems, the church of

---

8. Ibid., 198 points to the efforts of rural movements like the Grangers, Greenbackers, and Populists as evidence of the tension and efforts to reverse this trend.

9. Schlesinger, "Critical Period," 303.

10. Godbey, *Commentary*, 1:311.

11. Schlesinger notes that, from 1868 to 1888, while seventeen Protestant churches left the district below Fourteenth Street in New York City, 200,000 people arrived. From 1878 to 1888, 22,000 in Boston's thirteenth ward had no Protestant church, while in the heart of Chicago, 60,000 people had no church, either Protestant or Catholic ("Critical Period," 306–7).

12. Godbey, *Commentary*, 1:311.

13. Hudson, *Religion in America*, 220–21, citing McLoughlin, *Modern Revivalism*, 202–6, 262–67. See also Schlesinger, "Critical Period, 307.

this day was also experiencing the effects of an intellectual revolution. The confrontation occurred on several fronts: Darwinism, comparative religion, biblical criticism, to name three of the most significant. However, the underlying cause for this intellectual revolt was the movement of America from a traditional society to a modern society. This process had been underway for some time but the late nineteenth and early twentieth centuries appear to have occasioned a rapid movement forward in this transition to modernity.

Modernization, according to Peter Berger, has been brought about by recent technological innovations with profound economic, social and political consequences. Also significant was the revolution affecting how people thought, believed and felt.[14] Berger identifies several qualities of a modern society, all of which were increasingly evident in the period under consideration. Abstraction occurs when the institutions of society become more distant and removed, resulting in the development of urbanization, bureaucratization, and technologizing, all of which leave the individual feeling isolated.[15]

Futurity, where tomorrow rather than yesterday becomes people's primary focus, is part of the modernization process.[16] The concern for time as something to be mastered was evident in many ways in late-nineteenth-century America including its hectic pace of life. One observer of that scene wrote, "St. Martha is the patron saint of the women, and St. Vitus of the men. Nervous prostration is our characteristic disease. Leisure is a word for whose meaning we consult the dictionary. In the clatter of the train, in the click of the keys at the telegraph office, the spirit of the age finds speech."[17]

Modernization, says Berger, is further characterized by individuation, the separation of the individual from his or her community and the portrayal of that individual as complicated and distinct. It is perhaps this process coupled with the rugged individualism characteristic of American society that prompted holiness evangelist George Watson to write, "God works through persons, through individual souls, instead of committees, and federated bands, or great organizations. The strongest force on earth is

---

14. Berger, "Toward a Critique," 335.

15. Ibid., 337.

16. Ibid., 339.

17. Hodges, *Faith and Social Service*, 61. The importance of "progress" and "tomorrow" in this period is also pointed out by Carter, *Spiritual Crisis*, 157.

Introduction

the individual soul."[18] One result of this process of individuation has been to set the individual in opposition to society.[19]

The modern society is also one where what was once perceived as dominated by fate has now become a matter of choice. Such a liberated society now thirsts for the new and novel. Tradition has lost its authority; anything is possible.[20]

Finally, says Berger, the modern society has become secular, one where the religious explanation for things holds far fewer adherents and far less plausibility.[21] The tendency to remove God from Creator to First Cause can be seen as evidence for this secularizing tendency.

Within this rapidly secularizing society, Charles Darwin's *Origin of the Species* (1859) detonated an explosion of earthshaking proportion. What he intimated in 1859 he made explicit in 1871 with the publication of *Descent of Man*. Here Darwin traced the origin not of life in general but of humankind in particular.[22] His views stirred great opposition but gained such surprisingly quick acceptance in America that Richard Hofstadter can call this *the* Darwinian country from 1870 to the early twentieth century.[23]

The church's reaction to Darwinism took a variety of forms. Some, such as Charles Hodge of Princeton Seminary, categorically condemned these views as atheistic and contradictory to the Christian faith. These views, he contended, denied the argument for God's existence that had been based on the design of the universe, denied the traditional doctrines of sin and redemption, called into question the Genesis account of Creation, and with it, the Bible's credibility.[24] Another of the church's responses, one that might be called cautious acceptance, was illustrated by Princeton University President James McCosh who considered that Darwin's views may represent a portion of the truth.

---

18. Watson, *Our Own God*, 236.
19. Berger, "Toward a Critique," 342.
20. Ibid., 345.
21. Ibid., 347.
22. Brauer, *Protestantism in America*, 219–20.
23. Hofstadter, *Social Darwinism*, 5. Not all supporters of evolution were Darwinian. Some held views more like those of Herbert Spencer, whose interpretation led to what has been called Social Darwinism. Spencer was popularized by John Fiske, who combined evolution and idealism into a vision of a glorious future. See Welch, *Protestant Thought*, 2:207–9.
24. Hofstadter, *Social Darwinism*, 25. See also Carter, *Spiritual Crisis*, 49.

Some in the church were more enthusiastic in their acceptance of evolutionary thought and their readiness to synthesize it with their own views. George Frederick Wright, a professor of New Testament Language at Oberlin College, the editor of *Bibliotheca Sacra*, and an authority on glacial geology, was a notable example. The embrace of these new theories by scholars like Wright and by ministers like the influential Henry Ward Beecher, led to their acceptance as insights into how God created.[25]

A fourth reaction to evolution was to redefine the relationship between science and religion. Previously religion had been seen as dependent on facts, historical or scientific. In the redefined relationship, religion would be understood as outside the reach of scientific investigation, located within the heart.[26]

The late 1870s found the scientific world and much of the public squarely behind biological evolution with this trend continuing into the 1880s.[27] By that time, religion had been forced to share its traditional authority with science and American thought had been greatly secularized. Evolution had made its way into the churches themselves with no prominent figure to dispute it.[28]

What were the factors that paved the way for rapid acceptance of Darwin's views?[29] Hofstadter points out that the Civil War had so wearied the nation that further contention was to be avoided. Getting on with the work of settling the country and exploiting the industrial momentum was what was needed.[30] Also paving the way for Darwin's views was a rising interest in science brought on by the growing need for technicians and scientists in a nation of burgeoning industry and agriculture.[31] Hofstadter also observes how biblical criticism, comparative religion, and the shift away from traditional religious beliefs helped prepare many for the evolutionary theories.[32]

---

25. Schlesinger, "Critical Period," 303.
26. Marsden, *Fundamentalism*, 20.
27. Schlesinger, "Critical Period," 303.
28. Hofstadter, *Social Darwinism*, 30.
29. Hudson, *Religion in America*, 247.
30. Hofstadter, *Social Darwinism*, 5.
31. Ibid., 19.
32. Ibid., 14. To speak of a direct cause-effect relationship would be misleading since these were all manifestations of underlying processes at work at this time. As well, one could just as easily argue that Darwinism helped to foster higher criticism and comparative religion.

Introduction

The intellectual revolution made it necessary not only to reconsider humankind's place in the world process, but also Christianity's place in world religions. During this period, comparative religious study became very popular and for several reasons. Missionaries, brought into contact with other religions, learned that morality could be found outside their own religious framework.[33] As well there was an explosion of information during this time. Translations and editions of Oriental religious texts brought these to a wider audience while archeological discoveries made possible a clearer understanding of past civilizations.[34] Work in other disciplines such as mythology, psychology, and anthropology further explored the commonalities among religions, including Christianity.

The increased attention given to *Religionswissenschaft* can be seen in the popularity of the publications that described it. James Freeman Clarke's *Ten Great Religions* (1871) went through twenty-one editions in its first fifteen years.[35] A more graphic demonstration of the interest in this subject was seen in Chicago in 1893. Here, with thousands attending, the first World's Parliament of Religions took place, its motto drawn from Malachi: "Have we not all one Father? hath not one God created us?"[36]

The avalanche of information brought on by the intellectual revolution helped to make the late nineteenth century a time of suspended judgment. These lines from the English poet Arthur Hugh Clough (1819–1861) expressed the sentiment of the period on both sides of the Atlantic:

> Oh say it, all who think it,
> Look straight, and never blink it!
> If it is so, let it be so,
> And we will all agree so;
> But the plot has counterplot,
> It may be, and yet be not.[37]

Something of the complexity of the times and the reaction of one conservative movement is heard in this observation from a well-known

---

33. Schlesinger, "Critical Period," 304.
34. Welch, *Protestant Thought*, 2:104–7.
35. Schlesinger, "Critical Period," 304.
36. Ibid., 304.
37. Houghton, "Character of the Age," 37. This unfinished poem deals with the nature of humanity.

holiness writer, "We walk amid quagmires and crooked paths, but the sanctified believer walks on marble."[38]

The Battle for the Bible

The complexity of the situation only worsened with the battle that struck closest to the heart of American Protestantism, the battle for the Bible. Long regarded as the ultimate source of authority for Protestants, attacks here could and did have devastating consequences. The story of biblical interpretation in America is so important for this study of the Holiness movement that it will be taken up in chapter two.

The focus there, however, will not be on biblical scholarship, since in nineteenth-century America, the scholarly and critical study of the Bible played only a minor role. Much more important in American Christianity of that time was the use of the Bible by the average person, at home, at church, or elsewhere. Within the popular study of the Bible there was a very strong tradition, nourished from deep within the American psyche and supported by the upsurge in egalitarian sentiment between the Revolutionary and Civil War, that every person was capable of interpreting the Bible for himself or herself. The result is what we are calling the populist hermeneutic.

Populist is not being used here in its usual sense to describe a political movement that sought to oppose the shifting balance of power from country to city. The term is chosen to represent an approach to reading the Bible that is more than popular, but less than political. This approach to the Bible while popular in the sense of being widespread was not popular in the sense of being universally accepted. As we will see, a number of prominent figures opposed it with vehemence.

The populist hermeneutic was individualistic in that it granted to each person the right to interpret the Bible for himself or herself. It was not simply individualistic, however, for in many ways it actually exalted the common person above the scholar. This approach to the Bible was both democratic—it extended the right to interpret to all, and privatistic—referring to the intimate communion with God from which such interpretation would flow. We consider the populist hermeneutic in chapter two.

---

38. Watson, *Love Abounding*, 173.

Introduction

The American Holiness Movement

Without question, the last quarter of the nineteenth and the early decades of the twentieth century must be regarded as one of the most tumultuous periods in American history. What seems equally clear is that the storm spent its greatest fury on the Protestant Church in America. For many, she was a bastion of traditionalism in a day when traditions were seen no longer as ancient monuments to be cherished but as unsafe and unstable structures to be demolished. The changes she experienced in this period were significant, and many of their effects continue to shape American Christianity.

One group facing this storm was the Holiness movement which traced its roots from John Wesley through American Methodism. From the 1830s through the early postbellum period, Wesley's holiness message (with American alterations) was firmly upheld among Methodists. It could be found, as well, among other denominations, due, in part, to the work of Presbyterians Charles G. Finney and William E. Boardman, Congregationalist Asa Mahan, and Baptist A. B. Earle. The 1880s, however, saw tensions develop between Methodism and the Holiness movement for institutional and theological reasons. While many holiness advocates remained within the Methodist Episcopal churches, many others left to form new denominations. Their pronounced emphasis on holiness—what it is and how to get it—as well as their schismatic beginnings, made these new denominations sectarian in nature. The roots and development of the Holiness movement in America will be the topic for chapter three.

This study focuses on the biblical interpretation of the American Holiness movement in the late nineteenth and early twentieth centuries. The movement, like other elements in the church, was significantly shaped by the dramatic changes experienced at this time. The way they read and understood the Bible was also affected. How much it was influenced, and in what ways, is the heart of this study.

When analyzing biblical interpretation, it is wisest to begin with the premise, now widely accepted in biblical studies, that the interpretation of any literature, including the Bible, proceeds out of the context of the interpreter, and is thus shaped, to a greater or lesser extent, by that context. A careful reading and analysis of the biblical interpretation of this movement, seen against the tumultuous backdrop of late-nineteenth- and early-twentieth-century America, and in the clarifying perspective of the history of biblical interpretation, will enable modern readers to learn much about this movement, how it understood itself, its doctrine, and its time.

Seven authors have been chosen who were considered leaders and Bible teachers in the Holiness movement during the years 1875 to 1920. Daniel Steele (1824–1914) was a highly respected Methodist Episcopal educator and pastor. Born in Windham, New York, Steele was converted in 1842 and sanctified in 1870 under the ministry of A. B. Earle.[39] He pastored for thirty years and taught for twenty-five at Wesleyan University, Genesee College, Syracuse University (where he served for a short time as Acting President), Boston University and the New England Deaconess Training School. His areas of expertise were primarily New Testament Greek, systematic and practical theology. Among his many books are commentaries on Leviticus, Numbers, and Joshua (in Whedon's commentary series), as well as numerous popular works on the Wesleyan doctrine of entire sanctification. The most scholarly of the authors to be studied, Steele also maintained a loyalty to the Methodist Episcopal church and an irenic spirit that was not present among all others. It would also appear that, of these seven, Steele came closest to representing Wesley's doctrine on Christian perfection.[40]

Beverly Carradine (1848–1931) was also a loyal Methodist, representing the Southern branch of that church. He grew up in a well-to-do family in the South and attended college. Converted and called into pastoral ministry from a career in business, he became not only a pastor but a nationally known holiness evangelist and writer.[41]

W. B. Godbey (1833–1920), was one of the most colorful figures in the Holiness movement and perhaps its most prolific author. Godbey was born and raised in the South within a family that for several generations had abstained from the practice of slavery.[42] Graduating from Georgetown College in Kentucky in 1859, he became a Methodist Episcopal pastor as his father and grandfather had been. Godbey was serving as the president of Harmonia College in Perryville, Kentucky when he became entirely sanctified. His reaction was to give away his library, resign his presidency, and begin evangelistic work, a ministry which quickly grew to international

---

39. Steele, *Love Enthroned*, 275, 278–79.

40. Steele, *Half-Hours with Saint Paul*, 7.

41. Carradine, *Sanctified Life*, 59.

42. Some of this biographical material is available in Faupel, "Preface," vii–xvii. Other information was gathered from Godbey's *Autobiography*, and from his other writings.

Introduction

proportions. His publications numbered more than 200, including a complete commentary and new translation of the New Testament. During the late 1890s he left the Methodist Church and lent his aid to various radical branches of the Holiness movement.[43]

Martin Wells Knapp (1853–1901) also began his ministry in the Methodist Episcopal church but left in 1901 because of conflict over his holiness evangelistic work.[44] He attended Albion College in Michigan where he was converted at age 19, and he was sanctified nine years later while pastoring. Becoming active in evangelism, he established the monthly *Revivalist* in 1888, which he moved, four years later, to Cincinnati. Shortly after this he began God's Bible School and Missionary Training Home in that city. His leadership in the fledgling denomination which became the Pilgrim Holiness Church was cut short by his untimely death at 48.

Reuben Robinson (1860–1942), better known as "Uncle Buddy," rose from abject poverty in the South to become "one of the most loved and appreciated men" of his day.[45] Converted in 1880, he was sanctified ten years later through Godbey's influence. Robinson had very little formal education, although he briefly attended South Western University Preparatory school in Georgetown, Texas. He left after eight months to pursue evangelistic work, coming into contact with the Salvation Army. He left the Methodist Episcopal church over the issue of sanctification and joined the Church of the Nazarene in 1906. Robinson, with a very wide evangelistic ministry, by this time had preached in 40 states. In 1926 alone he worked in 42 states, three Canadian provinces, and preached 500 times. He calculated that in 47 years of religious work (1880–1926), he had traveled about one million miles, preached 18,000 times, prayed with more than 80,000 people at the mourner's bench, and written thirteen books.[46]

George D. Watson (1845–1924), carried on a world-wide evangelistic ministry as part of the Methodist Episcopal and Wesleyan Methodist churches. Born in Accomac County, Virginia into a Methodist family, Watson planned on a career in medicine.[47] The Civil War interrupted these

---

43. Cf. Hamilton, *William Baxter Godbey* for the definitive scholarly work on Godbey.

44. Biographical information drawn from Jones, *Perfectionist Persuasion*, 100–4. Knapp reveals his own spiritual pilgrimage in *Out of Egypt*, especially 187–92.

45. Robinson, *Chickens*, 3.

46. Robinson reveals much of this information about himself in his writings, especially his autobiography, *My Life's Story*.

47. Most of this biographical information was drawn from Watson's biography, *Glimpses*, by his wife, Eva.

plans and he enlisted in the Southern Army where he was converted under the influence of a Southern Methodist chaplain. Following the War, Watson attended the Methodist General Biblical Institute in Concord, New Hampshire, where he gained a rudimentary knowledge of Hebrew, Greek, and theology.[48] He joined the Philadelphia Conference of the Methodist church in 1868, moving later to Indiana. It was there in 1876 that he was sanctified and the very next year played a prominent role in a holiness conference in Cincinnati.[49] His outspoken defense of the doctrine appears to have soured his relationship with the Methodists. He left the church of his childhood and in 1896 joined the Wesleyan Methodist Church where he remained until his death.

Joseph H. Smith (1855–1946) grew up in the Philadelphia area where he was converted, sanctified, and called to preach in 1874.[50] After spending some time in Georgia as a missionary for the Northern Methodists, Smith returned home to pastor in that denomination from 1881 to 1886. In 1887 he was granted supernumerary relations with the Conference because of an illness. That same year his condition dramatically improved and with the freedom that accompanied his status, he began an aggressive evangelistic ministry. This ministry grew until his services were in greater demand than any other holiness evangelist.[51] He became a member of the National Camp Meeting Association for the Promotion of Holiness in 1883 and its president in 1925. Smith gave up the opportunity to acquire a college education to pursue home missions work in 1875, but did serve as the college pastor of Meridian College in Mississippi from 1907 to 1912.

The writings of these seven authors, representing the best of holiness interpretation, have been carefully studied to determine the presuppositions that underlay their interpretation. Chapters four, five and six will present this material.

Holiness interpretation will be examined in chapter four in light of Wesley's theological method, known as the Wesleyan Quadrilateral. By exploring how the movement understood the four elements of Scripture, reason, tradition, and experience, we can see how they differed from Wesley and how their own interpretations emerged. Chapter five will examine

---

48. Garrison, *Forty Witnesses*, 100–1.
49. Jones, *Study of the Holiness Movement*, 778.
50. The best treatment of Smith is Rose, *Theology of Christian Experience*.
51. Ibid., 117.

INTRODUCTION

what happened to the populist hermeneutic in the hands of the holiness writers, noting how it was maintained and altered.

The Holiness movement, as with all movements, interpreted the Bible using certain presuppositions. Four that played a very important role in shaping holiness interpretation were the immanence of God, the centrality of the Holy Spirit, the unity of the Bible, and its more-than-literal nature. These will be explored in chapter six. The final two chapters will provide summary observations on holiness biblical interpretation and will analyze the intersection between holiness interpretation and biblical criticism now taking place.

What can be gained by taking a close look at biblical interpretation in the Holiness movement, a relatively unknown paragraph in the story of American Church history? This movement significantly influenced Pentecostalism, which has become one of the most important forces in world Christianity. By identifying the elements of biblical interpretation used by the parent, greater understanding of the offspring can also be gained.

Those within the Holiness movement today continue to be affected by the methods and presuppositions of biblical interpretation employed during this formative period. Such a study allows these persons to become more critically aware of past interpretation, to understand the impact of the past on the present, and to make whatever changes are necessary.

Beyond a greater understanding of this movement and those influenced by it, this study also sheds further light on the controversy between the Fundamentalists and the Modernists in the early part of this century, a conflict whose effects continue to be felt. While much has been written about fundamentalism, one reaction to the "modernistic" influences in society and the church, the very different reaction of the American Holiness movement has not been adequately explored. That some holiness churches would come later to identify with the fundamentalist cause, while others would resist the impulse to do so all the while remaining staunch traditionalists makes the investigation even more intriguing.[52]

I hope this study will benefit both those within and without the Holiness movement. Under examination, those within can gain a clearer understanding of their past and how that past impacts upon their present. Those without can benefit from looking more closely into a movement which exerted at one time a recognizable impact on American society. Even its

---

52. Bassett, "Theological Identity," 108, note 106. Cf. Stanley, "Wesleyan/Holiness Churches."

lamentable recession to the fringes of that society is laden with insights into the workings of American Christianity in this period. As well, this study provides a case history of how one movement with sectarian characteristics interpreted the Bible, thereby providing more data for this broader topic which begs exploration.

2

The Populist Hermeneutic in American Biblical Studies

A CURSORY GLANCE AT American history reveals the influence of the Bible. It has helped to shape her national character, inspired American writers, and guided countless decisions, public and private. Robert Baird, writing in the early 1840s to defend the American religious system to Europeans, classified all denominations into evangelical Protestants and unevangelical, then characterized the former as "churches whose religion is the Bible, the whole Bible, and nothing but the Bible."[1]

The use of the Bible in America proceeded on two levels, one formal and the other informal. While some attention has been given to the formal,[2] the informal, popular side of American biblical studies has received little attention. Because the Holiness movement relied more on the informal variety, our focus will be on popular interpretation.

The Question of Authority in Biblical Interpretation

To recognize the Bible's importance in America is to be reminded that many of this country's founders were Christians, for whom the Bible has

---

1. Baird, *Religion*, 613.

2. For an excellent discussion on the rise and influence of the New England scholars such as Moses Stuart, see Brown, *Rise of Biblical Criticism*. Another aspect of American biblical studies that has received close scrutiny is the conflict between scholarly findings and traditional beliefs in the late nineteenth and early twentieth centuries, well-treated in Marsden, *Fundamentalism*.

always been very important. But also from the beginning, the church has disagreed about the proper interpretation of many passages. Two Christians have read the same text and come to almost opposite conclusions.[3] Thus there has always been the need to tether one's interpretation to some other authority. Paul rested his teaching on a revelation from Jesus (Gal 1:11–12). Irenaeus relied on the teachings of the apostles and the church they established.[4] His view was developed further by Tertullian, Augustine, and Vincent of Lerins, until the authority of apostles, councils, and ultimately the pope were regarded as the authority guaranteeing the correct interpretation of the Bible.[5]

For those born in the inspiring atmosphere of the Renaissance, exegeting within the confines of the authoritative interpretation was too restrictive. Nothing but a bold break with tradition would suffice if the Bible—standing alone as literally interpreted—was to confront the individual with its truth.[6]

However, by emphasizing "Sola Scriptura" and the Bible's perspicuity—that it is clearly expressed and clearly understood—the Reformers were not doing away with authority. Rather, they were handing over that authority to the individual Christian, as led by the Holy Spirit.

Critics pointed out that the Bible was a wax nose which one could easily manipulate to suit one's own purposes.[7] Sensitive to this charge, the Reformers safeguarded proper exegesis by specifying certain presuppositions that should guide interpretation. For Luther, the interpreter must recognize the centrality of Christ and justification by faith in order to truly understand Scripture.[8] John Calvin safeguarded the interpretation of the

---

3. Grant and Tracy, *Short History*, 73.

4. Irenaeus, *Against Heresies*, 508. Grant may be correct in calling him the patriarch of authoritative exegesis but it must be remembered that Irenaeus wrote to refute the Gnostics. With such opponents, appeals to inspired intuitions would carry little weight (cf. Grant and Tracy, *Short History*, 50).

5. Ibid., 74–82.

6. Ibid., 92. Grant points out that here was the Reformers' innovation in biblical studies; in their search for the literal and grammatical interpretation of the Bible, they only followed in the footsteps of Aquinas.

7. Albert Pighius, 1538, as cited in Ward, "To Be a Reader," 46n5.

8. See Runia, "Hermeneutics," 129, as well as Luther, *Works*, 34:337. So crucial was this truth to the proper understanding of the Bible that Luther criticized those books of the Bible where it did not appear prominently enough: "Therefore St. James' epistle is really an epistle of straw, compared to these others, for it has nothing of the nature of the Gospel about it" (Luther, *Luther's Works*, 35:362).

Bible through systematization, intending his *Institutes* to serve as a guide to help Christians understand the Bible.[9]

Clearly the Reformers doubted that common people could properly interpret the Bible without assistance from trained clergy. Luther included marginal notes and prefaces to most of the books in his translation of the Bible, as was the custom with vernacular translations of the sixteenth century. He also criticized the Enthusiasts for twisting the Bible to their desires.[10] Calvin, whose French translation also included marginal notes, acknowledged that, though the Bible is an overflowing source of wisdom, it does not say everything that anyone thinks it says.[11]

Protestantism, since the Reformation, has continued to vacillate between advocating the perspicuity or lucidity of the Bible for the individual believer, and fearing a narrowly individualistic interpretation. The Protestant Scholastics steered clear of private interpretations by further systematizing Reformation doctrines. Anglicanism, although embracing Sola Scriptura, continued to appeal to church tradition as a guide to interpretation.[12]

Puritans, reacting against Anglican traditionalism, reasserted the priority of the sermon over the Eucharist.[13] They called for "plain" preaching and rejected rhetorical display and "fine language" so that the power of the Holy Spirit could be felt.[14] The Quakers, under George Fox, accused the Puritans of bibliolatry, advocating a still more individualistic interpretation, and relying on the "Inner Light" of the Spirit.[15] The "Diggers," a mid-seventeenth-century movement in England, considered the Bible to have been used by the clerics, just as others had used the laws, to oppress the common man.[16]

Another movement which advocated an individualistic interpretation was Pietism. This amorphous reaction against Protestant

---

9. Calvin, *Institutes*, 1:7. Cf. Brown, *Rise of Biblical Criticism*, 5, for reference to the effects of systematic theology on the exegesis of Calvin.

10. Stout, "Word and Order," 22. Cf. Dammermann, "Continental Versions," 339.

11. Stout, "Word and Order," 22. Calvin's views are described in Hatch, "Sola Scriptura," 61.

12. Grant and Tracy, *Short History*, 97.

13. Stout, "Puritanism."

14. Knott, *Sword of the Spirit*, 4–6.

15. For a thorough treatment of George Fox, see Gwyn, *Apocalypse of the Word*.

16. Sabine, *Works of Gerrard Winstanley*, 474–75, as quoted in Knott, *Sword of the Spirit*, 89.

Scholasticism strove "after personal and individual religious independence and collaboration."[17] Although they did not carry the principle to the same extent as the Quakers, Pietists emphasized the importance of reading the Bible for its spiritual sense, discoverable only by those truly converted.[18]

Authority in American Biblical Interpretation

The question of who could interpret the Bible entered a new era when the first settlers stepped ashore in North America. While other movements had appealed to the right of private interpretation, America became a nation with "No creed but the Bible." The populist hermeneutic—"Everyone one's own interpreter"—came to characterize American Protestantism in the period between the Revolutionary and Civil Wars.

This populist hermeneutic considered the common person able to interpret the Bible for himself or herself. "Is the Bible written (like Caligula's laws) so intricate and high, that none but the letter learned (according to the common phrase) can read it? Is not the vision written so plain that he that runs may read it?" asked the radical Jeffersonian Baptist preacher, John Leland.[19] This understanding of the Bible's perspicuity built upon but far overreached the Reformers' original emphasis. They considered the Bible to be clear enough for the common person to read and understand matters necessary for salvation. They never gave carte blanche to commoners, as Leland and others were doing.

Now it was being argued that the common people could not only understand enough to be converted, but could even preach. Some went further to argue that the humility and simplicity of commoners made them *better* able to understand the Bible than the elite, whose vision was obscured by pride. Benjamin Austin, Jr., a late-eighteenth-century polemicist, pointed out that it was the common people who received Jesus gladly while "monarchical, aristocratical and priestly authorities cried crucify him."[20]

The view that the commoners could interpret for themselves empowered cobblers, blacksmiths, farmers and others lacking any formal

---

17. Carl Mirbt, quoted in Stoeffler, "Pietism," in *Westminster Dictionary of Church History*.

18. Frei, *Eclipse*, 177–78, 219.

19. Leland, *Rights of Conscience Inalienable*, 15–16, as quoted in Hatch, *Democratization*, 98.

20. Austin, *Constitutional Republicanism*, 173, as quoted in Hatch, *Democratization*, 26.

training in theology to preach and teach the Bible. Perhaps nowhere is this more dramatically evident than in the rise of women preachers during this period. Although lacking the social and educational opportunities enjoyed by men, and in spite of great opposition and controversy,[21] women were given the freedom to preach by Quakers, Methodists, "Christians," and other groups which exalted the common person.[22] That the populist hermeneutic continued to empower public roles for women up to and beyond the Civil War is illustrated by the importance of the Methodist lay-woman, Phoebe Palmer,[23] credited with helping to bridge the gap between the clergy-centered revivalism of Charles G. Finney and the lay-oriented variety of Moody.[24]

One form of the populist hermeneutic's attack on the authority of tradition and established religion was itinerant preaching, used with greater frequency during this time. Itinerants who entered a region where spiritual control was understood to rest with a member of the ruling elite and who began to speak for God were subversives, denying the right of the parish minister to serve as the sole spokesman for God. The itinerants' example and words claimed that the right to speak for God did not originate with an ecclesiastical body nor could it be limited to geographical boundaries. Like the Spirit, it could roam where it would.[25]

The common preacher could not appeal to the same objective standards of authority available to the established clergy. Few possessed a formal theological education; some ridiculed seminaries as "Religious Manufactories" set up to explain what is "plain" and make "easy things hard."[26] Seminaries and creeds, said Leland, were only the "Virgin Mary between the souls of men and the Scriptures."[27] While some common preachers might

---

21. The practice of allowing women to pray and testify was still considered one of Charles Finney's most radical "New Measures" in 1827, according to Dayton, *Discovering*, 88.

22. Hatch, *Democratization*, 78–79.

23. Palmer's *Guide to Holiness* at one point reached a monthly circulation of 37,000. See White, *Beauty*, 94. Cf. Smith, *Revivalism*, 124.

24. White, "Palmer, Phoebe Worrall."

25. For a further elaboration of the radical nature of itinerancy, see McLoughlin, "'Enthusiasm for Liberty,'" 47–73.

26. Elias Smith, editor of the *Herald of Gospel Liberty* newspaper, October 26, 1810, page 263, as quoted in Hatch, *Democratization*, 174.

27. John Leland, "The Modern Priest," as quoted in Hatch, *Democratization*, 97. The use of Catholic imagery to portray the Protestant establishment is significant in that it

A Holiness Hermeneutic

be able to appeal to the authority of ordination,[28] such accreditation only mattered if the granting denomination was accepted by the establishment. Far from acceptance, common preachers and their denominations were usually scorned by the established clergy.

Common preachers, lacking granted authority, had to find another way to prove their authority to speak for God. For proof they appealed to their persuasive power. The preacher who could produce the desired results in the audience was taken to be the true messenger; the one who could not returned to farming. Desired results included conversions, and better still, revivals. This need for practical results helps to explain why preachers were slow to suppress the emotional outbursts which were so prevalent in revivals; they demonstrated that God was at work through that preacher.

Common preaching was characterized by the use of the vernacular, not only because most preachers lacked a formal education, but also because they were confident that this was the best way to convey the truth of the gospel.[29] Their congregations were more easily persuaded when they heard the message in words they could understand and in a style they enjoyed. Hence storytelling and humor became important tools in the hands of the common preachers, enabling the demolition of carefully structured theological arguments with a well-placed anecdote. Some common preachers would at times locate their authority in dreams, visions or impressions. The prevalence of this practice prompted a troubled observer from the establishment to warn in 1805, "No person is warranted from the word of God to publish to the world the discoveries of heaven or hell which he supposes he has had in a dream, or trance, or vision."[30]

A populist hermeneutic required more than a common preacher. Untrained, often mobile, charismatic preachers only thrived because there were congregations that would accept them. Whatever else may have characterized such congregations, they shared with their preacher a strong confidence in the ability of the common person to think, decide and interpret the Bible for himself or herself. Democracy and individual rights pervaded

---

demonstrated the anti–Catholic sentiment which pervaded much of American Protestantism until recently. Anti-Catholicism probably helped to keep the fire of the populist hermeneutic burning among Protestants through the nineteenth century.

28. Mead, "Rise," 231–32 asserts that most denominations had some licensing process. The difference between churches was in part the emphasis to be placed on preparation.

29. Hatch, *Democratization*, 127. Baird described the characteristic plainness and simplicity of American preaching as well as its other qualities in *Religion*, 434–35.

30. As quoted in Hatch, *Democratization*, 10.

the atmosphere of that day. The individual conscience was regarded as the path by which God made known his truth to the human mind,[31] eliminating any need for the opinion of the elite. A parishioner in one such congregation expressed it this way:

> Know then that every soul is free
> To choose his life and what he'll be;
> For this eternal truth giv'n,
> That God will force no man to heav'n.
> He'll draw, persuade, direct him right;
> Bless him with wisdom, love and light;
> In nameless ways be good and kind,
> But never force the human mind.[32]

Concern about the Populist Hermeneutic

The notion that the commoner was able to interpret the Bible as well as if not better than the learned theologian came to be so widely held that John W. Nevin considered American religion to be characterized by the principle: "No creed but the Bible." This feature caused some concern among learned theologians, concern that turned to fear when commoners took to preaching their private interpretations. Nevin blasted this notion in "The Sect System."[33]

Nevin launched this attack on the populist hermeneutic in 1849 but others had lamented this quality of American Protestantism forty years earlier. Timothy Dwight, speaking at the founding of Andover Seminary in 1808, excoriated those "who declare, both in their language and conduct, that the desk ought to be yielded up to the occupancy of Ignorance." It takes a seven-years apprenticeship to learn to make a shoe or an axe, he observed, but these radicals suppose that God can make plain the "numerous, and

---

31. "Education in the Methodist Church," 534, 537.

32. Written by a nine-year-old parishioner of William Smyth Babcock, an itinerant minister in early-nineteenth-century New England with some connections to the Freewill Baptists, as quoted in Hatch, *Democratization*, 43. The full poem appears in the Appendix, 231–32. Hatch, in this section, describes and illustrates the "Individualization of Conscience" at work during this time.

33. Nevin, "Sect System," 144.

frequently abstruse, doctrines and precepts, contained in all the Scriptures, ... without learning, labour, or time."[34]

Six years later, in a Yale commencement address, Lyman Beecher bemoaned the same problem as he described preachers who were

> generally illiterate, often not possessed of a good English education, and in some instances unable to read or write. By them, as a body, learning is despised. With few exceptions they are utterly unacquainted with theology and like other men are devoted through the week to secular employment, and preach on the Sabbath, with such preparation as such an education and such avocations allow.[35]

Beecher also spoke affirmingly of the Bible's perspicuity; without it, "common people have *no Bible.*"[36] We have encountered this view before among the Reformers: the Bible is clear enough to lead the commoner to salvation, but to preach it required theological training.[37]

The Populist Hermeneutic and Popular Christianity

The early years of the republic were marked by the rise of popular religious movements,[38] especially the Baptists, Methodists, and "Christians."[39] These churches encouraged common folk to take the responsibility for their religion out of the hands of the church and its clergy.[40] They also made up the largest part of American Protestantism in the early nineteenth century.[41] The Baptist church with its militant localism grew at a tremendous pace after the Revolutionary War to become the largest denomination in America

---

34. Dwight, *Sermon Preached*, 7–8, as quoted in Hatch, *Democratization*, 19.

35. Beecher, *Address*, 7, as quoted in Hatch, *Democratization*, 18.

36. Beecher, "Faith Once Delivered," 74. This sermon, taken from his *Sermons Delivered on Various Occasions*, was preached in 1823.

37. While the primary reasons for the founding of Andover Theological Seminary in 1808 and Princeton Theological Seminary in 1812 seem to have been the quest for theological orthodoxy and the need to train men for ministry, the founders of both institutions were concerned about the anti-authoritarianism sweeping American Christianity. Cf. Hatch, *Democratization*, 19 and Noll, "Founding of Princeton Seminary," 87–88, 90.

38. Hatch, *Democratization*, 9–11.

39. The "Christians" were groups that rapidly grew into the denominational family that came to be known as Christian or Disciple churches.

40. Hatch, *Democratization*, 58.

41. Smith, *Revivalism*, 22–25.

by 1800. Twenty years later this title went to the mushrooming Methodists. The Christian movement of the Campbells and Barton Stone grew from non-existence to 450,000 by 1870.[42]

The most radical version of the populist hermeneutic that found institutional form was seen among the "Christians," which began with the expressed purposes of restoring the New Testament church[43] and giving everyone the right to interpret the New Testament for himself or herself. "We are persuaded that it is high time for us not only to think, but also to act for ourselves; to see with our own eyes, and to take all our measures directly and immediately from the Divine Standard."[44]

Methodists, as a whole, employed a less radical approach to biblical interpretation. However, because Methodism came to play a very important role on the religious scene in the nineteenth century they serve as a more significant example of the widespread influence of the populist hermeneutic.[45] Methodism was an ideal climate within which the populist hermeneutic could thrive. From its beginnings it had been a movement of the people and while it came to be embraced by all levels of society, its doctrines and methods first found readiest acceptance among the common people.[46] This was especially the case in America, under the leadership of Francis Asbury. Initiating changes which minimized liturgy and placed greater emphasis on preaching, Asbury sought an itinerant ministry that would reach the unchurched, maintain the faith of the converted, and minimize the complacency of Methodist ministers. "Next to the grace of God," he said, "there

---

42. Hudson, *Religion in America*, 117, 120, 122. See also Baird, *Religion*, 219–20, 264–70. The figure on the Disciples comes from Niebuhr et al., *Advancement*, 2.

43. Restorationism in American Protestantism was linked with the populist hermeneutic in its desire to return to the days when the religious leaders were common folk, like fishermen, and there was minimal religious establishment and (supposedly) no interfering creeds or tradition. Such views blended with the understanding that the Bible was to be interpreted normatively as a book whose characters and events are models to be followed today. Normativity is an important part of the populist hermeneutic since it makes the Bible so much easier to interpret.

44. "Declaration and Address of the Christian Association of Washington" (Washington, PA: Brown and Sample, 1809), as quoted in Hatch, *Democratization*, 162.

45. Hudson, *Religion in America*, 169. Hudson also traces the founding of the "Christian" movement, in part, to Methodism, citing Wesley's emphasis on peace among true believers of any theological persuasion, and the experience of Barton Stone where Presbyterians and Methodists worked together harmoniously in revivals in Kentucky in 1804 (ibid., 120–21).

46. Hatch, *Democratization*, 93.

A Holiness Hermeneutic

is nothing like this for keeping the whole body alive from the centre to the circumference, and for the continual extension of that circumference on every hand."[47]

Common people heard the gospel from common preachers who offered them "dignity of choice" and the chance to become a class leader, exhorter, local preacher, or circuit rider. Lay preachers became ubiquitous in American Methodism, reflecting the flattening of social distinctions.[48]

The widespread use of itinerants by Methodism was certainly not as radical on the nineteenth century frontier as it had been in mid-eighteenth-century New England. Nevertheless, its use symbolized a similar revolt against the authoritative patterns of a settled ministry as seen in one Methodist's retrospective look at itinerancy: "The itinerancy was born in a militant atmosphere, it rears fighters and expects its ministers to be in bondage only to the truth. The Methodist Church is the mother of moral radicalism in modern life."[49]

Methodist preachers were notoriously uneducated, at least by formal standards.[50] Peter Cartwright, one of the most famous Methodist itinerants, had little formal education and thanked God for it.[51] Not that he was opposed to colleges, in fact, he helped champion the cause of Methodist higher education. What he opposed was the assumption that a formal education was needed for effective ministry.

> A Methodist preacher in those days, when he felt that God had called him to preach, instead of hunting up a college or Bible institute, hunted up a hardy pony of a horse, and some travelling apparatus, and with his library always at hand, namely, Bible, Hymn Book, and Discipline, he started, and with a text that never wore out nor grew stale, he cried, "Behold the Lamb of God, that taketh away the sin of the world."[52]

---

47. Methodist Episcopal Church, *Doctrines and Discipline*, 42.
48. Hatch, *Democratization*, 85.
49. Hensey, *Itinerancy*, 55–56.
50. An informal system of education was in place from Wesley's day through the nineteenth century. In 1816, the General Conference authorized the Course of Study, wherein Methodist preachers would study assigned texts and be examined on them. See Chiles, *Theological Transition*, 32–33.
51. Cartwright, *Fifty Years*, 277.
52. Cartwright, *Autobiography*, 243.

An unsigned article in the *Methodist Quarterly Review* of October, 1842, edited by George Peck, responded to the criticism that Methodist Episcopal preachers were unlearned. The author admitted that the Methodists stood guilty as charged, although not before mentioning the great contributions that had been made to the field of theology by Methodists such as John Wesley, Richard Watson, Adam Clarke and others.[53] The goal of the church, he explained, is not education, but the spreading of scriptural holiness throughout the land. Learning or lack of learning does not bring preference among Methodists, but both are employed, where appropriate, for the greater purpose.[54]

Methodist biblical interpretation relied on those more subjective bases for authority—such as common sense, emotions, impressions, and the individual conscience—that characterized the populist hermeneutic. Freeborn Garrettson, converted under Asbury and an important figure in early Methodism, acknowledged that although the Bible was his infallible guide, "both sleeping and waking, things of a divine nature have been revealed to me."[55] One Methodist in 1842 exalted a divinely enlightened conscience to the level of an "inward moral dictator." "There is, therefore, one recipient

---

53. In addition to Wesley's *Notes* on the Bible, three other works from British Methodism shaped American biblical interpretation early on. The six-volume commentary on the whole Bible by Thomas Coke, one of the first superintendents of American Methodism, found its way into the Methodist course of study after its appearance in America in 1812. This was an important effort, even if, as Milton Terry pointed out, it is basically a reprint of William Dodd's commentary (1770) (Terry, *Biblical Hermeneutics*, 702). Adam Clarke criticized Coke's work in the General Preface of his commentary (1830), not for reprinting Dodd, but for omitting Dodd's marginal readings and parallel texts, and for failing to acknowledge the source of his material. While Joseph Benson's five-volume commentary appeared in America around 1820, Adam Clarke's commentary in eight volumes, appearing in America in 1811, was more influential. Richard Watson offered his *Biblical and Theological Dictionary* in 1831, as well as a commentary on Matthew and Mark, published in 1834. The next major commentary effort by the Methodists was begun by Daniel D. Whedon, editor of the *Quarterly Review*. Whedon authored a multi-volume commentary on the New Testament, the first part of which appeared in 1860. The project was originally intended to produce only a one-volume commentary to be distributed by the Methodist tract department. Plans were changed to meet the desire of the 1856 General Conference that a commentary be prepared, suitable for popular use. Whedon's series eventually included commentaries on the Old Testament written by other scholars, including Milton Terry and Daniel Steele. Cf. Whedon's "Preface" to his *Commentary on the Gospels*, 3. Cf. Chiles, *Theological Transition*, 32–33, 37–61.

54. "Education in the Methodist Church," 531–32.

55. Quoted in Hatch, *Democratization*, 10. Byrne, *No Foot of Land* contains a section on dreams, visions, voices and omens.

of truth within, and one source of truth without—a conscience and a Bible. The former, without the latter, is but an erring guide; the latter, without the former, is but a lifeless letter. But when both mingle their mutual light and influence, hope dawns upon the world."[56]

It might be argued with Nevin that a populist hermeneutic, loudly proclaimed by a man like Alexander Campbell, was only an illusion designed to allow authoritarian leaders to exert greater authority. Hatch asserts that the emergence of such leaders characterizes populist cultures.[57] Furthermore, these leaders, possessing extraordinary communication and organizational skills, arose from the ranks of common men and women and presented themselves as supporters of common values. Their emergence, not from the aristocracy or halls of learning, but from among commoners, strengthens the thesis rather than destroys it.

Puritan Roots for the Populist Hermeneutic in America

The populist hermeneutic, such an important part of American Protestantism from the Revolutionary to the Civil War, did not arise fully grown from the soil of the new Republic. Its main tap-root was nourished by developments within the Protestant Reformation.

Among the most important influences were those non-separating Congregationalists who settled in New England. Their goal was to create the Promised Land, a society that embodied the ideals of Christ[58] and would be "a model to the nations."[59] In this tightly controlled covenant community, the Bible was regarded as the self-authenticating authoritative word of God.[60] Public dissension including variant interpretations of the Bible was not tolerated because it would dim the light sent out from the "City Set on a Hill." Thus Anne Hutchinson, accused of antinomianism and "traducing the ministers" for emphasizing the sufficiency of the Spirit's work, was excommunicated from her church and banished from the colony in 1638.[61] The same fate was suffered by Roger Williams who believed that the right

---

56. "Education in the Methodist Church," 537–39.
57. Hatch, *Democratization*, 208.
58. Cherry, "Symbols of Spiritual Truth," 265.
59. Stout, "Puritanism," 964–66.
60. Cohen, "Two Biblical Models," 183–84.
61. Cooper, "Hutchinson." Cf. Rutman, *American Puritanism*, 106–7.

to interpret the Bible belonged, not to the church or covenant community, but to the private individual.

> In vaine have English Parliaments permitted English Bibles in the poorest English houses, and the simplest man and woman to search the Scriptures, if yet against their souls' persuasion from the Scripture, they should be forced (as if they lived in Spain or Rome itself without the sight of a Bible) to believe as the Church believes.[62]

Samuel Gorton sowed considerable controversy with his Quaker-like emphasis on the internal witness of the Holy Spirit and anti-clericalism. He was fined and banished from Boston in 1637 and lived for a time in Rhode Island.[63]

The treatment of Hutchinson, Williams, Gorton and others demonstrated the unwillingness of Massachusetts Puritanism to tolerate those who disagreed with the approved interpretation of the Bible. On the one hand, this was to be expected since the Puritans did not want to jeopardize their efforts, pursued at great personal cost, for the sake of private conscience. However, the Puritans lived with an internal tension between strict adherence to the revealed word and openness to new revelation from the Bible. ". . . [T]he Lord hath more light yet to break forth out of his Holy Word," said Puritan John Robinson, who encouraged his flock to be ready "to receive whatever truth shall be made known . . . from the written Word of God."[64] Congregationalism, according to Hudson, was shaped by this view.[65]

Furthermore, Puritanism carried with it an "innate dissidence." Born in opposition to the religious traditionalism of Anglicanism, it could never quite shed its opposing and protesting character. Such a quality functioned valuably so long as the Puritans remained a persecuted or barely tolerated

---

62. Quoted in Sykes, "Religion of Protestants," 3:186. Williams generally used the Geneva Bible, according to Garrett, *Roger Williams*, 42.

63. Taylor, "Gorton." Gorton's views were influenced by the radical Puritan preacher John Saltmarsh (c. 1612–1647), who taught the possibility of direct revelation from the Spirit and deemphasized the letter of the Bible on behalf of a more allegorical approach. A contemporary and kindred spirit to Saltmarsh, John Everard (himself influenced by the German Lutheran mystic Jakob Boehme), encouraged readers to penetrate the outward court of the tabernacle (the letter of the Bible) and proceed to the Holy of Holies that lay beyond the letter (Knott, *Sword of the Spirit*, 88–89).

64. Mather, *Magnalia Christi Americana*, 64.

65. Hudson, *Religion in America*, 33.

A Holiness Hermeneutic

minority. Once they became the "establishment," however, this innate dissidence nourished disagreement. While the Puritans stoutly resisted private interpretation, their innate dissidence combined with their openness to new revelations from the Bible. The result, because of their position of influence on the future of American Christianity, was to nourish the soil from which the populist hermeneutic would blossom.

The Puritans fostered private interpretation in another way, having to do with their choice of Bible translation. English Puritanism in its infancy was nurtured on the Geneva Bible, a plain-styled version, completed in 1560, which came quickly to be the Bible used in the homes of English-speaking Protestants.[66] The Geneva Bible contained a marginal commentary, the work of Olivetan revised by Calvin.[67] The commentary concentrated, almost exclusively, on a Calvinistic understanding of justification by faith in Christ alone.[68]

The Authorized Version, appearing in 1611, replaced the Geneva Bible among Puritans after a generation. This change had far-reaching implications, mainly precipitated by the lack of a marginal commentary in the "King James" version. It was now easier for the Puritans to discover the biblical blueprint for the new society which they sought. New insights were drawn from passages, insights more relevant to seventeenth-century Puritanism. The slate had been wiped clean and it was upon this blank slate that a new authority, the Puritan clergy, wrote their new interpretation, covenant theology.[69]

However, once the slate was wiped clean, others felt free to write their own interpretations there. It is somewhat ironic that while the Authorized Version liberated Puritans to carry out their vision of a new society in which public dissension was not tolerated, it also liberated others in Puritan society to disagree with the establishment and arrive at their own interpretations.

The American Puritans contributed indirectly to the populist hermeneutic of a later generation in a third way, their use of typology. This exegetical method had been employed by the church almost continuously

---

66. Stout, "Word and Order," 21.
67. Ibid., 21–22.
68. Ibid., 22.
69. Ibid., 25–26.

from the New Testament period to the present and formed a very important part of the Puritan consciousness in America.[70]

Typology, like allegory, finds the significance of an event beyond the bounds of the event itself. The two differ, however in that typology considers both the event (type) and its fulfillment (archetype) as fully historical. The typological interpretation of the Puritans was clearly based on the practice of the Reformers for whom typology was as important as allegory had been in the Middle Ages.[71] It was perpetuated by its prevalence in the Geneva Bible.[72] Typology enabled the Puritans to place their New World experiment within a biblical and historical context, thus providing evidence for others and assurance for themselves.[73]

Puritan typology was an important influence on the populist hermeneutic. Typological exegesis is very flexible and subjective in that similar interpretations result only if similar presuppositions are shared. The Puritans endowed this flexible and subjective method with a noble heritage and bequeathed it to future generations. In doing so they placed into the arsenal of American interpreters a tool whose use could be staunchly defended by its heritage but whose results were widely dissimilar. For example, Roger Williams used the typological method to argue against the idea that New England was a New Israel.[74] The Puritans thus unintentionally built into American biblical interpretation a certain proclivity for subjectivity which would later come to fruition in the populist hermeneutic.

The writings of Jonathan Edwards (1703–1758) played a part in the progression from Puritan typology to the populist hermeneutic. Edwards, like his Puritan forebears, employed typology,[75] but with a significant difference. Instead of finding types only in the Bible, Edwards looked for them

---

70. Bercovitch, "Introduction," 3.

71. Davis, "Traditions of Puritan Typology," 28. Numerous examples of typology can be found in Luther's interpretation. Calvin considered that the law should be understood using some form of typology (Calvin, *Institutes*, 2:7, 349).

72. Stout, "Word and Order," 24.

73. Reinitz, "Separatist Background," 107.

74. African-American slaves also referred to Scripture's types, but they reversed the identifications that Puritans had made. America, with its enslaving institutions, was not the Promised Land, but Egypt, from which the slaves sought an Exodus. Noll, "Image of the United States," 49. Williams' use of typology is discussed in Reinitz, "Separatist Background," 108.

75. Another difference between Edwards and the earlier Puritans was his use of allegory. See Stein, "Quest for the Spiritual Sense," 109, 111–12.

both inside and outside the Scriptures. Influenced by the newer scientific epistemology, nature became a particularly rich source of types.[76] This adaptation influenced the populist hermeneutic in two ways. First, Edwards' typology was even more subjective than it had been in the hands of the Puritans.[77] Second, his legacy of extending typology to nature has been seen as an influence on the Romanticism of Emerson.[78] If so, then the encouragement that Romanticism gave to the populist hermeneutic (which we will consider shortly) can be traced in part to Edwards.

The irony of this indirect influence on the populist hermeneutic is that Edwards was very critical of "Enthusiasts,"[79] itinerant evangelists without any official sanction who authenticated their message with subjective experiences.[80] Edwards, like the Reformers and Puritans before him, both criticized private interpretation of the Bible and indirectly contributed to the widespread acceptance of this practice in the nineteenth century.

The First Great Awakening and the Rise of the Populist Hermeneutic

Edwards' life and work was closely connected with what has been called the First Great Awakening, a series of semi-connected revivals that swept up and down the American colonies in the early to mid-1740s. The catalyst for these revivals were the preaching tours of the "Grand Itinerant," George Whitefield. These revivals significantly furthered the coming populist hermeneutic in several ways. Whitefield's tours prompted uneducated itinerant preachers to follow his example and (although lacking his education and skill) launch out into service for God. This surge of itinerancy, while causing untold controversy and division, also challenged the notion that the ordained clergy were God's only spokesmen in town, and set a pattern of commoner preaching that was influential in the Second Great Awakening and beyond.

76. Lowance, "Images or Shadows of Divine Things," 211, 238 suggests that nature may have served, for Edwards, as another source of revelation for the regenerate. Elsewhere, however, Edwards asserts that Christians should be wholly dependent on the Scriptures (Miscellany No. 535), as cited by Stein, "Quest for the Spiritual Sense," 105.

77. Jonathan Edwards, "Miscellany No. 362," as cited in Lowance, "Images or Shadows of Divine Things," 225.

78. Ibid., 243.

79. Stein, "Quest for the Spiritual Sense," 102.

80. Ibid., 102–3. Cf. Hatch, "*Sola Scriptura*," 62 for Edwards' reservations about the ability of the commoner to interpret the Bible.

The controversy stirred by the lay preachers set clergy against clergy in a bitter dispute[81] that created a vacuum of clerical leadership. In this vacuum, the laity found it necessary to "take responsibility for their religious lives to retain God's special favor for America." The result was the creation of new, more democratic religious movements, where the populist hermeneutic could thrive.[82]

The Revolution and Beyond

The American Revolution caused the older world of order and authority to collapse. In its place stood a self-confident people, armed with the newly-acquired vocabulary of freedom and passionate about the sovereignty of the common person.[83] In law, medicine, politics, economics, and religion, there was a crisis of authority as common people extended the arguments used against the British to question the rights of a small elite to overpower the rights of the many. Fiery blasts of anti-authoritarian rhetoric poured from the burgeoning popular press. Political groups organized, built on principles opposed to Federalism, which was the party of the elite. The conflict even erupted into violence as Daniel Shay led a rebellion of farmers against the urban elite in 1786–87.

It was during this period in America that the populist hermeneutic took definite shape and spread most widely. Men like John Leland and Lorenzo "Crazy" Dow denied the right of any one class of people to speak for another and defended the right of private judgment and individual conscience as the proper way to interpret the Bible.[84] These leaders were not so much anti-intellectual as they were anti-elite. It was the common sense of the people, not the classical education of a few, that was the sure route to truth. Consensus, more than theological coherence, was now the litmus test of right doctrine. From this time until after the Civil War the right of private interpretation of the Bible became one of the definitive characteristics of American Protestantism.

---

81. Within this debate, the Old Lights opposed the greater emphasis on the theology of the New Lights by asking why they may not go directly to the Bible to learn Christian theology, rather than asking the Assembly of the Divines (Hatch, "*Sola Scriptura*," 62), a question much to the liking of the supporters of the populist hermeneutic.

82. Stout, "Great Awakening."

83. Hatch, *Democratization*, 6.

84. Ibid., 14.

Reasons for the Dominance of the Populist Hermeneutic in Nineteenth-Century America

It is possible to identify four influences on nineteenth-century American Christianity that helped maintain the dominance of the populist hermeneutic during this time: the Second Great Awakening, the rise and dominance of Methodism, the philosophy of Scottish Common Sense Realism, and Romanticism. The Second Great Awakening was a series of revivals that extended over most of the United States and lasted from the end of the eighteenth century to around 1840. These revivals, characterized by a strongly plebeian flavor, were ideal climates for the populist hermeneutic. Both in the cultured East and the wild West, revivalists placed a greater emphasis on the ability of humans to respond to God than they had in the First Great Awakening. Such a populist hermeneutic was especially prominent in the frontier phases of the revivals which encouraged common preaching, appeals for immediate decision, and the presence of strong emotions.

Americans, recognizing the revivals as successful evangelistic tools, sought to reproduce them, populist hermeneutic and all. Finney, the leader of evangelical revivalism in the late 1820s, did not begin his preaching career as an ordained minister with formal theological training. His emphasis on human ability, egalitarian methods, and emotional religion helped to maintain the populist hermeneutic.[85]

The Second Great Awakening also delivered many members to the more democratic denominations, most especially the Methodists. They were already accustomed to Arminianism, emotionalism and lower ministerial standards, and possessed, in the itinerant system, a ready tool to corral and cultivate converts.

Earlier we demonstrated the possession and promotion of the populist hermeneutic within Methodism. We turn now to trace back the sources of this stream. These roots lead us back to John Wesley himself who believed that the Bible should be interpreted using reason, tradition and experience.[86] By reason, Wesley meant the ability of individuals to search out truth using logic. Not simply a rationalist, Wesley always maintained that true understanding required assistance from the Holy Spirit. In his commentary on the phrase, "All Scripture is inspired by God" (2 Timothy

---

85. Cf. Finney, *Lectures*, 248–49 for his defense of protracted meetings based on their past success.

86. An excellent treatment of Wesley's theological method is Thorsen's *Wesleyan Quadrilateral*.

3:16), Wesley spoke of the Spirit inspiring both the authors and those who read it in pursuit of God's wisdom.[87] Wesley also relied on tradition, the thoughts of great Christians in the past. As tradition represented the effect of God's work in earlier days, Wesley considered the experience of salvation to represent that effect on souls in his day.[88] This emphasis on experience is considered one of Wesley's more significant contributions to theology. Wesley's hermeneutic, emphasizing as it did human experience, human ability, and the ongoing work of the Spirit, left room for a more subjective interpretation of the Bible.

Wesley's subjectivity may be partly due to his contacts with Pietism.[89] His view of the Spirit as inspirer of both the original authors and present-day interpreters he owed to the work of seventeenth-century Pietists, such as Johann Jacob Rambach (1693–1735)[90] and Johann Albrecht Bengel (1687–1752). Wesley relied heavily on Bengel's *Gnomon* for his *Explanatory Notes* in part because of Bengel's blend of high quality scholarship, high regard for Scriptural authority, and practical use for the Bible.[91] Wesley transmitted these pietistic influences to American Methodism in a lasting way through his *Standard Sermons* and *Notes*, which served for years as the guides for biblical interpretation.[92]

---

87. Wesley, *Explanatory Notes*, 794.

88. Cf. Chiles, *Theological Transition*, 80.

89. Stoeffler, "Pietism," 191–95. Stoeffler considered the Moravians to have helped Wesley personalize the Anglican doctrines of salvation by faith alone and the Spirit's assurance of salvation. They were also one source for the doctrine that perfection could come instantaneously and as a gift from God. Cf. also the chapter on "Inner and Outer Word" in Brown, *Understanding Pietism*, 64–82.

90. Frei, *Eclipse*, 38.

91. Stoeffler, "Pietism," 198–201. Johann Albrecht Bengel (1687–1752), "one of the foremost religious scholars of the day," originated South German (Swabian) Pietism, and was "the one expositor of the Bible whose authority on biblical interpretation was well-nigh universally acknowledged by Continental Pietists" ("Pietism," 199). Wesley also consulted the Dissenter Philip Doddridge's *Family Expositor*, Calvinist John Guyse's *Practical Exposition of the New Testament*, and mystic and high-churchman John Heylin's *Theological Lectures at Westminster Abbey with an Interpretation of the Four Gospels*.

92. Of course, Methodists did not bring Pietism to America. Its influence had been felt here for more than a century, and had helped to shape the unique character of American Christianity with its emphases on personal piety, practicality, and an aversion to polemics. American Christianity had seen the merging of Pietist and Calvinist traditions, the blending of heart and intellect. According to Marsden, *Fundamentalism*, 44–45, pietistic sympathies could be found among "Old School" Presbyterians.

A Holiness Hermeneutic

The presence of pietism is one important reason why Methodism thrived in its new home and became one of the most dominant influences in American Christianity. Methodism arrived speaking the language of the heart, a language that pietism had made America's mother tongue. Thus, when Methodists spoke about experiential religion, the individual's relationship with God, and the role of the Spirit in interpretation, America listened and agreed.

The populist hermeneutic was also maintained by a pervasive emphasis on "common sense." The reigning philosophy of the day, Scottish Common Sense Realism, argued that the common person had the capacity, through the physical senses and an innate moral sense, to gain knowledge of the natural world and the moral universe. Designed to refute the skepticism of Hume and the idealism of Berkeley, it was widely embraced in nineteenth-century America where it gave philosophical support to this country's innate self-confidence.[93]

Common Sense Realism emphasized that basic truth is essentially the same for all persons of all times and places.[94] This meant that the Bible could best be understood through inductive study, using the same method proposed for the study of science by the seventeenth-century English philosopher Francis Bacon.[95] One should look carefully at the evidence to determine what Scripture actually said then classify these "facts" to determine its meaning. The goal of nineteenth-century American theologians was to make biblical interpretation a scientific exercise.[96]

A scientific interpretation of the Bible was needed because nineteenth-century American biblical scholarship found itself fighting on two fronts. From abroad they had to defend the Bible against the onslaughts of German rationalistic criticism while at home they faced common people demanding the right of private interpretation.[97] Because Common Sense philosophy was presented as anti-philosophy, it was used to oppose Germanic

---

93. Pointer, "Scottish Realism."

94. Marsden, *Fundamentalism*, 111.

95. Marsden, "Everyone One's Own Interpreter?", 93, offers as an example James W. Alexander (Alexander, "On the Use," 171–90). Alexander, son of one of the founders of Princeton Theological Seminary, Archibald Alexander, graduated from there in 1824, pastored, taught at Princeton University, and then taught church history at the Seminary from 1849–1851 before returning to the pastorate.

96. Ibid., 93.

97. Ibid., 94.

speculation. Because it represented the transparency of truth to any honest seeker, it was used to oppose the perceived anarchy of individualism.[98]

Moses Stuart of Andover Theological Seminary, the greatest American biblical scholar in the early part of the nineteenth century, was firmly committed to the Common Sense philosophy.[99] Because God wanted to reveal himself to humanity, and because the original recipients of the revelation were common people, the Bible must be clear enough for commoners to understand. Those passages difficult to understand should be interpreted by reading the obscure in light of the clear.[100] In a further bow to "Sola Scriptura," Stuart criticized creeds which have some didactic value, but can be overly confining and entangling. "Above all," he writes, "let Protestants beware how they speak of any other *standard* than that of God's holy word."[101]

However, Stuart's defense of the Bible's perspicuity was not unqualified; it came with warnings against overly subjective interpretation. He criticized those who took verses from their contexts and from the original author's intent. The Bible, he argued, must be understood in its original context and in its original language.[102]

While the Common Sense philosophy was used by some like Stuart to prevent private interpretations, it was also used by those who argued the opposite point. Like John Leland they could ask the rhetorical question, "Is not a simple man, who makes nature and reason his study, a competent judge of things?"[103] Common Sense Realism, popularly understood, filled nascent, unschooled theologians with self-confidence. So inspired, they lampooned carefully reasoned dogmas, such as predestination, as logically incomprehensible, to be dismissed with crude doggerel:

> You can and you can't,
> You will and you won't;
> You'll be damned if you do,
> And you'll be damned if you don't.[104]

---

98. Ibid., 82–83.

99. Ibid., 92.

100. Stuart, *Elements of Interpretation*, 17–18, as quoted in Brown, *Rise of Biblical Criticism*, 98.

101. Stuart, "Have the Sacred Writers," 99.

102. Ibid., 99–100.

103. Leland, *Rights of Conscience Inalienable*, 15–16, as quoted in Hatch, *Democratization*, 98.

104. Francis, *Old New York*, 147–49, as quoted in Hatch, *Democratization*, 130.

A Holiness Hermeneutic

This attack of "enlightened common sense" on Calvinism represented a revolt not simply against a theology that devalued human ability but against the perceived scholasticism of the educated elite and a preoccupation with theology.[105] Thus it was that the tool so highly valued by biblical scholars for attacking radical "proof-texting" individualists, was being used by these same radicals to deny the need for biblical scholars.

A fourth force which permitted the populist hermeneutic to survive until the Civil War was Romanticism. Transplanted from abroad, it was influential in American religion through the middle third of the 1800s.[106] Romanticism fostered the notion that truth could be intuitively perceived through one's feelings.[107] Common Sense Realism, said the Romantics, had overemphasized reason to the neglect of intuition. Each one had the God-given capacity to directly comprehend spiritual truth. There was thus a greater willingness to rely on subjective appeals to the heart, feelings, imagination, and emotions.[108] Such subjectivity bolstered the populist hermeneutic with its emphasis on the individual conscience as a means of perceiving God's truth. It appealed to pietistic America's aversion to dogma. The power to persuade became even more important than theological acumen, and common preaching thrived. Individualism, already prized by many Americans, became a national treasure, thanks in part to Romanticism. The American is not "dragged along, . . . by forces independent of himself," but moves "the machine entrusted to him by his Creator by his own free volitions."[109]

The populist hermeneutic that had been a characteristic of American Protestantism since the Revolution lost much of its prominence after

---

105. Hatch, *Democratization*, 173.

106. George Perkins considers American Romanticism to have been more than a simple imitation of European Romanticism. It was Romantic
> by virtue of the abounding strangeness of this new continent, and the experience of a way of life in which, for a time, it seemed that the theoretical possibility of uninterrupted human progress might be concretely realized. And then, slowly revealed, the tragic flaw in the American state came into view, the widening, unhealing breach between the sections—and the appalling catastrophe of the Civil War rang down the curtain on an epoch. (Perkins, "New Nation," 461)

107. McLoughlin, "Introduction," 14. Cf. Perkins, "New Nation," 463. According to Marsden, these views were both fostered by revivalism and helped shape an important manifestation of revivalism, the mid-nineteenth-century Holiness movement (Marsden, *Fundamentalism*, 227).

108. McLoughlin, "Introduction," 15–16.

109. Dixon, *Personal Narrative*, 182–84, as quoted in Review of *Personal Narrative*, 654.

the Civil War. Its collapse was due in part to inherent problems that had long been eroding its supports. Earlier it was supposed that the practice of everyone interpreting the Bible according to the dictates of his or her own conscience would lead to unity and harmony. In fact, it led to a multiplication of sects and divisions. Movements like the "Disciples of Christ," which began with a populist hermeneutic, grew into denominations which resisted such treatment of the Bible and promoted their own sectarian theology.

It would also appear that the more respectable a denomination became, the less support it gave to a populist hermeneutic and the more interested it became in a formally trained clergy. Baptists embarked upon this path late in the eighteenth century and, between 1830 and 1860, established over twenty colleges. Methodism, which founded thirty colleges in this same period, also traveled the path to respectability away from the earlier popular hermeneutic. They were prodded along by Nathan Bangs whose position as editor of several denominational papers allowed him to steer the denomination toward middle-class respectability.[110]

In addition to these internal factors, American Christianity suffered several shocks in the period from 1860 to 1900 which dampened enthusiasm for the populist hermeneutic. The most important of these shocks was the Civil War. As President Lincoln observed in his second Inaugural Address, the North condemned slavery using the Bible while the South used the same Bible to defend it. By Appomattox, Americans had to be suspicious of a hermeneutic that allowed both sides to encourage and defend such a bloody conflict.

The decades of struggle over slavery and the Civil War exhausted the churches and led to fear of further division. When controversy did arise, there was strong pressure to make peace. This probably contributed to the rapid acceptance of biblical criticism.

The populist hermeneutic, although more radical and anti-traditional in its early stages, had by this time become conservative and dependent on a traditional society. The "freedom" to seek out one's own path was actually done within carefully delineated boundaries. All private interpretations which emerged were judged against the standards of orthodoxy upon which Christianity agreed. Thus the Mormons, whose hermeneutic was quite similar to that of the democratic denominations, were forced out of respectable society for their unacceptable views.

---

110. Hatch, *Democratization*, 204.

A Holiness Hermeneutic

With modernization came the end of traditional society. Industrialization, urbanization, immigration, and the new intellectualism crashed like a giant wave on postbellum America. The carefully delineated boundaries and societal consensus were swept away. With it went the sense of homogeneity, familiarity, and Protestant hegemony, in short, the conditions that fostered the "individualization of conscience."

The element of the intellectual revolution that dealt the severest blow to the church was biblical criticism. European scholarship, especially that from Germany, had been influencing formal American biblical studies for more than a century. Prior to the Civil War, men like Moses Stuart and Edward Robinson would make some contribution to the field, but their work aroused little interest among their contemporaries. "In matters of religion," writes Brown, "Americans would rather depend on their pious hearts than upon scientific study."[111]

Up until the last third of the nineteenth century, there was a consensus that the Bible was the word of God and that it could be interpreted using common sense. This consensus eroded, thanks to the assured results of biblical criticism, until by 1900, many were not so sure.[112]

A resurgence of American interest in biblical criticism occurred in the decades following the Civil War. Scholarship raised questions about Genesis and the Pentateuch, the place of the miraculous, and the uniqueness of Judaism and Christianity. Some scholars, committed only to scientifically verifiable truth, found the questions intriguing and probed for answers. The information they discovered led more and more of them to question the authority and infallibility of the Bible. Others became troubled by the questions being raised and by the answers their colleagues proposed. The issues were debated in scholarly publications, in classrooms, and in denominational assemblies.

In 1879 C. H. Toy was forced out of his position as professor of Old Testament Interpretation at Southern Baptist Theological Seminary for teaching Wellhausenian and evolutionary views.[113] Charles A. Briggs, professor of Hebrew and Cognate Languages at Union Theological Seminary for many years, was charged with heresy in 1891. The basis for the charge arose from an address he delivered that year at his induction into Union's chair of biblical studies. In "The Authority of Holy Scripture," Briggs

---

111. Brown, *Rise of Biblical Criticism*, 169.
112. Noll, *Between Faith and Criticism*, 11.
113. Ibid., 27.

attacked such treasured doctrines as the infallibility and verbal inspiration of the Bible. The uproar resulted in Briggs and Union leaving the Presbyterian Church.[114]

The Methodists were also affected by the conflict. Hinckley G. Mitchell of the Boston University School of Theology was charged with heresy by the Bishops for questioning Mosaic authorship of the Pentateuch. Trial proceedings lasted from 1895 until 1905 with Mitchell eventually being removed from his position.[115] It would appear, however, that such heresy trials did not have the effect desired by their conservative opponents, but instead accelerated the embrace of the new ideas.[116]

The intellectual revolution, including the controversy over biblical criticism, made the late nineteenth century a very bewildering time. Some discarded the compass of a populist hermeneutic and hired a trained expert to guide them along unfamiliar paths. Others saw value in having both a compass and a guide. Still others, suspicious of the guides for hire, chose instead to bring along a trusted friend to help read the compass.

Those who left behind the compass hired guides well-versed in the new scientific approaches. Academics like Shailer Mathews fell in step with the presuppositions of the new views, and many others followed along. The Bible was carefully scrutinized and its doctrinal statements regarded simply as reflections of the culture of the biblical author and thus, not authoritative.[117]

Others continued to maintain confidence in the compass, the ability of each individual to interpret the Bible, but joined with it the need for biblical criticism as a trained guide. Such was the argument of Milton S. Terry, a Methodist scholar and author of *Biblical Hermeneutics* (1883).[118] "The professional interpreter of Scripture needs more than a well-balanced mind, discreet sense, and acuteness of intellect. He needs stores of information in the broad and varied fields of history, science and philosophy." Terry proceeded to inventory these "stores of information:" a knowledge of geography, politics, chronology, natural science, philosophy, the sacred tongues, and comparative philology. Perhaps with a nod

---

114. Marsden, *Fundamentalism*, 117; Longfield, "Briggs, Charles Augustus"; Noll, *Between Faith and Criticism*, 28–29.

115. Ibid., 28.

116. Wright, "Study of the Old Testament," 19.

117. Hudson, *Religion in America*, 257–59.

118. Tyson, "Terry, Milton Spenser."

A Holiness Hermeneutic

to his circuit-riding progenitors, Terry conceded that some have been able expositors without these; nevertheless, they are now indispensable to maintain and defend against skepticism. Yet Terry insisted that more than education was required to properly interpret the Bible. One must also possess spiritual qualifications, including a desire to know the truth, a love and enthusiasm for it, and a "living fellowship and communion with the Holy Spirit."[119]

Some chose to continue to trust the compass of the popular hermeneutic. The most prominent such group, fundamentalism, represented an uneasy coalition of theological and social conservatives as diverse as B. B. Warfield of Princeton Seminary and the former shoe salesman turned evangelist, Dwight L. Moody. Fundamentalists appealed to the traditional evangelical faith which had characterized American Christianity throughout the nineteenth century. They accused the higher critics of operating with anti-supernatural, historicist presuppositions. Worse still, they felt the critics had removed the Bible from the common reader and placed it into the hands of the scholars.

Fundamentalism maintained that it was common sense rather than scholarship that was needed to understand the Bible. Moody counseled his followers to avoid arguing with those who do not believe the Bible since convincing them is the Spirit's job. The task of the true believer is to "give them the Word of God; not to preach our theories and our ideas about it, but just to deliver the message as God gives it to us."[120]

Many fundamentalists came, in time, to be closely associated with Dispensationalism.[121] Growing out of the work of the Plymouth Brethren clergyman, John Nelson Darby (1800–82), dispensationalism taught that history was divided into periods of time, each characterized by a different way God chose to offer salvation. The Bible, especially prophecy, was interpreted in strictly literal fashion. This view gained popularity in the United States through the prophecy conferences of the 1880s and 90s and through C. I. Scofield's annotations of the Bible (1909).[122]

Dispensationalism appealed to fundamentalists, in part, because both understood truth as static. While other interpretive methods might

---

119. Terry, *Biblical Hermeneutics*, 154–57.

120. Moody, *Secret Power*, 37.

121. Dispensationalism is discussed in Sandeen, *Roots of Fundamentalism*, and Weber, *Living in the Shadow of the Second Coming*.

122. Noll, *Between Faith and Criticism*, 57–58.

be complicated and hard-to-understand, the fundamentalists considered theirs to be simple and easily accessible through common sense.[123] Based on Common Sense Realism and Baconian science, the authority of the Bible was located in its scientific verifiability. This was one reason why inerrancy became so important to fundamentalism, because it guaranteed the scientific accuracy of the Bible.

The blending of fundamentalism and dispensationalism suggests that fundamentalists were not entirely content to follow only the compass of private interpretation. Timothy Weber observes that fundamentalist leaders assured believers that scholarly assistance was unnecessary, but then initiated their followers into an interpretative approach that was very difficult to follow without help like that provided by the notes in the Scofield Reference Bible.[124] Fundamentalism continued to assert that private interpretation was the compass by which anyone could find the true paths, but dispensationalism was the trusted friend they brought along to help read the compass.

Others who continued to maintain the priority of private interpretation were the American Holiness movement and its younger cousin, Pentecostalism. Both were conservative in theology, like fundamentalism, although they lacked the scholastic element that fundamentalism received from its Princeton Seminary connection. The populist hermeneutic embraced by the Holiness movement and Pentecostalism also differed in that it was based on a more subjective authority, that of spiritual experience. The commoner was the one who was best qualified to read, understand and proclaim the Bible, but not simply because he or she had common sense and the Bible was perspicuous. Rather it was the experience of entire sanctification—the "Baptism of the Spirit" which occurred subsequent to regeneration—which truly opened the eyes of the believer to behold wonderful things in the word of God. In these movements, the Spirit (and sanctified preachers) acted as trusted friends who come alongside to help read the compass.

Phineas Bresee, who left the Methodists to begin the Church of the Nazarene in 1895, expressed it this way:

> In this baptism the Holy Spirit becomes also a revealer of the Word of God. The Holy Ghost is the Great Teacher. Under the light of His fire the Word yields up its mysteries. By His presence, the

---

123. Marsden, *Fundamentalism*, 61.
124. Weber, "Two-Edged Sword," 113–14.

veil is taken away, and we are initiated into the blessed mysteries of redemption. To eyes not anointed, the Bible is largely a sealed book.[125]

We will return in future chapters to examine holiness biblical interpretation more closely. First we must describe its origin and development in America.

---

125. Bresee, "Baptism with the Holy Ghost," 334–35.

3

The History of the American Holiness Movement

WILLIAM G. MCLOUGHLIN IDENTIFIES three stages in the development of the American Holiness movement.[1] It began in the early nineteenth century as a pietistic effort to preserve the Wesleyan doctrine of entire sanctification within Methodism. When this effort met with resistance later in that century, holiness advocates were forced to make the difficult choice between toned-down perfectionism and schism. Many chose the latter, marking the second stage of development. The movement entered the third stage as it became institutionalized in the early twentieth century and denominations sought to preserve their gains through organization and administration.

Wesley and Early Methodism

The story of the American Holiness movement begins, not in America, but in England, with the Anglican cleric and founder of Methodism, John Wesley (1703–91). Wesley's ministry was devoted to describing and defending humanity's ability to do good and avoid evil by grace and the power of God's Holy Spirit. He called people to lead new lives, pressing on toward the goal of perfect love. He structured Methodism to foster this spirituality through class meetings, lay ministry, and other means. Wesley's theology centered on God's grace, while his ethic centered on love. God has

---

1. McLoughlin, "Introduction," xvii–xix. McLoughlin acknowledges his debt to Ernst Troeltsch, who most ably described the development from sect to church.

mercifully extended prevenient grace to every person, not only an elect few. This grace restored the freedom that humanity had lost in Adam's sin and permitted love for God and one's neighbor.

Once the Christian was converted by God, Wesley considered his or her potential to love to be almost limitless. The significance given to human ability is evident in Wesley's theological method, the Wesleyan quadrilateral. With the assistance of the Holy Spirit, the Christian is able to understand the Bible by relying on his or her own experience, the experiences of believers in other ages (tradition), and human logic or reason.

Wesley challenged Christians to go beyond conversion to be perfected in Christ, one of the most distinctive aspects of his theology.[2] In sanctification, God restored the defaced image of creation. Even though Wesley described this experience as Christian perfection, he was not referring to sinless perfection, but to perfect love for God and humanity. "Entire sanctification, or Christian perfection, is neither more nor less than pure love; love expelling sin, and governing both the heart and life of a child of God. The Refiner's fire purges out all that is contrary to love."[3] Whether such an experience would be early in the Christian's walk with God or toward the end, whether it was accomplished instantaneously, gradually, or by some synthesis of the two, and the method by which this grace would be bestowed, these were questions about which Wesley remained ambiguous.[4]

Wesley drew from several sources in the development of this doctrine. He was dependent on Pietism, with its quest for perfection and the confidence that such could be attained. He shared an Enlightenment-era confidence in the ability and potential of humanity. That it was an optimism of grace, not an optimism of nature, preserved it from Pelagianism.

Given the elevated place of tradition in his theological method, it is not surprising that Wesley drew something of his doctrine of Christian

---

2. A fine treatment of the development and scope of Wesley's doctrine of sanctification can be found in Peters, *Christian Perfection*.

3. Wesley, "Letter to Mr. Walter," 432.

4. Peters, *Christian Perfection*, 31, 48, 57. Discussion continues among Wesleyan scholars about these issues. Charles Edwin Jones and others argue that Wesley did not emphasize the instantaneous reception of sanctification, but rather the seeking of it (Jones, *Perfectionist Persuasion*, 4; cf. Dieter, *Holiness Revival*, 31). Timothy L. Smith asserts that Wesley did emphasize the crisis while never completely eliminating the possibility of growth toward it ("Holiness Crusade," 608–27). According to Peters, Wesley's early years saw an emphasis on the process of sanctification. In time, he became more convinced of its reception in an instant, coming finally to see it as a synthesis of process and crisis.

perfection from the early church fathers, especially from the East, among the most influential being Gregory of Nyssa.[5] Wesley found in the writings of Gregory and others a perfection prepared for by discipline and devotion, and set out as the goal of the Christian life.[6]

According to Peters, the search for holiness was a common theme in the religious literature of Wesley's day. Of this literature, three authors of devotional works particularly influenced Wesley: Jeremy Taylor, Thomas à Kempis, and William Law. Two works of the latter, *Treatise on Christian Perfection* and *Serious Call to a Devout and Holy Life*, were very influential on Wesley.[7] Wesley also placed great weight on what he could observe of the experiences of Christians. For this reason, the revivals he witnessed from 1759 to 1763 convinced him of the possibility of perfection and its attainability in an instant.[8]

Wesley's most important interpreter was his chosen successor, John Fletcher, in whose hands Wesley's doctrine of Christian perfection underwent some crucial adjustments. Fletcher viewed history as divided into dispensations; the present period being characterized by the ministry of the Holy Spirit. To Wesley's disapproval, Fletcher spoke of entire sanctification as a baptism of the Holy Spirit and a personal Pentecost experience.[9]

The Holiness Revival Comes to America

Methodism, transplanted to America prior to the American Revolution, grew rapidly in the years following the War. These early years, while witnessing staggering growth, also saw a decrease in the emphasis on holiness

---

5. Recent scholarship has demonstrated that the writings Wesley attributed to Macarius the Egyptian were, in fact, the work of Symeon of Mesopotamia, whose views were heavily influenced by Gregory of Nyssa. Cf. Outler, "Introduction," 9–10. Cf. "Macarius the Egyptian."

6. Outler, "Introduction," 9n26, 10.

7. Peters, *Christian Perfection*, 19.

8. Ibid., 30–31.

9. Cf. Letter by John Fletcher to Mary Bosanquet, 7 March 1778, reprinted in Tyerman, *Wesley's Designated Successor*, 411, as cited by Dayton, *Theological Roots of Pentecostalism*, 50. Here, too, there is some disagreement about whether Wesley was more Christocentric or Pneumatocentric. Timothy L. Smith contends that Wesley did not object to Fletcher's pneumatocentricism ("How John Fletcher," 68–87). Dayton points to the writings of the two men to reveal their disagreement over this matter (*Theological Roots of Pentecostalism*, 51–54).

A Holiness Hermeneutic

among Methodists, primarily for two reasons. Methodist preachers were compelled to emphasize evangelism rather than sanctification, since they were addressing largely unconverted crowds.[10] Secondly, Wesley's tracts, including his comments on Christian perfection, were removed from the 1812 *Discipline*. Although they were to be published separately, this was not done until 1832, sharply curtailing circulation of Wesley's views on the subject. When reprinted, these tracts occupied a less authoritative status than previously.[11]

The beginning of the renewed emphasis on the doctrine of entire sanctification can be traced to Timothy Merritt, a Methodist Episcopal pastor from New England. In 1825, he published *The Christian's Manual; a Treatise on Christian Perfection*,[12] and continued to emphasize the doctrine with the founding and editing of the monthly periodical, *Guide to Christian Perfection* in 1839.[13]

Wesley's writings reveal his understanding of sanctification as being the result of both crisis and process. Throughout this period, however, there was a growing tendency to see sanctification as the product of an instantaneous crisis, rather than a long process, as evidenced by the writings of Merritt. Also contributing to this trend was the work of Adam Clarke, whose commentary on the Bible was a standard resource for Methodist ministers throughout much of the nineteenth century. "We are to come to God as well for an instantaneous and complete purification from all sin, as for an instantaneous pardon." Clarke reasoned that just as the field does not produce its proper crop until the thorns and thistles are removed, so the soul cannot produce a crop of righteousness until entire sanctification does its instantaneous work of cleansing.[14]

The emphasis on the instantaneous nature of sanctification was also shaped by the American revivalist milieu. Evangelists were calling sinners to a present salvation; it was only a small step further to speak of a present sanctification, one available in an instant.

The most important revivalist of his time, and another very important figure in the resurgence of the holiness message was Charles G. Finney. Although he began with the revitalized Calvinistic ethic of Samuel Hopkins

---

10. Dunlap, "Tuesday Meetings," 85.
11. Peters, *Christian Perfection*, 98.
12. Ibid., 101.
13. Dieter, *Holiness Revival*, 3.
14. Clarke, *Christian Theology*, 208.

rather than the Anglican moralism and pietism lying behind Wesley's doctrine, the end result—Oberlin Perfectionism—was similar to Wesleyan perfectionism.[15] The non-Methodist origins and context of Oberlin Perfectionism created a bridge whereby Christians of other denominations could understand and adopt the Methodist doctrine of entire sanctification. Finney's revivalism not only furthered acceptance of sanctification as a crisis, but also provided new methods for its promotion.[16]

A major figure behind the mid-nineteenth century revival of holiness in America was the Methodist lay woman, Phoebe Palmer.[17] Personal tragedy and the influence of her sister, Sarah Lankford, led Palmer into a period of soul-searching which culminated, on July 26, 1837, in an experience of entire sanctification.[18] Three years later she took over the leadership of the Tuesday Meeting for the Promotion of Holiness which Sarah had begun in 1835. For the next several decades, Methodist pastors and lay people learned of God's sanctifying power at these meetings in the Palmer's home in New York City.[19] Methodist leaders like Nathan Bangs and George Peck, Bishops Edmund S. Janes and Leonidas L. Hamline, and educators Stephen Olin, Willbur Fisk and John Dempster were among the Palmer's friends and supporters.[20] The presence of non-Methodists helped to cultivate an interdenominational air about the growing holiness revival.[21]

Phoebe Palmer's influence extended well beyond the walls of her parlor. She and her husband, Walter, purchased Merritt's *Guide to Christian Perfection* and merged it with another holiness paper into the *Guide to Holiness*, Phoebe serving as editor. Circulation grew to 37,000 in 1870, a figure higher than probably 90 percent of all magazines published in the United States at that time.[22] This periodical, brimming with testimonies of

---

15. Smith, "Doctrine of the Sanctifying Spirit," 92, 104. Finney's version is often referred to as Oberlin Perfectionism because it was developed while at Oberlin College and in collaboration with Asa Mahan, Oberlin's first president.

16. Dieter, *Holiness Revival*, 22.

17. White provides a thorough study of Phoebe Palmer in *The Beauty of Holiness*.

18. White, *Beauty*, 9, 22.

19. Peters, *Christian Perfection*, 111.

20. Smith, "Holiness Crusade," 610. Olin and Fiske were the former and current president of Wesleyan University, respectively, while Dempster founded Concord and Garrett Seminaries (Dieter, *Holiness Revival*, 37).

21. Ibid., 38.

22. White, *Beauty*, 92–94.

entire sanctification, served as a bond which helped to unite the revival.[23] Palmer's pen also produced more than fifteen popular books on the topic of holiness.

Many requests for speaking engagements came to Walter and Phoebe Palmer. By 1850, they were spending half the year at Methodist revivals and camp meetings in the United States and Canada. From 1859 to 1863 they traveled and spoke in England and Europe.[24]

Promoted in her Tuesday Meetings, in her writings, and in their public appearances, was her "altar" theology. She taught that Christ is not only the sacrifice for sin, but also the altar on which Christians must offer themselves to him. By presenting oneself on that altar in an act of total consecration, the altar sanctifies the gift. Struggle and long delay was unnecessary. If God wanted his people to be sanctified, which he surely did, one need only take this "shorter way" and claim it by faith.[25] Sanctification, given by God's grace in response to one's consecration by faith, would issue in freedom from all inclinations not springing from love. To maintain the experience required a continuing measure of faith, obedience and testimony.[26]

The most dominant influences on Palmer's thinking were the writings and example of John Wesley.[27] Like him, Palmer made the Christian life her main concern, especially the life of holiness. In his writings, Palmer found numerous calls to press on to perfection, take it by faith, and testify to the same.

Her theological method was similar to Wesley's, with some modification. Like the "man of one book," Palmer wanted to be known more than anything as a "Bible Christian."[28] Palmer place a greater emphasis on experience and broadened it to include impressions received from God.[29] She also understood reason as common sense, and extended tradition to include early Methodists like Hester Rogers.

---

23. Dieter, *Holiness Revival*, 35–36, 48; Jones, *Perfectionist Persuasion*, 3.

24. Smith, *Revivalism*, 123–24.

25. White, *Beauty*, 129–30.

26. An excellent summary of "altar" theology can be found in Dieter, *Holiness Revival*, 27–28.

27. Palmer's father had been converted under Wesley's ministry (White, *Beauty*, 9). White also includes a very helpful comparison of the thought of Phoebe Palmer and John Wesley (ibid., 106).

28. Dieter, *Holiness Revival*, 44.

29. White, *Beauty*, 111–12.

While claiming to carry on the message of Wesley, Palmer clearly carried it beyond Wesley. Her emphasis on the need to testify or lose the experience cannot be found in him. Wesley saw sanctification as important and occurring at a point later in the life of the Christian, but Palmer's "shorter way" made the crisis crucial and necessary at the beginning of the Christian life. Wesley produced a generation of seekers after holiness, Palmer produced holiness professors. Those who followed Wesley focused on how to seek for holiness; Palmer's followers focused on how to live the holy life.[30]

Some of Palmer's modifications of Wesley were derived from two of Wesley's interpreters, John Fletcher and Adam Clarke. From Fletcher she took the understanding of entire sanctification in pneumatocentric terms.[31] Clarke's influence can be seen in her emphasis on sanctification as a crisis that can and should occur early in the life of the Christian and according to a certain method. It was also from Clarke that Palmer gained the connection between holiness and power.[32]

Palmer's theology also shows the influence of the American milieu. Shades of the Puritan covenant are evidenced in her assertion that the altar sanctifies each gift.[33] Oberlin perfectionism contributed the emphasis that God enables instantaneous submission to his will.[34] Pietistic revivalism not only contributed the methods by which Palmer's teaching was spread, but also the emphases on immediacy and experience, the universal invitation, and the view of grace as dynamic.[35]

Also influencing Palmer's altar theology was her own experience of sanctification. Because she and her sister were both sanctified in a definite crisis, she was encouraged to think that the experiences of others could and indeed should be just as definite.[36]

Permitting Palmer's ministry as well as influencing it was the populist hermeneutic described in the previous chapter. Without this it is doubtful that the writing and speaking of a lay woman and the testimonies of countless lay people would ever have been heard.

---

30. Jones, *Perfectionist Persuasion*, 4.
31. White, *Beauty*, 120.
32. Ibid., 120. Peters, *Christian Perfection*, 106.
33. Jones, *Perfectionist Persuasion*, 5.
34. White, *Beauty*, 124–25.
35. Dieter, *Holiness Revival*, 19–20.
36. White, *Beauty*, 23.

Palmer's altar theology aroused opposition, even from her supporters. She was accused of blurring the distinction between entire sanctification as an encounter with the Holy Spirit (as Wesley taught it) and as the exercise of faith in the word of God.[37] Even Bangs challenged her to consider whether the presence of perfection should not be determined by the flowering of the fruit of the Spirit, rather than on the basis of "naked faith."[38] She replied that procrastinating seekers needed her theology to prod them on toward full consecration.[39]

It would be difficult to overestimate Palmer's influence on the later Holiness movement. Her Tuesday Meeting set the pattern, not only for other such meetings, but for later holiness bands and camp meetings as well.[40] Her editing and writing, in addition to explaining the doctrine of entire sanctification, promoted a non-theological, anecdotal, experiential style for expressing it. Her life and ministry encouraged the involvement of lay people, and especially women in the work of the church.[41] Due in no small measure to her influence on Methodist Bishops and leaders, holiness remained an important element in official Methodism into the twentieth century.

Palmer's altar theology was as influential as its creator. It was taken up and institutionalized by the National Camp Meeting Association for the Promotion of Holiness organized in 1867.[42] Denominations that later formed with holiness as their watchword took Mrs. Palmer's theology as their own. The Pentecostal movement adopted her theology as they found it in the holiness denominations, added the doctrine of glossolalia, and proclaimed it with vigor.[43]

---

37. Ibid., 141. Langford, *Practical Divinity*, 94.

38. Smith, "Holiness Crusade," 611. Bangs could still pronounce her teaching orthodox and Wesleyan (Dieter, *Holiness Revival*, 30).

39. Smith, "Foreword," xii.

40. Jones, *Perfectionist Persuasion*, 49.

41. Two women whose lives were influenced by Palmer and who proceeded to accomplish a great deal in Victorian society were temperance leader Frances Willard, and the co-founder of the Salvation Army, Catherine Booth. A third woman touched by Palmer's ministry exerted great influence, but indirectly. Methodist pastor's wife Martha Inskip was sanctified during a Palmer meeting at Sing Sing, New York in 1864. Her husband, John, found the experience only a short while later, and went on to be one of the founders and first president of the National Camp Meeting Association for the Promotion of Holiness (Dieter, *Holiness Revival*, 41–44. Jones, *Perfectionist Persuasion*, 100).

42. White, *Beauty*, 157–58.

43. Ibid., 157–58.

The doctrine of Christian perfection, in terms of its cultural impact and widespread support, reached its zenith in the mid-nineteenth century. It was instrumental in fostering the urban revivals of 1857 and 1858 where huge mid-day prayer meetings sprang up in cities around the country. Methodists embraced their "peculiar doctrine," but were joined by other denominations also. Presbyterian William E. Boardman wrote about the *Higher Christian Life* in 1858, while A. B. Earle, a prominent Baptist, sought to lead people into *The Rest of Faith* (1859) he had discovered.

Several factors converged to bring about this high-water mark for holiness. Revivalism rode the crest of a wave across almost all denominations. Entire sanctification was added to the call for conversion as the logical next step. Pietism, an important element of this revivalism, prepared the way with its emphasis on perfection as the goal of Christian maturity.[44]

Timothy Smith also attributes the rise of the holiness message to the optimism, idealism, and moral seriousness of this period, evident in the perfectionistic tendencies of Romanticism and Transcendentalism. Entire sanctification, says Smith, offers to the common person the ethical ideals to which Emerson aspired on a more sophisticated level. Perfectionist teaching also appealed because it was practical and produced results, qualities admired by American Christians who wanted a faith that did something.[45]

Social Ministries of the Holiness Revival

Evangelicals with holiness convictions were very active in social reforms in ante-bellum America. Wesley had taught that Christian perfection issued in perfect love and active involvement in the betterment of one's world. Those who carried the message of perfection sought to express that love for all, even to produce a perfect society, if possible.

Finney was an important influence which helped to steer the movement in this direction. There could be no revival, he wrote in his *Lectures on Revivals of Religion*, unless people worked for social reforms like temperance and abolition.[46] Both as revivalist and educator, Finney put holiness to practical effect.

Holiness advocates were actively engaged on behalf of the poor. Crusades against alcohol and prostitution characterized efforts to remove

---

44. Dieter, *Holiness Revival*, 14.
45. Smith, "Holiness Crusade," 610.
46. Finney, *Lectures*, 272.

poverty's causes. The Five Points Mission in New York City, co-founded by Phoebe Palmer, pioneered efforts to restore the poor to self-sufficiency by providing housing, jobs, food, clothing, and schooling.[47] One holiness denomination was founded, in part, as a protest against pew rental, a practice felt to exclude the poor from Methodism.[48]

There was also a strong abolitionist sentiment among holiness adherents. Slavery was antithetical to their true freedom in Christ and their understanding of holiness as perfect love. Furthermore, those who had experienced entire sanctification through complete consecration to God threw themselves into abolitionism with the same absolutist mindset.[49]

An example of such radical abolitionism can be found in the Wesleyan Methodist Connection, organized in 1843, primarily in opposition to Methodism's ambivalence on the slavery question. Led by Orange Scott, an abolitionist Methodist Episcopal pastor from New England, the new denomination promoted its radical sentiments in print and in person, even sending missionaries into the slave-holding states. Wesleyan Methodists were also clearly committed to Christian perfection, becoming the first denomination to adopt an article of faith on entire sanctification.[50] There could be no separation, they maintained, between piety and radicalism, for only by their holiness could their radical goals be achieved.[51]

Recent scholarship has demonstrated that it was the antebellum holiness revival, more than any other branch of Christianity, that elevated feminism to a matter of principle.[52] Here again, considerable credit must go to Finney whose most controversial New Measure was to permit women to pray and speak in public. Feminism was also fostered by the holiness revival's commitment to abolitionism. The same scriptures that blasted slavery, promoted egalitarianism, and breathed courage into the souls of the reformers were easily adapted for use by the early feminists.[53] They could also point to early Methodists for support. Wesley had appointed women

---

47. Smith, *Revivalism*, 170–71.

48. The Free Methodist Church was begun in 1860 to proclaim holiness and share the gospel with the poor. For this reason, all the pews in their churches would be free of charge. Cf. Dayton, *Discovering*, 102 from an early Discipline of the Free Methodist Church.

49. Dieter, *Holiness Revival*, 24–25.

50. Ibid., 25.

51. Dayton, *Discovering*, 79; Dieter, *Holiness Revival*, 70–71 n38.

52. Dayton and Dayton, "Your Daughters Shall Prophesy," 67.

53. Dayton, *Discovering*, 88.

as class leaders and lay preachers, while Adam Clarke's influential commentary defended the right of women to minister.[54]

Although she might have balked at the label "feminist," Phoebe Palmer's writings and example helped to promote the equality of the sexes. In *Promise of the Father* (1859), she built her defense for the ministry of women on Acts 2:17–18 as the fulfillment of Joel 2:28–29 which predicts that women as well as men will be filled with the Holy Spirit and prophesy. Anticipating her critics, Palmer explained that Paul's prohibitions of the public ministry of women were entirely cultural and no longer binding on the church today, especially on the church liberated by the sanctifying Spirit.[55]

Feminism flourished in the antebellum holiness revival for several reasons. Its theology, centered on experience and emphasizing the Holy Spirit, permitted a greater measure of freedom and equality than did the more traditional, doctrinally-oriented theologies. A theology which emphasized perfection was itself a criticism of the status quo and a platform from which further critiques could flow, such as those offered by feminism.[56]

The Antebellum Holiness Revival's Transatlantic Connections

The call of the American holiness revival to christianize Christianity was heard across the Atlantic and left an impression on Protestant evangelicalism in Europe and England. One of the first of the holiness evangelists to travel from the United States to Britain, and certainly one of the most successful, was James Caughey. Born in Ireland in 1810, Caughey grew up in New York State where he came under the influence of Finney. In 1845 he began a successful career as a Methodist evangelist in America and England, reinvigorating established churches and preaching sanctification to British Methodists. His crowds were large and his popularity widespread but so was the controversy that surrounded him, eventually causing him to be barred from preaching in Methodist Churches in England.[57]

---

54. Hardesty et al., "Women in the Holiness Movement," 227–29; Dayton and Dayton, "Your Daughters Shall Prophesy," 70; Clarke, *Holy Bible*, 279.

55. Dayton and Dayton, "Your Daughters Shall Prophesy," 73; Dayton, *Discovering*, 96; Hardesty et al., "Women in the Holiness Movement," 233.

56. Ibid., 242–47.

57. Carwardine, *Transatlantic Revivalism*, 107–33.

The message of Finney was also heard in Great Britain although it came first in print and only later in person. Distribution of Finney's *Lectures on Revivals of Religion* led to revivals in Wales in the 1840s.[58] When Finney finally visited England from 1849 to 1851, his success was primarily among middle-class moderate Calvinists in England. He returned in 1859 to meet with somewhat fewer triumphs.[59]

Walter and Phoebe Palmer arrived that same year to minister in the British Isles and enjoyed considerable success.[60] As with Caughey, the message and methods of the Palmers stirred up no little controversy. Official Methodism was offended by attacks on the use of alcohol and on the formalism of the church. Some objected to having a woman in the pulpit.[61] The Palmers were also banned from conducting revivals among Methodists in England and returned home in 1863. They came back to a nation weary of war and to a holiness revival that was about to enter into a new phase.

1867–1879: Holiness Organization

Slowed by the Civil War, the holiness revival gained momentum in the years following. Small meetings held in urban areas of the Northeast fueled the growing sentiment that a special means was needed for the organized and widespread promotion of sanctification. For decades, the church had known the value of the camp meeting for providing fellowship, spiritual renewal, and evangelism. Now the novel idea was conceived to use the camp meeting as the chief means to promote holiness.[62]

John S. Inskip, a leading Methodist Episcopal pastor in New York City who was greatly influenced by Phoebe Palmer, led the way in this new phase of the holiness revival. He and other Methodists determined that a "National Camp Meeting for the Promotion of Holiness" would be held in Vineland, New Jersey from July 17 to July 26, 1867. Vineland was chosen for its easy rail access from other major Eastern cities and because it was the seat of Vineland Seminary, the center of Methodist activity in Southern

---

58. White, *Beauty*, 68.

59. Carwardine, *Transatlantic Revivalism*, 134–81.

60. White, *Beauty*, 50; Carwardine, *Transatlantic Revivalism*, 182–97, especially 185.

61. Hardesty et al., "Women in the Holiness Movement," 233. It was a pamphlet written to attack Mrs. Palmer's presence in the pulpit that prompted Catherine Booth, later co-founder of the Salvation Army, to reply with *Female Ministry*.

62. Dieter, *Holiness Revival*, 99, 104.

New Jersey. It was laid out as a model town with a forty-acre park, and both the village and surrounding townships had ordinances banning the sale of liquor.[63] The ten- day meeting occasioned sermons and exhortations on holiness by twenty-six speakers, mostly Northern Methodists, and even Bishop Matthew Simpson. The meeting drew 10,000 people, mostly urban, middle class Methodists who could afford a vacation in the country.[64]

The tremendous success at Vineland led to the formation of the National Camp Meeting Association for the Promotion of Holiness.[65] Another National Camp Meeting was planned for the next year, 1868, to be held in Manheim, Lancaster County, Pennsylvania. This meeting attracted enormous crowds and influenced many denominations, including two Pennsylvania German groups, the Evangelical Association and Mennonites. The leaders of the meeting, sensitive to the criticism that they were opening the door to schism, decided to confine their efforts to regular Methodist camp meeting grounds by invitation of local camp meeting administrators.[66]

By the 1870s, the holiness revival had become a nationally organized movement, popular with a large segment of Methodism, including many of the denomination's leaders.[67] The National Camp Meeting Association was a recognized institution in the church, while a popular religious press was effectively spreading the holiness message.

This message clearly showed the influence of Phoebe Palmer's theology with its emphasis on crisis over process, on assurance and promotion over seeking, and intolerance of other methods. It also demonstrated Pentecostal imagery. This placed even greater emphasis on the crisis, assurance, and evidence of sanctification, as well as focusing attention on the pneumatic themes of power, gifts, and prophecy.[68]

There were some who were reluctant to accept the Holiness movement. Southern Methodists remembered that some of the same Bishops who were now promoting holiness had been responsible for placing Northern Methodist pastors in Southern Methodist churches in the wake of Union victories during the War. Several prominent Methodists objected to

---

63. Jones, *Perfectionist Persuasion*, 19; Dieter, *Holiness Revival*, 106.
64. Jones, *Perfectionist Persuasion*, 19.
65. Dieter, *Holiness Revival*, 106.
66. Ibid., 108.
67. 1872 saw the election of five of eight new bishops in Northern Methodism who were supporters of holiness (Jones, *Perfectionist Persuasion*, 15).
68. Dayton, "Asa Mahan," 64–65.

the methods of the movement. Ironically, among the methods questioned was the role of the itinerant holiness evangelist, who came in for the same criticisms that were directed by the established churches at the early Methodist circuit riders decades earlier.[69]

The International Holiness Movement

After the War, the holiness revival spread from America to many other parts of the globe. The German church, at all levels of society, was influenced by the holiness message of Robert Pearsall Smith.[70] In 1880, several evangelists from the National Camp Meeting Association for the Promotion of Holiness met with good success in their travels to Great Britain, India, and Australia.[71]

The Holiness movement in England took a distinctive turn in what came to be known as the Keswick movement. Gaining a foothold primarily among Low Church Anglicans, it was similar in many respects to the American Holiness movement, the chief differences arising from its more Calvinistic orientation.[72]

Social Dimensions of the Postbellum Holiness Movement

After the Civil War removed the need for abolitionism, the Holiness movement continued to work on behalf of the newly freed African-Americans, the urban poor and the rights of women, spurred on by their belief in the perfectability of humanity through the power of God's grace.[73] Denominations like the Christian and Missionary Alliance and the Salvation Army were formed specifically to reach the poor with the gospel.[74] Rescue

---

69. Peters, *Christian Perfection*, 145.

70. Dieter, *Holiness Revival*, 156–203 has a very fine overview of the European and English dimensions of the Holiness revival and Smith's part in it.

71. Jones, *Perfectionist Persuasion*, 23.

72. Dieter, *Holiness Revival*, 156–69, 174–89; Thompson, "Appraisal," 12–14; Cf. Marsden, *Fundamentalism*, 77.

73. Smith, "Holiness Crusade," 618.

74. Dayton, *Discovering*, 113, 117–19.

missions and homes for "fallen women" operated outside denominational boundaries to serve the poor.[75]

The best-known instance of the Holiness movement's support of women's rights during the late nineteenth century is the Salvation Army.[76] There were other examples as well, such as Amanda Smith, an African-American evangelist with an international itinerant evangelistic ministry, and Alma White, who served as the self-proclaimed Bishop of the Pillar of Fire church, a small holiness denomination in New Jersey. Large numbers of women were ordained and installed as pastors in the Church of God, Anderson, the Church of the Nazarene, and the Pilgrim Holiness Church.[77] By the early twentieth century, feminism's strong support within the Holiness movement began to fade, due in part to concerns for respectability and the association of the movement with fundamentalism.[78]

1880-1900: Conflict and Division

In the last two decades of the nineteenth century, the conflict between Methodism and the holiness adherents worsened. While still supporting the doctrine of sanctification, even advocating its value in countering the rise of liberalism, denominational officials were becoming more suspicious of the methods employed.[79] There was growing criticism of the doctrine as it was being proclaimed at the camp meetings, with its emphasis on crisis, and on claiming the experience by faith. Some Methodists even criticized Wesley and the very idea of entire sanctification.[80]

Fueling the fires of conflict was the rising level of Methodist respectability. Methodists had become solidly middle-class; not a few were rich. Increasingly the trend was toward more elaborate churches, formal worship, and seminary-educated clergy.[81] This sophisticated, citified Methodism left little room for the ruralism of the camp meeting with its emotionalism, strict external standards, and exclusiveness.

---

75. Dayton, *Discovering*, 116.
76. Ibid., 94–95.
77. Hardesty et al., "Women in the Holiness Movement," 236–41.
78. Dayton and Dayton, "'Your Daughters Shall Prophesy,'" 91–92; Hardesty et al., "Women in the Holiness Movement," 249.
79. Smith, "Holiness Crusade," 616.
80. Ibid., 620–24.
81. Dieter, *Holiness Revival*, 205.

A Holiness Hermeneutic

The Methodist leaders also found it increasingly difficult to understand where the National Camp Meeting Association and itinerant holiness evangelists fit in the denominational structure. This uncertainty was exacerbated when, in 1881, the Northern Bishops vetoed the proposal of several respected and moderate holiness leaders for a national convention to promote holiness. The Bishops felt holiness could be better promoted and controlled within established structures. In so doing, many in the Holiness movement felt forced to make a very difficult choice. They had to decide whether to continue to promote the doctrine through methods proven successful, or give up those methods and allow the "central idea of Christianity" to be promoted by a church that seemed to have little use for the doctrine.[82]

Which direction they chose is evident in the proliferation of local holiness associations modeled after and encouraged by the National Camp Meeting Association. These associations, while providing to holiness converts the fellowship and nurture lacking in the local church, dismayed Methodist leaders. This was especially the case in the South and Midwest, where more radical holiness associations pushed the movement toward schism.[83]

Leading the way in this direction were men like Daniel S. Warner and John P. Brooks. Brooks left the Methodist church in 1885 and two years later published *The Divine Church*, an attack on denominationalism.[84] Warner was forced out of the Church of God, Winebrenner in 1878 because of his views on holiness. His radical anti-sectarian message led to the founding of the Church of God, Anderson in 1880.[85]

Those in the movement who wished to oppose Methodism's resistance found ample encouragement in holiness theology. Like Peter and John before the Sanhedrin, they had to obey God rather than man.[86] Furthermore, with a theology where the greatest works of God—conversion and sanctification—were accomplished as crisis experiences and were available to all by faith, there was little sympathy for those who would not go on to perfection. Nor was there any question in the minds of holiness folk as to

---

82. Smith, "Holiness Crusade," 620; Jones, *Perfectionist Persuasion*, 35.
83. Ibid., 47. Smith, "Holiness Crusade," 618–19.
84. Ibid., 619.
85. Dieter, *Holiness Revival*, 260–63.
86. Acts 4:19. Jones, *Perfectionist Persuasion*, 87.

who was and was not sanctified since the tests were clearly visible: either strict standards of dress and behavior or intensely emotional worship.[87]

For many in the movement it became clear that preserving the authenticity of the holiness message would require a break with Methodism. New converts were returning home from camp meeting to wither in their local Methodist churches.[88] Converts to holiness from other denominations found an even more hostile environment in their churches.[89] Some who desired to stay and maintain a strong holiness witness within Methodism found themselves being squeezed out by a denomination resistant to the independent methods on which the movement grew and thrived. Most of these "come-outers" and "put-outers" joined the new holiness denominations.

The new churches attracted many both for their clear support for holiness and because they offered a conservative, protective environment in a culture that was rapidly changing.[90] The Holiness movement stood for the "plain old truth" with the "Old Book" against the new theologies. As W. B. Godbey wrote, "all truth is as old as the Bible, and everything new is false."[91] Ironically, these groups did not join together into one large holiness denomination, partly due to the resistance of the National Camp Meeting Association to "come-outism."

The Holiness Movement in the Early Twentieth Century

By the turn of the century, the holiness denominations had begun to enter McLoughlin's final stage: the institutionalization of the spiritual movement. Holiness churches were called upon to ordain and support preachers, nurture converts and children, build churches and Sunday Schools suitable for the suburban environment to which they had relocated, and support missionaries and educational institutions. None of these could be done without

---

87. Smith, "Holiness Crusade," 618.
88. Dieter, *Holiness Revival*, 225.
89. Jones, *Perfectionist Persuasion*, 54–55.
90. It has been suggested that the radical holiness associations that eventually produced denominations were shaped by the same factors that produced the late-nineteenth-century political movement known as populism (Dieter, *Holiness Revival*, 276; cf. Synan, *Holiness-Pentecostal Movement*, 52–53).
91. Watson, *Coals of Fire*, 60; Godbey, *Commentary*, 2:195.

money and organization.⁹² As the churches climbed the ladder toward the middle class and paid more attention to their own preservation, like the church from which they had separated, they gave less attention to the poor and neglected. They continued to describe themselves as poor long after that was no longer strictly true. From their new vantage point further up the socio-economic ladder, they attended less to the truly poor and more to the status quo.⁹³

Growing out of the Holiness movement in this period was Pentecostalism. Donald Dayton, in *Theological Roots of Pentecostalism*, describes how this process was facilitated by the earlier association of entire sanctification with Pentecost and by the similarities between the teaching of both movements: salvation, the baptism of the Holy Spirit, healing, and the second coming of Jesus. The chief difference was Pentecostalism's addition of glossolalia.

Holiness adherents remained within the Methodist Episcopal Church into the twentieth century. In spite of the fact that the "come-outers" and "put-outers" numbered approximately 100,000, they represented only a small percentage of those holiness adherents who remained within the Methodist church.⁹⁴ Weary from the controversies of the previous decades, those who remained showed little toleration for disputes. As a result, sanctification as a process, for which there was widespread support, came to be emphasized over the crisis.

Having set the context of the late nineteenth and early twentieth centuries, described the history of popular biblical studies in America, and provided an overview of the American Holiness movement, we can now look more closely at particular holiness writers and their interpretation of the Bible.

---

92. Jones, *Perfectionist Persuasion*, 121–42.

93. Ibid., 127, 133, 135.

94. Dunlap estimates the total holiness adherents at half of Methodism's four million members ("Tuesday Meetings," 101).

4

The Wesleyan Quadrilateral and Holiness Biblical Interpretation

Introduction

AT LEAST TWO DANGERS are possible when analyzing the use of the Bible by the American Holiness movement. One is to focus only on their methods of biblical interpretation and neglect the presuppositions underlying those methods. Such a focus would reveal little of the uniqueness in the Holiness movement's use of scripture, since many of their methods were widespread among Christians of the late nineteenth and early twentieth centuries. To focus instead on the presuppositions underlying those methods allows greater insight. It is far more revealing, for example, to examine their assumption that the Bible is one unified piece of divine revelation than to ask whether they always interpreted a passage in its historical context.

A second danger is to oversimplify the analysis. Just as the movement was diverse, so was its use of the Bible. Some interpreted the Bible quite literally, while others found types and allegories wherever they turned. All three major millennial views were represented. Some gave greater place to reason than others. Nor did this diversity result simply from the passage of time. Daniel Steele, writing in the 1870s, is very similar in some of his presuppositions to Joseph H. Smith, writing in the 1920s, while Smith's work is quite unlike that of "Uncle Buddy" Robinson, his contemporary. Standing at the proper angle, however, one can see certain patterns within this diversity.

This analysis begins with an overview of the movement's use of Scripture, examining how the Holiness movement's use of Scripture compares to what has been called the Wesleyan quadrilateral and how they continued to use the populist hermeneutic.

We will then look more closely at the major presuppositions underlying their biblical interpretation. Bypassing those they held in common with nineteenth century Protestantism—inspiration, Christocentricity, etc.—we explore their understanding of the immanence of God in relation to the Bible, as well as their view of Scripture as Spirit-centered, unified, and more-than-literal.

Holiness Interpretation and the Wesleyan Quadrilateral

Wesley's theological method involved the interplay between scripture, tradition, reason, and experience, with the Bible always serving as the final authority.[1] Richard Lovelace compares it to a baseball diamond, with Scripture represented by home plate, then tradition, reason, and experience.[2] In order to adequately interpret a passage—hit a home run—one must begin at home plate and touch all the bases before returning home to scripture.[3]

To change the metaphor, if the Bible is the lode from which gold is mined, the other three are furnaces in which that gold is purified. The purpose is refinement, the perfection of what has been discovered. Wesley saw these four elements as integral to a proper understanding of the Bible. While not all four were systematically employed each time he interpreted a passage, Wesley considered no interpretation sound if it could not stand up to the heat from all of the furnaces.

While these same four elements were present within the theological method of the Holiness movement, changes occurred in the definitions of some of the components, the emphasis on each, and the interplay between them. What emerged was less a quadrilateral and more a bilateral between the Bible and experience. The "furnaces" of reason and tradition, having produced questionable workmanship in the past, were avoided and at times vilified.

---

1. The idea of the Wesleyan quadrilateral was first proposed by Albert Outler in the late 1960s. A good account of Outler's intention can be found in Thorsen, *Wesleyan Quadrilateral*, 21–24.

2. Lovelace, "Recovering Our Balance," 80, as cited in Thorsen, *Wesleyan Quadrilateral*, 72.

3. Ibid., 72.

Scripture

Wesley's words in his preface to "Sermons of Several Occasions" are well-known: "O give me that book! At any price, give me the book of God! I have it: here is knowledge enough for me. Let me be homo unius libri," or a man of one book.[4] Just as for Wesley, the Bible represented the final authority for the Holiness movement. If scripture was found to address a doctrine or issue, the last word had been spoken.

The authority of the Bible rests on its divine inspiration, an inspiration largely assumed rather than argued. The Holy Spirit was called the "Spirit of inspiration," and the Bible called the "breath of God's mouth"[5] and the "grand thesaurus of inspired truth."[6]

When the authors turned their attention from the inspired truth to the process of inspiration itself, they refer to it as plenary and verbal.[7] For Steele, the authors were not simply stenographers for the Spirit; they even exercised the freedom to coin new Greek words to express that message. Godbey, on the other hand, believed God dictated the message. He encouraged those preparing for ministry to master Greek and Hebrew so that "they can read the identical words used by the Holy Ghost in the revelation of the glorious plan of salvation."[8] When discussing the authorship of Hebrews, Godbey wrote,

> Of course the reader understands the utter insignificance of the whole question appertaining to human authorship, since the letter is actually indited by the Holy Ghost. Consequently we should not consider it the revelation of Paul, or Apollos, or any other man, to the Hebrews, but God's letter straight from heaven to us.[9]

In fact, Godbey writes, "plenary inspiration . . . forever annihilates the importance of human authorship."[10]

---

4. Wesley, "Preface," 51.

5. Godbey, *Commentary*, 1:154.

6. Ibid., 2:375.

7. Steele, *Milestone Papers*, 165; Steele, *Substitute*, 186–87; Steele, *Leviticus and Numbers*, 368, 385. Godbey refers frequently to plenary inspiration. See Godbey, *Commentary*, 2:205; ibid., 4:11, 4:184. On numerous occasions Godbey asserted that verbal inspiration occurred only in the original. See ibid., 3:317; ibid., 5:211; *Bible*, 11.

8. Godbey, "Spiritual Gifts and Graces," 43.

9. Godbey, *Commentary*, 2:4.

10. Ibid., 205.

A Holiness Hermeneutic

All of the authors understood, to one degree or another, that this inspiration was questioned by "critics." Partly because of his role in higher education, Steele may have been more aware of the critical issues than the others. He informed his readers that his commentary on Leviticus and Numbers was written with "Bishop Colenso's 'Pentateuch Critically Examined,' and his recent diatribes in review of the 'Speaker's Commentary' lying open before us."[11] Martin Wells Knapp was less willing to dialogue, considering questions about the inspiration of the Bible to arise from Satan.[12]

When these authors did decide to defend the inspiration of the Bible, their ammunition was drawn from the usual sources: fulfilled prophecies, the purity of Jesus' life and the effect of his teaching on society, the Bible's enduring universality, profundity (especially considering its unlettered authors), superhuman content, and self-testimony, as well as its effects on the life of the individual reader. Special note should be taken of this final argument, both because of its significance for Wesley, and because it may have been most important to this movement.[13]

It was not the text of the Bible alone which spoke with authority to the Holiness movement but the text as it was employed by the Holy Spirit. It was the Spirit's job to confirm the authority of the text to the believer, not with new revelations of truth, but by making the believer "perfectly assured of the Divine origin of truths already accredited as inspired."[14]

The most important theological distinction of the Holiness movement was its belief that subsequent to regeneration God's Spirit cleanses the heart from inbred sin. It was this same sanctifying Spirit who guaranteed the authority of the Bible and other important doctrines. As a result, "we are never again troubled with doubts of the inspiration of the Bible. The hungry man, when he finds bread that perfectly satisfies and nourishes him, has no difficulty with the sophistry which would prove that it was made of chaff and not of wheat."[15]

When the Holy Spirit sanctifies, "the enemy is no longer able to keep you in doubt about the divinity of Christ or the inspiration of the Holy Scriptures; . . . Nothing but the Holy Ghost can make all of these things real

---

11. Steele, *Leviticus and Numbers*, 213.

12. Knapp, *Holiness Triumphant*, 247.

13. Knapp, *Out of Egypt*, 22; Rose, *Theology of Christian Experience*, 146; Thorsen makes this point in *Wesleyan Quadrilateral*, 145–46.

14. Steele, *Jesus Exultant*, 290.

15. Steele, *Love Enthroned*, 261.

to us, but, bless the Lord! He can do it."[16] It is in sanctification that one has rest from theological problems and is able to live oblivious to the howling winds of temptation and worldliness.[17]

In the hands of the Spirit, the text was enlivened. George Watson compared the Bible to Moses' rod that became a serpent after being cast down, asserting that "the Word of God as a mere letter, held in the grasp of human reason, is lifeless; but when under a Divine commission, cast forth upon human hearts, it becomes a living truth," a sharp, two-edged sword.[18]

The Spirit-enlivened word could illuminate the mind of the interpreter. "It takes the Holy Spirit to unlock the book," wrote Beverly Carradine. "He who reads simply with the eye of the Intellect will miss the glory of the book, and never realize the soul-food with which it is stored. It is well to ask the light and blessing of the Holy Ghost upon us each time that we read."[19]

They claimed a "double-inspiration" took place as the same Spirit who inspired the authors to write the Bible inspired the interpreters of those passages. As noted earlier, Wesley taught this in his exposition of 2 Timothy 3:16. Godbey implied such double-inspiration when, at the end of his commentary on Colossians, he confessed, "The Blessed Holy Spirit, who gave to Paul this wonderful epistle, has illuminated the foregoing expositions."[20]

It should be said again that while the Spirit inspired the interpreter, the Spirit neither gave a new revelation beyond the Bible nor guided contrary to the Bible. Such caveats were offered frequently as if the authors recognized that their emphasis on the activity of the Holy Spirit might lead to abuse and charges of fanaticism.

Perhaps they also wanted to guard against the assumption that, since the Spirit inspires the interpreter, it is no longer necessary to study the Bible. Encountering such an assumption, Steele wrote, "The unwise query has been raised why I write my sermons if I am conscious of the indwelling of the Holy Spirit, the fountain of spiritual light." He answered that the "grace of the Spirit, while it floods the soul with light on its personal relations to God, communicates no dogmatic truth . . . Hence the Holy Spirit

16. Robinson, *Honey*, 176.
17. Watson, *Love Abounding*, 327; Robinson, *Honey*, 113.
18. Watson, *Coals of Fire*, 145.
19. Carradine, *Sanctified Life*, 117.
20. Godbey, *Commentary*, 3:159–60.

affords no dispensation from hard work. He is not bestowed as a premium to laziness."[21]

Unlike later fundamentalists, the Holiness movement did not have an unbreakable loyalty for the King James Version. Their willingness to employ other versions and even make a new translation is reminiscent of Wesley's attitude on these lines.[22] Carradine used the King James Version, but sharply criticized its translators for their unfamiliarity with the doctrine of entire sanctification and their cowardly concessions to King James' temper. Steele also criticized it and seemed to favor the Revised Version of 1881. While considering the English and American revisions to be improvements over the Authorized Version, for Godbey they still fell short of desirability. Due to ecclesiastical shackles, the Revised Version only corrected 904 of the 2000 errors (by his count) in the King James Version. To make matters worse, higher criticism had slipped in to taint the ASV. Godbey's counsel was to occupy the middle ground between the higher critics and the fanatical and "superstitious rabble" who are stuck on the KJV. Best of all was to do as he did and read it in the original languages.[23]

Historical criticism, by this time fairly widespread in the United States, had brought with it questions about the inspiration and authority of the Bible. While Wesley had maintained his confidence in the face of the rationalistic criticism in his day, the challenges facing the late nineteenth century were much greater and more sweeping. How did the Holiness movement face these? The responses of our authors to historical criticism represent a wide spectrum. Perhaps the most accommodating was Daniel Steele who distinguished between constructive and destructive higher critics. The former are "studious to conserve all the truth that the Holy Spirit has inspired" while the latter are "madly attempting to sweep out of the universe every vestige of a supernatural revelation, and to beat down to the dead level of naturalism every religious truth that stands a foot above that level."[24] As one can see from his commentaries on Leviticus, Numbers, and Joshua, Steele was familiar with the work of critics like De Wett and Colenso.

---

21. Steele, *Love Enthroned*, 295.

22. Cf. Wesley, *Explanatory Notes*, 5–10.

23. Carradine, *Second Blessing*, 18, 20–21. Steele's preference can be found scattered throughout his writings, especially *Milestone Papers*, 35, 88, 94, 96, 128–29, 220. Godbey, *Higher Criticism*, 14, 18, 41–43; *Commentary*, 1:288; *Bible*, 17.

24. Steele, *Gospel of the Comforter*, 239.

Godbey appears less aware of the work of the critics themselves and less tolerant of higher criticism in general. He acknowledged the positive work of biblical criticism but considered higher criticism to be "that specious, occult form of infidelity which is so detrimental to Christianity from the fact that it sails altogether under Gospel colors." The problem with these "present-day Sadducees" is that they have become too rationalistic, eliminating the supernatural for the natural. They have substituted pure intellectualism for the pure spiritual gospel, becoming intellectual giants, but spiritual dwarfs.[25]

Even less familiar with the work of the critics and more denunciatory were Robinson and Watson. Robinson considered many "of the great leaders of our leading denominations" to be "woefully tainted with higher criticism, and worse still, even with destructive criticism." Higher critics only believe part of the Bible, and "reserve the right to go through God's book, and tear out all that don't just suit them, and by the time they all get through tearing out what don't suit them, we have no Bible left."[26] Generally, whenever Watson mentions criticism, it is with the adjective "higher," and with a negative association.

Joseph H. Smith, familiar with the work of critical scholars, could not accept their evolutionary, naturalistic presuppositions and conclusions. These "Modern Sadducees" base their philosophy on "science falsely so called," and practice destructive criticism. To neglect holiness meant carnality in the church and an increasing tendency to follow professors, philosophers, and other "authorities" rather than the Bible.[27]

Generally speaking, the Holiness movement, like Wesley, felt it was far better to present a living example of Christianity than to debate the critics. This was true even of Steele, who, as a practicing scholar, had the greatest opportunity and resources for such debate. For those without an adequate education and whose rigorous preaching schedules deprived them of time and access to the work of the critics, a living witness rather than a logical argument was the only strategy.

---

25. Godbey, *Higher Criticism*, 10–11; Godbey, *Commentary*, 5:103, 5:296.

26. Robinson, *Chickens*, 34; Robinson, *Pitcher of Cream*, 141.

27. Rose, *Theology of Christian Experience*, 142; Smith, *Pauline Perfection*, 13–14, 22, 73.

Reason

Reason occupied an important role in Wesley's theological method. While he was very conscious of the dangers of rationalism, he maintained that the truths of Christianity were rational; there was no essential contradiction between reason and faith. Methodists were insistent, he said, "that to renounce reason is to renounce religion, that religion and reason go hand in hand, and that all irrational religion is false religion."[28]

The American Holiness movement of the late nineteenth century, as a whole, was far less enthusiastic about reason's potential for good. They still employed it, being neither irrational nor anti-rational. But this movement, like other conservative groups of the day, was wary of reason. Wesley had warned against the dangers of rationalism; these groups felt they had witnessed reason's traitorous activities against the army of the Lord.

As expected, some within the Holiness movement appreciated reason more than others. Steele saw no contradiction between faith and reason. For him, "faith in Christ, on the ground of his unique and sinless character and supernatural works, crowned with his own resurrection from the dead, is the highest reason."[29] Even the Christian's experience of being guided by the Holy Spirit would not be "repugnant to the divine endowment of reason" since the two gifts from God, the Spirit and reason, would not conflict.

> There may be a conflict between faith and the erroneous deductions of reason, but there can never be hostility between intuitive truth in the domain of the intellect and intuitive truth in the realm of the spiritual nature illumined by the Spirit divine. The spiritual intuitions may be far above the merely intellectual, but they can never contradict them.[30]

Steele believed reason had its place, this place was important, and people should understand what that place is, so he included a section in *Love Enthroned* on "The Psychology of Christian Assurance." However, as a concession to some of his audience, he included this footnote:

> If the reader abhors metaphysics, he would do well to skip this and the following section. Yet we have tried to practice the advice of our college preceptor, Dr. Olin: "Students, if you put metaphysics into your sermons, be sure that you make them luminous." We

---

28. Wesley, "Letter to Dr. Rutherforth," 354.
29. Steele, *Jesus Exultant*, 241.
30. Steele, *Milestone Papers*, 166–67.

trust that much skepticism will be dispelled by showing that a degree of certitude in spiritual knowledge, higher than even that of material things, is attainable by every believer in Jesus Christ.[31]

There is a place for reason, Steele argued, but not reason only. He cautioned his readers to remember that since Christianity is addressed to both the intellect and feeling, preaching should aim for both the head and the heart. The "tendency of the schools," he writes, "is to repress feeling and to intensify the dry intellect; whereas few people reason while all feel."[32]

Steele was certainly not the only one in the Holiness movement who saw the benefits of reason. Carradine considered it "blessed to be sanctified, and even more blessed to be intelligently sanctified." "He who reads, thinks and compares," wrote Carradine, "has always an advantage over the thoughtless man or the mere creature of impulse."[33] If one were in doubt about the possibility of being entirely sanctified, Carradine encouraged a scientific approach, what he referred to as the "experimental method in the discovery of truth."[34]

But this same author considered reason and intellect to be inadequate apprehenders of divine truth. "It is not by reasoning that the world knows God or the things of God." Nor can reason bring the experience of entire sanctification because the person "involved in tenses and moods and Greek roots, and who is worried about psychology and theology, does not get it."[35]

Godbey considered the intellect to be a good thing, but intellectualism to be "one of the worst forms of modern infidelity." "The diluted heterogeneity of science, metaphysics, history, literature and eloquence does not feed the flock at all. People who are spiritually dead are delighted with it, as the vulture with carrion, but your live members starve to death and backslide into intellectualism under such preaching."[36]

"There is a place for reasoning and theological instruction," conceded Watson, but God's work goes beyond what can be grasped by "mere brains and carnal reason."[37] Far better than the "slow process of reasoning" is the

---

31. Steele, *Love Enthroned*, 214. Steele is quoting Stephen Olin, President of Wesleyan University in Connecticut from 1842–1851.

32. Steele, *Jesus Exultant*, 135.

33. Carradine, *Sanctified Life*, 167.

34. Carradine, *Better Way*, 179.

35. Carradine, *Old Man*, 262–63.

36. Godbey, *Holiness or Hell*, 17, 23.

37. Watson, *Love Abounding*, 77, 352.

God-given ability to discriminate between truth and error,[38] when the Spirit of God speaks to the inner spirit of the Christian through intuitions and "instinctive perceptions of divine verities" which are "superior to logic."[39]

There are at least two factors which made reason less valuable for the Holiness movement than it was for Wesley. Since the Enlightenment, Christianity had suffered at the hands of reason. Wesley saw some of this in his day but by the late nineteenth century the damage was even greater with the perpetrators sometimes arising from within the church. Wesley wrote as a correspondent living within earshot of the battle. These authors believed the assassin lurked inside the house.

This devaluing of reason also occurred because the Holiness movement was composed of individuals who, generally speaking, were not well-educated, even by the standards of that day. This perspective meant less willingness to trust reason. It also reflected an anti-intellectualism that characterized the American Holiness movement, if not society in general.

The Holiness movement was far more comfortable speaking about common sense than it was about reason. Reason almost never receives unqualified praise; common sense almost always does. Reason was associated with those who were intellectual giants and spiritual dwarfs; common sense belonged to the nineteenth century's hero, the common person. Neither was touted as a direct route to God, but common sense would get you closer, faster, and safer.

Tradition

Tradition was very important to Wesley and one of the means by which he sought to connect his renewal movement and the early church. He valued it for reflecting a Christianity which was both intellectually rigorous and spiritual alive. It was Wesley's appreciation for tradition, says Thorsen, that enabled Wesley to maintain his catholic, tolerant spirit.[40]

By the late nineteenth century, tradition suffered a redefinition and reemphasis. Few in the Holiness movement considered tradition to be helpful, and many saw it as harmful. Steele came the closest to affirming tradition with references to Augustine, Ignatius, and Bede, the eighth-century English theologian. He criticized the Plymouth Brethren for not

---

38. Watson, *Pot of Oil*, 32.
39. Watson, *Steps to the Throne*, 29.
40. Thorsen, *Wesleyan Quadrilateral*, 168.

being more faithful in their doctrine to the ancient creeds. "If it is true that all men are wiser than one man, it is true that all churches are more correct in a doctrine held in common than one small sect which sets up a doctrine inconsistent with it."[41] Although at times Steele spoke disparagingly of creeds and other vestiges of tradition, his opposition was not to liturgy or tradition, but to formalism and sacramentalism.

One must look long and hard throughout the rest of the movement to find even this much support for tradition as an aid in theological methodology. More often one encounters criticism of almost everything that happened after the end of the New Testament period. Influential writers, such as Knapp, criticized the use of creeds and "church history" to defend unbiblical doctrine.[42]

Godbey was more explicit in his condemnation. "Martyr blood and fire had kept the Church humble, poor, unpopular, and despised three hundred years. Meanwhile she had no creed but the Bible." With the conversion of Constantine came popularity, influence, wealth, the paganization of Christianity, and the first human creed. This was the first of many, "thus recognizing and inaugurating human authority, going off into ecclesiasticism, no longer content with New Testament simplicity."[43]

Godbey and others did use a form of tradition, but one far different from Wesley's. Unlike Wesley, they did not draw eclectically from many traditions—Greek Orthodox, Roman Catholic, Lutheran, Moravian, and others. Instead, convinced that "God has always had a true people on the earth,"[44] they traced a narrow line that snaked its way forward from the "golden days" of New Testament purity—considered the "incipiency" of the Holiness movement[45]—across a narrow ridge of orthodoxy, through periods of persecution, to the present. Godbey's line traced through the Waldenses in the third century, through the Moravians to the Methodists, also including others such as à Kempis, Fenelon, and George Fox.[46] Less important than knowing the identity of each element in this pure lineage

41. Steele, *Substitute*, 190.
42. Knapp, *Lightning Bolts*, 155.
43. Godbey, *Commentary*, 3:209.
44. Ibid., 210.
45. Knapp, *Lightning Bolts*, 72.
46. Godbey, *Sanctification*, 10. Godbey likely considered the Waldenses to be the predecessors of those who followed the teaching of the twelfth-century Peter Waldo. Steele would add the Lollards, Mystics, and Quakers to this slender line of piety (*Milestone Papers*, 154).

was knowing that such a lineage existed . . . and that the modern Holiness movement was a direct descendant.

Wesley considered tradition as the work of God among his people in the past, drawing from it insight and correction. The Holiness movement considered tradition primarily as God's way of keeping the truth of holiness alive until their day.

When the Holiness movement did draw from tradition, it was almost never from ancient church tradition but usually from the previous few hundred years. Frequent reference can be found to Madame Guyon, John Bunyan, John Fletcher, Richard Watson, Hester Rogers, and of course, John Wesley and his brother, Charles, among others. What is also noteworthy is that tradition was not used primarily as a source of writings to guide the interpretation of the Bible but as a source of examples to illustrate it.

The devaluation of tradition from Wesley's lofty estimation began, for American Methodists, as far back as Asbury himself whom Outler considers to have had little time for tradition.[47] So important a figure as Asbury could not fail to influence the later Holiness movement. As well, the movement, due to its lack of formal education, was less familiar with the sources of tradition.

More important, however, was the movement's reluctance to be associated with any past that was not part of this pure line traced back to Pentecost. The message of holiness was so central and delineated by this slender line of piety they had no interest in looking outside the line for help to guide their interpretation. Only from the pure, persecuted minority throughout the ages, but especially from the ranks of early Methodism, came the examples of the sanctified life that meant so much.

The denigration of tradition by the Holiness movement should not be surprising for yet another reason. The modernization process underway at this time meant less value was placed in the past and more placed in the future.[48]

Experience

According to Thorsen, Wesley's understanding of the role of experience as a reliable source for theological insight may be one of his most important

---

47. Outler, "Biblical Primitivism," 150.
48. Berger, "Toward a Critique," 339, 345.

contributions to Christian thought.[49] While aware of the limitations of experience, he found reason and tradition to be essential checks to maintain a proper balance.

While the Holiness movement found less room for reason and tradition than had Wesley, they wholeheartedly embraced his emphasis on experience. Their failure to maintain his balance resulted in occasions where experience became equal to or greater than the Bible.

Experience was an important part of the epistemology of the movement. While they agreed reason was helpful in gaining certain types of information, some things could only be known by experience. "One experience in the converted or sanctified life," said Carradine, "is worth ten thousand theories."[50] By experiencing God's love we can know him "with a swiftness, a certainty and a personal communion, that surpasses all the boasted knowledge of science, and furnishes the only true interpretation of creation and providence." Watson goes on to say that such love "has a quick art of knowing, and seeing, and interpreting all things by a sort of lightning flash of intuition, that leaps over the plodding process of slow reason and knows things more surely without learning them, than reason does with all its logic."[51]

Theological truth was to be found in what was "written in the Word and experienced in the lives of those who gain and retain this baptism from above."[52] Frequently one finds expressions pairing "the Bible and experience." According to Steele, it was "an open Bible, interpreted in the light of a spiritual experience" that was one of the secrets of Methodist success.[53] When it comes to scriptural interpretation,

> it will not do to lean on the authority of a majority of experts; but on the practical question of the extent of gospel salvation from sin, through the power of the Holy Spirit, the unlearned minority who have put the doctrine to experimental proof may be very much wiser than the learned majority of the magnates of the modern church, who have never subjected the question to the test of personal experience. Here the testimony of some Uncle Tom or Amanda Smith of the slave plantation may outweigh the opinion

---

49. Thorsen, *Wesleyan Quadrilateral*, 201.
50. Carradine, *Sanctification*, 8.
51. Watson, *Our Own God*, 3.
52. Knapp, *Revival Kindlings*, 323.
53. Steele, *Milestone Papers*, 155.

A Holiness Hermeneutic

of a whole faculty of German theological professors. Experience outweighs theory; faith makes philosophy kick the beam.[54]

Carradine found "Some scripture passages can only be unlocked by experience. We may think we understand; but it requires more than a knowledge of grammar, rhetoric, and the laws of exegesis to clear up the mystery." The relative values he ascribed to exegesis and experience can be seen in his reference to the former as "exit Jesus" and to the latter as "Commentary Life."[55]

Experience is so important to the interpretation of the Bible that in order to understand it, one must be willing to obey it. Obedience is to understanding what learning one's letters is to reading, explained Knapp, citing John 7:17: "If any man will do his will he shall know of the doctrine."[56] Steele quoted Bengel's dictate:

> Te totum applica ad Textum;
> Rem totam applica ad Te.
> (Apply thyself wholly to the Text;
> Apply the subject wholly to thyself.)

"The most cultivated intellect refusing to bow to God's commands inevitably misses that knowledge which the humble and God-fearing slave easily receives, because his nature is open God-ward." An obedient will "puts eye-salve upon men's eyes and they clearly see."[57]

The Holiness movement was certainly not the first group to believe experience was important for the interpretation of the Bible. The church has long maintained that the experience of conversion provides insight into the Bible. However, the Holiness movement took this one step further, considering the truest understanding of scripture to await, not conversion alone, but the experience of entire sanctification.

Steele spoke of this experience as providing "an astonishing insight into the Holy Scriptures and a daily hunger for the word of life." For the entirely sanctified, "Gospel truth ceases to be vague and shadowy. It becomes real. A mysterious power unveils its meaning, and applies it to the soul. There is a voice within which attests the objective truth. An invisible interpreter attends the reading of the sacred page and 'we discover wonders in

---

54. Steele, *Half-Hours with Saint Paul*, 239–40.
55. Carradine, *Heart Talks*, 207; *Better Way*, 244; *Golden Sheaves*, 30.
56. Knapp, *Out of Egypt*, 32–33.
57. Steele, *Jesus Exultant*, 244, 281.

God's law.'"⁵⁸ Like Jesus' second touch on the eyes of the blind man, writes Carradine, "We see into the Word of God as never before. Passages that were obscure and mysterious become luminous with a deeper and truer meaning. The Bible becomes a new book and an illuminated one at that."⁵⁹

Godbey counseled those who would understand the Bible to

> get all the rocks of depravity eliminated from your heart, leaving it soft, tender, and filled with perfect love. Then you can go down into the profound mysteries of revealed truth, flooded with new spiritual illuminations, and progressively edified by fresh revealments of the Divine attributes in glory, though you never saw a college nor inherited Solomonic genius.⁶⁰

So important was this experience to the proper interpretation of the Bible that Watson considered "a plain man entirely sanctified, without learning, and with the Bible in his hands, has an understanding of the divine promises, sees farther into the prophecies of God, gets a firmer grasp on God's Word, than all the doctors of divinity that are not sanctified."⁶¹

Within the Holiness movement there appears to have been widespread acceptance of the subjective experience whereby one receives an impression from God, is guided by a dream, or even has a vision. Through these God provided guidance regarding a choice to be made, instructions as to what to say to another person, a new truth from the Bible, or a vision of Heaven. Knapp found sufficient interest in these matters to offer a book-length treatment entitled *Impressions* which he claimed to have written by impression from God.⁶²

He wrote this not only to explain how such impressions come to the believer, but also to guard against abuses.⁶³ Many others joined him in warning that while God may choose to provide such experiences, not every experience is from him. Nor should such experiences convey anything that supersedes Scripture. Of the authors studied, only Watson suggested that

---

58. Steele, *Love Enthroned*, 261.
59. Carradine, *Second Blessing*, 212.
60. Godbey, *Commentary*, 6:403.
61. Watson, *Love Abounding*, 167.
62. Knapp, *Impressions*, 2.
63. Hynson argues that Knapp moved from this more moderate position to one more radical, where he "did not hold steadfastly to the tests of Scripture, but allowed Pentecostal tornadoes, and floods of experience to become dominant" (Hynson, "Wesleyan Quadrilateral," 30).

A Holiness Hermeneutic

such "extraordinary revelations" accompany spiritual maturity. He believed God gives us, "when we are perfectly dead to self, spiritual apprehensions of heavenly companionships and visions of the coming glory and reign of Christ on this earth."[64]

The importance they attached to experience is evident from their understanding of the Bible's purpose. For them it was not primarily literature to be studied. Those who approach the Scriptures this way, Smith wrote, "gaze at the frame instead of looking into the glass." Or else they engage in "investigating and analyzing the texture of the glass," instead of "contemplating the object it reveals." Such practices are foolish for "The literature of the Word is not the Word. The critical examination of texts and translations is not the beholding of the glory of the Lord." This type of examination has its place but the reader must not stop until he or she has turned from contemplating the frame and the glass, to seeing Christ pictured therein.[65] Even the comments of these holiness authors on textual matters were designed primarily to better enable the Bible to speak to our experience rather than to determine the proper text of the passage for its own sake.[66]

Scripture was not simply literature, it was God's way of producing right experiences in the reader, God's scissors to cut away self. It was considered a source of healing. "The Bible presents every shade, every step and degree of the soul's disease and its marvelous and compound cure; but the Bible is a book from God's heart to man's heart; it is addressed emphatically to man's spiritual nature, and therefore can only be unlocked with the key of spiritual experience."[67]

The goal of Christian experience is evident in Godbey's intention that his New Testament commentary be an experimental commentary designed to prepare the common person for service to Christ and his description of

---

64. Watson, *Pot of Oil*, 46.

65. Smith, *From Glory to Glory*, 41–43.

66. Such comments on the Greek text include Steele, *Saint John's Epistles*, 136 and Godbey, *Higher Criticism*, 6, 8–9, 15; Godbey, *Bible Theology*, 304, 306; Godbey, *Commentary*, 7:30, 7:497, 7:528. Godbey was especially fond of the manuscript discovered by Tischendorf in 1859, the very year Godbey graduated from college. He considered Codex Sinaiticus the "pure, inspired original" and "a copy of the first volume ever compiled," dating "far back in the very blaze of the Apostolic age" (Godbey, *Bible*, 14–16) and preserved by God until the time was right (Godbey, *Higher Criticism*, 15). Tischendorf himself dated Codex Sinaiticus to the middle of the fourth century (Kepler, "Sinaiticus," 378). Godbey used this as the source of his translation of the New Testament.

67. Watson, *Coals of Fire*, 71; Watson, *White Robes*, 18.

the Bible as the source of spiritual nourishment.[68] Knapp also emphasized the Bible's experiential effect when he described it as a harrow to stir the soil of the soul, a guide to teach us to be holy, and a looking glass under the electric light of the Holy Spirit.[69] He and many others spoke of the Bible as God's promises to humanity. Watson considered that the 32,000 promises in the Bible "cover every condition and every case that can be imagined in this world, and every single promise is secured by the atonement."[70] A book of promises is meant to be experienced, both by "claiming" them and living out their fulfillment.

The importance of experience is evidenced not only in the purpose for which God wrote his word but in the purpose for which our authors wrote their words. Nearly everything they wrote was intended, either directly or indirectly, to bring their readers into some sort of Christian experience, usually "full salvation," or entire sanctification. It was not uncommon for them to close a chapter with a call for commitment like the following, "If, as I have shown by God's word, the blessing of a holy heart can be secured instantaneously, and is to be obtained through faith, why not have the pearl of great price right now?"[71]

At times their purpose was primarily informational or explanatory, such as in Knapp's biography of the evangelist, Joseph Webber. However, as its preface reveals, even this was written to indirectly promote Christian experience:

> It is humbly hoped and prayed that this book may be used of God in confounding the enemies of gospel truth, leading its readers to accept of forgiving grace; in detecting spurious revivals; in pointing to the secrets of success in revivals that are true; in inspiring evangelists, pastors and all other workers with new and more zealous efforts for the salvation of the people; and that it may prove to be a "tornado," destructive only to that which Christ came to destroy, but a blessing to all that is precious in His kingdom.[72]

---

68. Godbey, *Commentary*, 5:283; Godbey, *Higher Criticism*, 5; Godbey, *Bible*, 4; Godbey, *Commentary*, 7:3.

69. Knapp, *Christ Crowned Within*, 65; Knapp, *Rescued*, 87; Knapp, *Holiness Triumphant*, 45.

70. Knapp, *Revival Kindlings*, 186, 188, 326; Watson, *Love Abounding*, 274, 398; Smith, *Things of the Spirit*, 33; Steele, *Love Enthroned*, 212.

71. Carradine, *Sanctification*, 81.

72. Knapp, *Revival Tornadoes*, 6.

A Holiness Hermeneutic

It appears that the Holiness movement placed such great emphasis on experience that they allowed it, at times, to shape their interpretation of the Bible. Of course, they would dispute this claim and assert they were simply reading the passage as God intended it to be read. They even warned against this practice. Prior to exegeting a passage, Watson asserts, "I will give a simple exegesis of the words. I do not wish to add anything to the Word or to take anything from it, but simply explain the Word as it lies there." However, in the sentence just preceding this quote, we find him confessing, "I never knew how to read that text in my life until the Lord gave me the experience which the text contains."[73]

Evidence of such shaping can be found scattered throughout the writings of the movement. Knapp's distrust of "chance happenings" caused him to criticize the early church for choosing Judas Iscariot's successor by casting lots. Had they tried a more spiritual means they would "have been saved the mortification of choosing a man who never was heard of afterwards, and of forestalling the Spirit, who put Paul in the place of Judas." Their Pentecost and our own prevent such "religious gambling."[74]

When a passage did not quite fit the experiences being promoted, some explanation must be forthcoming which brings the text into line. For example, when Watson wanted to teach that true prayer needs to be preceded by sacrifice and commitment, he turned for proof to the sacrificial system of the Old Testament where the priest first offered the sacrifice and then the incense, which Watson understood to symbolize prayer. Unfortunately for Watson, Deuteronomy 33:10 reverses the order and puts incense before sacrifice. He brought the passage into line with experience by explaining that this is a "poetical climax, which accounts for reversing the order of terms. Both in the order of history and experience, first comes the sacrifice, then the incense, then the teaching."[75]

The Holiness movement, at this time, was often criticized for its demonstrativeness which included shouting, weeping, running around the tabernacle, jumping pews, or falling prostrate. Knapp shaped his interpretation of Rev 5:14 to defend this expressiveness. Referring to the scene in Revelation 5 as a "model holiness-meeting," he pointed out the vocal response to the truth ("and the four beasts said, Amen") and the physical

---

73. Watson, *Love Abounding*, 304.
74. Knapp, *Impressions*, 38–39.
75. Watson, *Coals of Fire*, 31.

demonstrations ("And the four and twenty elders fell down and worshipped him"). Such shaping continues in his comments on Revelation 19:

> These holiness meetings in the skies are characterized by "hallelujahs" and "Amens," by their subjects "rejoicing and being exceedingly glad," and even by "falling down" under the mighty influence of the gathering. The very demonstrations that are here derided as "fanaticism," and "wild-fire," and "extremes," are clearly the normal attendants of worship in the skies. Unsaved formalists advertise their deplorable blindness by opposing demonstrations that are of celestial birth. The hallelujahs and Amens of the holiness movement here below are simply scintillations which fly down from similar meetings above.[76]

Not surprisingly, when experience shaped interpretation, it was usually in the mold of the movement's understanding of entire sanctification. Because they considered holiness to be "the great central pervading idea of the whole book of God from beginning to the end,"[77] they read the Bible through the lens of their own experience of holiness.

Their understanding of full salvation led them to find sanctification in places where others had not. Watson was complimented by his publisher for being able to find entire sanctification "in many portions of the Old Testament where few people have ever thought to look for either the doctrine or the experience."[78] One such place was Genesis 28 to 32, which contains the account of Jacob's experiences between Bethel and Peniel. "If we candidly peruse the progressive steps of the religious experience of Jacob, we shall see reflected, as in a mirror, the New Testament teachings of adoption, consecration, and the baptism of power."[79]

Another example of the experience of sanctification shaping biblical interpretation is found in Carradine's treatment of Ezekiel 36:23–28. He took this to refer, not primarily to God's promised restoration of Israel as it appears, but to entire sanctification when God would remove all filthiness and the "stony heart" from Christians. "A stone is something cold, hard, and heavy. Has the converted man at times a cold, hard, heavy feeling in his soul? Who will dare to deny it?" Carradine did not, for he had heard

---

76. Knapp, *Holiness Triumphant*, 101, 209–10.
77. Joseph H. Smith as quoted in Rose, *Theology of Christian Experience*, 138.
78. McDonald, from the introduction to Watson, *Coals of Fire*, 3.
79. Ibid., 113.

and would recount how converted but not yet sanctified people admitted to having such a stony heart.[80]

Why did the movement place so much emphasis on experience, even to the point of having experience shape their interpretation? Precedent for the use of experience could clearly be found in Wesley, although not to the extent employed here. Such a precedent, however, was important in defending the use of experience.

This emphasis also drew nourishment from the pragmatic American milieu in which the Holiness movement flourished. In a society that had practically canonized Baconian science, the pragmatic, experiential method was highly prized. Carradine even encouraged his readers to "try the Baconian or experimental method" to discover the sanctified life.[81]

The Holiness movement was a movement built on one doctrinal distinctive, the experience of entire sanctification. This being true, a greater reliance on experience is not at all surprising.

One final reason can be suggested. As we noted earlier, the Holiness movement was composed primarily of persons without much formal education. Carradine observed that "so many poor, obscure, illiterate and uncultured people are harnessed to the great Holiness movement of today."[82] Knapp acknowledged he "has not written for the learned and the critical, but to aid the 'poor in spirit' and the 'hungry-hearted,' those who long for light and have been hindered from receiving the glad experience herein magnified by erroneous views in regard to it."[83]

Those lacking formal education would be more comfortable with a methodology that gave a large place to experience. "In many instances," writes Knapp, "a simple word or tear or metaphor or illustrative incident has done more to kindle a fire in a cold heart than a whole ton of the cold coal of logical argument would have done."[84]

Summary

When the ecclesiastical offspring of John Wesley took his theological method in hand, they modified it significantly. For the most part, Scripture

80. Carradine, *Old Man*, 55–58.
81. Carradine, *Better Way*, 179.
82. Carradine, *Sanctified Life*, 194.
83. Knapp, *Double Cure*, 2.
84. Knapp, *Revival Kindlings*, 10.

remained the final authority for the movement as it had been for Wesley. Its divine inspiration rested primarily upon the witness of the Holy Spirit to its authority. This same Spirit enlivened and illumined the Bible, especially for the sanctified. Secondarily, biblical inspiration rested upon internal testimony about itself and the external testimony of history. Treatment of biblical criticism varied from toleration to vehement opposition but the movement, like Wesley, preferred presenting a living example of Christianity to debating the critics.

While some in the Holiness movement considered reason an ally, it was more commonly suspected than respected because of the damage caused by rationalism. Unlike Wesley who considered reason, particularly logic, an indispensable component in his theological methodology, his offspring, lacking Wesley's appreciation for formal education, preferred common sense.

The Holiness movement had little time for tradition as Wesley understood it. The only tradition they trusted was a narrow band of piety that stretched back through the centuries to the early church. Everything else was in various stages of apostasy. Tradition for them was this narrow band, especially the last two hundred years of it.

Experience, already an important methodological element for Wesley, became even more important for the Holiness movement, especially when the experience in view was entire sanctification. God's purpose in his word was to produce such an experience. These authors wrote to lead their readers into these such an experience. Reason and tradition faded in importance with the new formation becoming Scripture and experience. This, according to Outler, continued a trend begun by the movement's American Methodist forbearers.[85]

At times, experience became more important than the Bible and shaped its interpretation. This emphasis on experience arose from the movement's Wesleyan and American roots, the importance it placed on experience of sanctification, and its lack of formal education.

---

85. Outler, "Biblical Primitivism," 151.

5

The Populist Hermeneutic in the American Holiness Movement

ONE OF THE CHARACTERISTICS of nineteenth century American Protestantism was the widespread use of the populist hermeneutic in biblical interpretation. Rooted in the Reformation, this approach to scripture thrived in America's democratic climate. Methodism, whose message and methods were well-suited to this climate, grew at an astounding rate, helping the populist interpretation to be the standard approach to Scripture prior to the Civil War.

The end of the nineteenth century saw the populist hermeneutic fall on hard times. By then it was perpetuated primarily among those who still possessed something of the democratic spirit, method, and message of early American Methodism and those who were theologically conservative. Both of these being true of the Holiness movement, it is not surprising that it continued to employ the populist hermeneutic.

At issue was who had the authority to interpret the Bible. Must it be the theological elite, the ecclesiastically powerful, the formally trained clergy, or could everyone be one's own interpreter? The Holiness movement chose the last option and this chapter explores that choice in detail.

Subjective Interpretation Permitted

The populist hermeneutic exalted those bases for authority that are generally considered subjective such as dreams, visions and impressions. As well, it permitted interpretations that were more-than-literal, especially typology. Holiness exegesis demonstrated its place in the trajectory of the populist hermeneutic by making great use of subjective interpretation.

It was noted in the previous chapter that impressions, visions, and dreams were important to the Holiness movement. To pray for special insight into a passage of scripture, to recount one's dream, to speak of the guidance of God by an inward voice would have raised no eyebrows within a holiness audience. To do so in the secularized society of that day would have raised a cry of disapproval and accusations of subjectivity.

One of the most noticeable elements of holiness interpretation was the widespread use of typology and allegory. This will be examined in more detail in the sixth chapter. What is interesting to note here is that the typologizing carried out by the Holiness movement is similar to that employed by the Puritans. The presuppositions certainly differ, but the methods do not.

The freedom to discover types outside those mentioned in the New Testament, and even outside the Bible, noted in our discussion of the Puritan roots to the populist hermeneutic, also appeared in the Holiness movement. Robinson can turn to nature and find the ant teaching us about works and the spider teaching about faith.[1]

While they may have been familiar with the typologizing of the Puritans, the Holiness movement did not defend its use by appealing to historical precedent. As we will see, the holiness interpreters offered little rationale for their more-than-literal interpretation. What is being suggested here is that by employing typology, the Puritans, albeit unwittingly, encouraged its use by later movements, like this one.

Formal Education Suspected

One characteristic of the populist hermeneutic was the suspicion that formal education was not needed to interpret the Bible and may in fact be more harmful than helpful. This suspicion was right at home in the Holiness movement. That they were not completely opposed to formal education is evident from the fact that the Holiness movement itself founded many schools, and most of the authors under consideration completed college. Generally speaking, they followed a moderate position, one illustrated by Knapp's counsel on ministerial preparation:

1. Robinson, *Chickens*, 16, finds these types in Proverbs, but takes them outside the Bible to discover their meaning to us.

> There are two extreme and mistaken views in regard to preparation for the pastorate. One is that no man is fitted for it without a complete college course; the other is that if one is called to it he needs no special drill, but at once by the Holy Ghost is prepared for the service. Both of these views are unscriptural, and the truth lies between them.[2]

Those who took a moderate view, such as Carradine and Smith, considered that formal education was fine so far as it went, but it could not provide all that was needed for ministry and should never be expected to do so. Although Smith did not attend college, he spoke positively of the value of formal education. His support needs to be qualified by his observation that a ten-day camp meeting is equivalent to one year in seminary.[3]

Some, like Godbey, were even more critical of formal education. When he became sanctified, he left his position in higher education, gave away his library, and remained ever after suspicious of formal learning. Those like Godbey who criticized did so for various reasons. Some considered that formal education provided what is useless and possibly what is harmful. Spending four years studying "heathen authors" is worthless and a "shame on the escutcheon of Christianity."[4] Spending any time studying higher criticism is dangerous. As Godbey saw it, there was only one consolation relating to higher criticism, that "avenging spectre which in these latter days has eloped from the pit and is now peregrinating the earth with the tread of a giant. That consolation is that it has not reached the little preachers who have never rubbed up against a college. If you are one of them, thank God and take courage."

Godbey followed this statement with a word of comfort to the "little preachers," and a warning to those striving to be big: "The bolt that strikes the poplar dead, passes harmless over the gentle hazel's head."[5] As if such a warning is not frightening enough, we are told that those with a formal education who are not regenerated and sanctified will find that "their boasted education and profound Biblical culture will only augment their damnation, giving them a vastly more awful hell than if they had lived and died ignorant Hottentots."[6]

---

2. Knapp, *Revival Tornadoes*, 54–55.
3. Rose, *Theology of Christian Experience*, 99.
4. Godbey, *Commentary*, 3:114.
5. Godbey, *Higher Criticism*, 24–25.
6. Godbey, *Bible Theology*, 69.

Formal education was faulted for failing to provide what is really needed for the ministry. So long as it emphasized "heathen classics" instead of the Bible, it was not preparing preachers to offer the Bread of Life. Nor did it prepare preachers with the skills needed to minister. Godbey observed that

> As a rule the most intellectual people are not the most efficient soul-savers. A prominent doctor of divinity told me that in a ministry of thirty years he did not know that he had been instrumental in saving a soul . . . General observation confirms the conclusion that preachers who have received a collegiate education, as a class, are the most inefficient soul-savers.[7]

Spiritual gifts such as boldness, patience, gentleness and wisdom are available from God "and not handed out from the gray walls of the great university," according to Robinson, who had no college and almost no formal education. While he conceded that "a good education is a great blessing to anybody on earth," he added, "the most learned of the land are the least spiritual and seem to know the least about God and the working of the Holy Ghost."[8]

Knapp grew concerned about the church's willingness to substitute a trained mind for a true Christian. "An alarming symptom of apostasy in the churches is the advancing of men without these experiences [i.e. regeneration and entire sanctification] to places of control, and the requirement of a college diploma instead of a Pentecostal experience as a condition of ministerial acceptability."[9]

No educational institution could manufacture the fervor that Godbey considered crucial for ministry. "A collegiate testimony is not the qualification to preach the gospel; but a tongue of fire, ringing out a red-hot testimony."[10] This testimony sounds forth from "Pentecostal preachers, no matter how inexperienced and uneducated," but rarely from "titled schoolmen." To be able to tell one's experience of regeneration and entire sanctification is "a qualification worth more in a soul winner than all the learning of all the ages, human and angelic, without it."[11]

---

7. Godbey, "Spiritual Gifts and Graces," 6.
8. Robinson, *Honey*, 120–21.
9. Knapp, *Lightning Bolts*, 199.
10. Godbey, *Commentary*, 1:234.
11. Knapp, *Lightning Bolts*, 199.

A Holiness Hermeneutic

The best environment would be a school where formal education was combined with practical training and where the flames of spiritual vitality would be fanned. To this end, Knapp opened God's Bible School and Missionary Training Home in 1900,[12] one of many such schools begun by the Holiness movement and other conservative groups.[13]

The Holiness movement's criticism of formal education appears rooted in the belief that such an education was fundamentally unnecessary. All that was really required was the Holy Spirit who would equip the preacher. With the Spirit's enabling gifts, says Godbey, "and no learning you can preach with the Holy Ghost sent down from heaven. If you possess the lore of the ages and have not this gift, while you may be an able speaker, you are utterly incompetent to preach the gospel."[14]

Godbey expressed this even more graphically: "An illiterate old negro, full of the Holy Ghost, has more Gospel in his own soul ready to transmit to others through his great thick dictionary-and-grammar butchering lips than a whole car-load of plug-hatted theologians without the dynamite of the Holy Ghost."[15]

Not only does the Spirit grant the gifts to preach, the Spirit also provides the knowledge of God's word to the average Christian. "The blessed Holy Spirit will invariably shed the light on His precious Word, necessary to guide the honest, humble soul in the way of all truth and righteousness."[16]

Laity and Women in Ministry

The populist hermeneutic resisted hierarchical structures within ministry, preferring to allow lay people and women to minister, and sometimes preach. This was also true of the Holiness movement, perhaps to a degree greater than other movements of this period.

The use of lay ministers was necessitated, said Godbey, by the apostasy of the ordained. "If the cultured clergy will not be true, God will excuse them and fill their places ten to one with the rustic laity, uncouth, from the

---

12. Jones, *Perfectionist Persuasion*, 103.

13. Other works detailing the establishment of Bible colleges by those within and without the Holiness movement include Carpenter, "Fundamentalist Institutions," 62–75; Ringenberg, "Bible Institutes"; Brereton, *Training God's Army*.

14. Godbey, *Work of the Holy Spirit*, 67–68.

15. Godbey, *Commentary*, 5:18.

16. Ibid., 72.

slums and jungles, washed in the blood, and baptized with fire, filled with perfect love, which makes them like Gideon's braves, competent to put to flight one thousand to one."[17]

For Godbey, the value of ordination was chiefly in commissioning persons for ministry. He defended the right of the Holiness movement to ordain,

> as it is utterly impossible for the grand army of preachers, male and female, whom God is now raising up from the rank and file of the uncultured populace, and even from the slums and jungles, to prevail on the popular churches to ordain them; though God has called and commissioned them to preach the everlasting Gospel to all nations.[18]

Godbey strongly denied any New Testament warrant for the "pompous, papistical, prelatical, and clerical ordination, which was foisted upon the Church during the Dark Ages" and which makes "ministerial privileges dependent on church ordination."[19]

Women in the Holiness movement were given the opportunity to preach.[20] Knapp and others believed that in the spirit-filled church, "Women divinely called, preach, and prophesy, and witness, while the unlearned in human lore are wise in the things divine." Citing Psalm 68:11, Joel 2:28–32, and the example of Philip's daughters (Acts 21:9), Knapp contended that "Women may be Pentecostal preachers" and referred the reader to Godbey's pamphlet, "Woman Preacher, where their right to preach is defended.[21] Godbey stopped short of appealing for women's ordination because he did not consider ordination all that important and because he felt such credentials would only be burdensome and restrictive for the women.[22]

---

17. Godbey, *Commentary*, 2:60.
18. Godbey, "Church-Bride-Kingdom," 75–76.
19. Godbey, *Commentary*, 7:406.
20. A fuller treatment of the importance of women in the Holiness movement can be found in Dayton and Dayton, "Your Daughters Shall Prophesy"; Dayton, *Discovering*, 85–98; and Hardesty et al., "Women in the Holiness Movement."
21. Knapp, *Lightning Bolts*, 177, 231.
22. Godbey, *Woman Preacher*, 6.

A Holiness Hermeneutic

Scripture as Plain

One of the hallmarks of the populist hermeneutic was the conviction that the Bible was so clear that even an uneducated lay person could discover truth within it. This note was frequently sounded throughout the holiness writings. Like the adherents of the populist hermeneutic that preceded them, they described the Bible as "plain," by which they meant it was simple, used unsophisticated language, and could be clearly understood. "Nobody can make a thing plainer than the Bible has already made it," said Robinson.[23] The Bible is its own expositor, "its own dictionary."[24] "How many there are," said Watson, "who think they cannot understand the deep things of God! . . . The Bible is not merely a book for learned men, but for you, and the Holy Ghost can make it as plain as the daylight."[25]

Assuming the plainness of the Bible, what did the Holiness movement do with enigmatic passages? Because they did not believe the Bible ever contradicted itself,[26] they were left to explain those things which appear contradictory.

Some of these are due to our limited understanding, we are told. For example, Steele thought many of the difficulties in harmonizing the Pentateuch "might all vanish if we had the vast volume of details of which the Mosaic books are only the synopsis."[27] Godbey considered it the "very climax of rationalistic infidelity for us to reject the plain revelation of God simply because our poor little gourd-heads can not comprehend it."[28] Our own limits are compounded by the inaccuracies that abound in the English translations, such as the Authorized Version, a problem Godbey sought to correct by translating his own version.[29]

Many of these contradictions could be solved with proper and careful interpretation. Such interpretation included a prayerful "tarrying" or

---

23. Robinson, *Honey*, 140; Cf. Watson, *Love Abounding*, 55; Godbey, *Commentary*, 1:122, 1:164; Knapp, *Holiness Triumphant*, 17; Carradine, *Sanctification*, 73.

24. Godbey, *Commentary*, 2:76; Godbey, *Bible Theology*, 70.

25. Watson, *Love Abounding*, 74. Such plainness, of course, depended on being part of the Holiness movement so as to accept the legitimacy of the holiness hermeneutic and be familiar with code words like pentecostal, naked faith, and second blessing.

26. Godbey, *Commentary*, 4:206.

27. Steele, *Leviticus and Numbers*, 184.

28. Godbey, *Commentary*, 4:44.

29. Godbey, *Bible Theology*, 213; Godbey, *Translation of the New Testament*.

"brooding" over the passage for although God may choose to reveal the proper meaning, it would not be to the "careless and hasty reader."[30]

It may be necessary at times to reconcile two conflicting accounts, as in the suicide of Judas. Robinson displayed not only reconciliation but imagination in his explanation. He placed Judas on a limb overhanging a cliff with the noose around his neck, thoughts of the previous three years with Jesus in his mind and the activities surrounding the crucifixion within his line of vision. At the precise instant when Jesus dies, "Judas leaps off of the limb and down his body goes to the end of the rope, and the crash was so fearful that the rope broke, and down over the cliff goes the flying man, and worse still, the dying man, and worse still, the lost man."[31]

Because the authority of the Bible rested not on the solution of all interpretive problems but on the witness of the Spirit, not all contradictions need be resolved. If the Bible left something unexplained and apparently inexplicable, it is safest to "leave everything where the Holy Ghost leaves it."[32] After all, "spiritual things, like their author, are far beyond the reach of the human understanding."[33]

It is our experience of sanctification that puts our hearts at rest concerning these difficulties. Watson confessed, "I would rather be a simpleton with a heart full of love than to be a philosopher with an ice-house in my breast." With this experience, "your intellect finds rest. You are not disturbed or annoyed by theological problems."[34] One day all these mysteries will be made clear.[35]

More than one of our authors actually indicated that difficult passages were desirable. Difficulties represented God's intention to reveal the true meaning of his word, not all at once, but in successive waves on each new generation. In this way, his people will have the light needed to understand contemporary events.[36]

Such enigmas are used by God to test our faith,[37] "sharpen our wits and impress the truth more vividly." They inspire us to investigate fur-

---

30. Carradine, *Sanctified Life*, 117.
31. Robinson, *Honey*, 256–57.
32. Godbey, *Sanctification*, 88.
33. Watson, *Love Abounding*, 38.
34. Ibid., 38, 327.
35. Watson, *Coals of Fire*, 105.
36. Godbey, *Commentary*, 1:85.
37. Steele, *Leviticus and Numbers*, 213.

ther and are useful in "illuminating our perspicacity and intensifying our assiduity."[38] God gave us the Bible, difficulties and all, as the "grandest intellectual gymnasium in the world." It is not the college educated whose minds are fit but "the assiduous Bible students."[39]

Evident in their treatment of biblical difficulties is the movement's view that scholars are expendable. While they might be helpful in determining the proper translation of the original, the common person is capable of handling even the "dark passages" of the Bible without scholarly assistance. Of course, one might expect this from a book so plain.

Essential Common Sense

As we observed in an earlier chapter, one of the most important elements of the populist hermeneutic was common sense, the ability of the ordinary often unschooled person to understand the Bible using only the innate sense God had given. Common sense was a theme that appeared frequently in the writings of the Holiness movement. Godbey spoke for many when he said, "The Bible is a plain book, needing nothing but common sense and the Holy Ghost to understand it."[40]

Occasionally, these writers would describe common sense in such a way as to demonstrate its advantage over modern philosophy. Steele criticized Idealism and Positivism by noting that the Bible was written "for people of common sense, who believe that consciousness attests that we live in a world of realities, and not of illusions."[41] Elsewhere he noted that the Apostle Peter was willing to go to the home of Cornelius, even though he did not fully understand the vision given him on the rooftop (Acts 10:9–23). "Thank God that he was a man of sound common sense, and not a Hegelian philosopher."[42]

---

38. Godbey, *Commentary*, 1:207; 2:371; 6:344.
39. Ibid., 7:79.
40. Ibid., 2:232.
41. Steele, *Love Abounding*, 236.
42. Steele, *Milestone Papers*, 162.

Scripture as Normative

Supporting the premise that the Bible could be understood using only sanctified common sense was the basic assumption that the Bible presented a normative picture by which the Christian should live. While such an assumption was not unique to this movement, it was here wholeheartedly embraced and employed without reservation. Old and New Testament characters were treated as models that we should emulate or avoid. For example, "Enoch's walk with God is recorded twice, as something indeed extraordinary, but not impossible to every man in every age. It is put on record for universal imitation."[43] The same was true concerning Abraham, Daniel, Paul, Peter, and of course, Jesus. There are also negative examples, figures worthy of attention so we could "avoid their faults."[44] Within this rogues gallery appeared men like Diotrephes (3 John 9) and Samson. Robinson's frequent sightings of Alexander the Coppersmith (2 Timothy 4:14) bear special mention:

> St. Paul was greatly troubled with a fellow he called "Alexander the Coppersmith." I see some marks of similarity between Paul and myself. I have been bothered with that same fellow. I notice he is still a great drawback to the churches. When I see the collectors coming back with only a few pennies in the hat, I know Alex. is on hand. When a man puts in a copper when he should put in 5, 10, 25 or 50 cents, he is an Alexander Coppersmith. Alex. has a mighty following today.[45]

Not only characters, but many Old and New Testament events should be repeated in our lives. The prominent Old Testament example is the exodus from Egypt and the entrance into Canaan. This should be repeated in the life of each Christian as he or she escapes sin's bondage and enters the promised land of full salvation.

The prominent New Testament example is Pentecost when the Holy Spirit came on the believers in Jerusalem. Each believer was expected to experience his or her "personal pentecost," when the Spirit would come in entire sanctification. So important was Pentecost to the Holiness movement, that the term found frequent usage as an adjective. There were pentecostal meetings, pentecostal papers, pentecostal preaching, pentecostal

---

43. Steele, *Gospel of the Comforter*, 219.
44. Steele, *Saint John's Epistles*, 180.
45. Robinson, *Sunshine and Smiles*, 56.

publishing houses, pentecostal churches, and frequently, God would be implored to send down the "Pentecostal Power."[46]

Standing out above all the periods of history, including biblical history, was the model epoch, the time of the New Testament church. Often the reader was called to return to primitive and apostolic Christianity, to live according to New Testament simplicity or New Testament discipline, or to live according to the book of Acts. Watson considered it "absolutely essential, when we are converted, to take the examples given us in the Bible and be in the apostolic succession." He goes on to affirm, "I believe in the apostolic succession; in believing as the apostles believed, and praying as they prayed, and acting as they acted. If you want to follow the example of the apostles settle it to-night, that God's Word requires you to go on to a personal Pentecost."[47]

The Holiness movement, by modeling itself after the New Testament church, was better able to understand the opposition it faced from Methodism. Had not the early church been opposed by Judaism, the very soil in which Christianity first took root? For Godbey, "The logical sequence is irresistible. Just as the leaders of Judaism blindly resisted the Holy Ghost, so the leaders of fallen Christianity at the present day ostracize and interdict the holiness people, who are preaching just what the apostles preached."[48]

What was it about the New Testament period that made it a model for the Holiness movement? Godbey referred to it as a time of simplicity. Such an identification, while reflecting a nostalgia for a period less complex than his own, meant more than a desire for a slower pace and clearer choices. Simpler, for Godbey, meant purer. He saw the New Testament church as representing the pure fountainhead of the gospel stream, coming as it did immediately after the time of Christ. Human creedal additives, from Constantine's day to the present, flowed into this unpolluted stream which now

---

46. Homer, "Pentecostal Power," 382. There were also several denominations organized in this period which took Pentecostal as part of their title, including the Association of Pentecostal Churches of America, the Pentecostal Mission of Tennessee, the Pentecostal Church of the Nazarene, the Pentecost-Pilgrim Church, the Pentecostal Union, and the Pentecost Bands of the World. See Jones, *Perfectionist Persuasion*, 121–25, 173, note 11.2.

47. Steele refers to "primitive Christianity" in *Jesus Exultant*, 181, and Watson to "apostolic" Christianity in *Our Own God*, 211. Godbey often uses "New Testament" as an adjective, including *Commentary*, 3:94, 3:227, and calls us to return to the book of Acts in ibid., 5:281. Watson's reference to apostolic succession is found in *Love Abounding*, 58.

48. Godbey, *Commentary*, 5:121.

stagnates in "human ecclesiasticism" and denominational schism.⁴⁹ The Holiness movement will fail, he counseled, if it does not return to "New Testament simplicity, and there abide. The departure of the Apostolic Church from primitive truth and simplicity, revealed in the New Testament, has developed the horrors of Romanism."⁵⁰

Watson's assumption that "the volume of historic Christianity is, by the Holy Ghost, reproduced in spirit when we are born of God" is foundational to the message of the Holiness movement. The dove that came down on Jesus at his baptism is repeated in our adoption as sons of God as we receive the inward assurance of salvation. Gethsemane and Calvary are repeated when we die to self and the world. We are buried in consecration and raised from the dead "by an act of perfect sanctifying faith (Rom. vi. 4, 5,) into victory over all sin and the world." "The day of Pentecost is truly and actually repeated in us when our purified hearts receive the instantaneous incoming of the personal fullness of the Holy Spirit to abide with us forever." That the Spirit fell on all classes of people––converted Jews, Samaritans, Romans, and Greeks—"shows that every Christian ought to be baptized with the Holy Ghost."⁵¹ When we realize that God is not only "transporting the history of redemption across the ages into the actual present," and when we testify that "these things are taking place in our own experiences," we are forwarding the kingdom of God.⁵²

To read the Bible as a portrayal of model characters and events and to locate the New Testament era as a model period is to greatly simplify the process of interpretation. This eliminates any need to resolve historical-critical questions that often prove so vexing. The common person in touch with reality, whose mind is not clouded with theoretical conundrums, who is endowed with a normal measure of "horse sense," and who is in fellowship with God, is fully equipped to interpret the Bible.

"No Creed but the Bible"

The populist hermeneutic is most clearly characterized by the watchword, "No creed but the Bible." Continuing in this tradition, the Holiness movement generally opposed human creeds, at times quite forcefully. Steele's

---

49. Ibid., 5:329.
50. Ibid., 3:333.
51. Watson, *Love Abounding*, 52–53.
52. Watson, *White Robes*, 123–24.

opposition is perhaps the mildest of the authors under consideration. He finds creeds inadequate to maintain orthodoxy, something only the Holy Spirit can really accomplish. "If men draw up these creed statements in the heat of theological controversy, we are not sure that they have excluded all error and included all saving truth," he observes.[53] Without proper care, such creeds can warp and inhibit one's ability to correctly understand the Bible.[54]

Creeds were treated favorably by Knapp and found their way into his arguments, but only when they agreed with the word (as Knapp understood it). Those which did not agree were like quicksand in which "sham religionists" perished. They are utilized in "sham churches" where "committees, conferences, cardinals or popes" are put in the place of Christ, where the Holy Spirit is ignored, where Scripture is twisted to suit creeds, and where human opinion is substituted for God's word.[55]

Watson and Smith are also willing to grant some place to creeds. While creeds are not entirely wrong, said Watson, "It is not for us to formulate God's infinite Bible into an inflexible creed."[56] To do so and bind oneself to such a creed would blind one to the truths of God's word.[57]

The most severe critic of creedal statements is Godbey. The only tolerable creeds were those that agreed with the Bible, and if they agreed with the Bible, why mention the creed at all?[58] Godbey considered the formulation of the very first creed, the Nicene, the greatest mistake in the history of the church. The dark ages, what he calls "Satan's millennium," proved to be "the prolific hot-bed of human creeds."[59] He conceded that in the days of widespread illiteracy, there may have been a need for such human encapsulations of biblical truth. Once the Bible—all the creed God's people need—became widely available to a literate audience, creeds became useless.[60]

In fact, because of the dangers associated with their use, creeds are worse than useless. They obstruct a true understanding of the Bible. The "creedistic shackles" of popery and priestcraft must be broken to find

---

53. Steele, *Gospel of the Comforter*, 272.
54. Steele, *Half-Hours with Saint Paul*, 92.
55. Knapp, *Lightning Bolts*, 55, 184.
56. Watson, *Steps to the Throne*, 90.
57. Watson, *God's Eagles*, 146; Watson, *Pot of Oil*, 9.
58. Godbey, *Commentary*, 4:241.
59. Godbey, *Bible Theology*, 5.
60. Godbey, *Commentary*, 2:89.

God's truth. The "fogs of creedism" must be burned away if we would truly find God's path to be a light for our feet.[61] Creedism also leads to sectarianism, something Godbey vehemently opposed. "There is no doubt but the creeds have had more to do with originating and perpetuating the divisions in the Church than anything else. Creed making has been the fatal mistake of Christendom."[62] If only the church had retained the Bible as its only creed, those breaches that might have occurred would have been gently healed by time alone, greater unity being the inevitable and happy consequence.

Godbey warned the Holiness movement against ever formulating a creed, for if they do, "it will prove a death knell."[63] The outcome for the Holiness movement would be what had happened to so many churches: heresy, heterodoxy, then, finally, dead formality and sect-idolatry.[64] The unfortunate devotee to an unbiblical creed would experience eternal destruction. As Godbey warned, "If your creed is true, you do not need it, as the Bible includes it; if untrue, throw it away, lest it lead you to hell."[65]

Clearly the concern with creeds was their human origin, unlike the Bible which was held to be of divine origin.[66] At times this concern became explicit and the various manifestations of human authority were openly rejected. Follow Jesus only, instructed Godbey, not human leaders. "Roman Catholic priests and carnal preachers want the people to be dependent on them for leadership." Such slavish obedience is inappropriate for the sanctified, who "are no longer tossed about by human creeds and cunningly manipulated by priestcraft; but, free as angels, they take the Bible for their only authority, and Jesus for their only companion, . . ."[67] One reason entire sanctification is being attacked is because it is the "only grace adequate

---

61. Ibid., 1:295, 298; 2:225.
62. Godbey, "Church-Bride-Kingdom," 61.
63. Ibid., 61.
64. Godbey, *Bible Theology*, 6–7.
65. Godbey, *Commentary*, 5:70–71; 7:480.
66. It is not coincidental that Godbey, whose theory of inspiration left the least room for human involvement, was the most adamant opponent of human creeds of those authors studied.
67. Ibid., 2:132; 3:39–40. The strong anti-Catholic sentiment, noted in the discussion of the populist hermeneutic in chapter 2, can be seen in this passage and others from the pens of writers in the Holiness movement.

to fortify . . . against human leadership," placing the Christian where God alone can lead by his Word, his Spirit, and providence.[68]

Creeds and other predetermined theological conclusions should not be permitted to guide interpretation. A commentary, depending on its perspective, could easily steer a person away from the proper interpretation of a passage.[69] Church loyalty could also prevent a clear reading of the Bible. You will not be fully able to understand the Bible unless "you utterly and eternally die to all of your creeds, confessions, dogmatisms, and preconceived notions and hereditary intuitions."[70]

Godbey believed that an interpreter could voluntarily set aside his or her preconceptions and engage the text with a completely open mind. While modern interpreters would scoff at such a claim, Godbey believed it was possible. It was true of himself, he said, for he had consciously refused to allow his denominational affiliation to inhibit his interpretive conclusions. "Though I have been a Methodist preacher all my life, I am as dead to Methodism as to Romanism or Mormonism." He claimed to have translated the New Testament without any encumbering ecclesiastical "shackles," unlike the translators of the Revised Version of 1881. He was free of such shackles because, though he was a "life-long member of the Methodist Church," he in fact belonged only to God.[71]

Such confidence to be able to interpret objectively and accurately arose to a great extent from the illumination he and others claimed to have received from the Holy Spirit in entire sanctification. While the vision of some might be obscured by sin or dogma, the sanctified interpreter received a clear picture of biblical truth.

One criticism leveled against the populist hermeneutic was the potential for schism. Steele argued that just the reverse was true. How was it, he asked in 1878, that Methodism had been able to retain its orthodoxy in all its branches without a doctrinal schism for nearly 150 years? "Not by papal anathemas, but by an open Bible, interpreted in the light of a spiritual

---

68. Ibid., 5:284–85.

69. Smith, *Pauline Perfection*, 73.

70. Godbey, *Commentary*, 4:155.

71. Ibid., 155; Godbey, *Bible*, 17. That the Holiness movement interpreted the Bible with their own set of presuppositions is a foregone conclusion. Several specific assumptions will be considered in the next chapter.

experience. These, instead of disintegrating the Church into individualism, bind it into a spiritual unity animated by freedom."[72]

As we have seen, the Holiness movement believed that holiness was the central truth of the Bible. Having grasped this central truth, they felt they occupied the privileged position for interpretation. Those human authorities who failed to see the centrality of holiness only demonstrated their blindness at the most important point.

True to the populist hermeneutic, the Holiness movement defended this anti-authoritarian approach to interpretation by appealing to the right and power of the conscience. If first "transformed by the Holy Ghost," conscience can serve as "the highest moral tribunal, and pertinent to be followed under all circumstances simply as the best alternative."[73] Elsewhere Godbey referred to the sanctified conscience as "this noble God-given faculty, the voice of God in the soul."[74]

There are times, however, when the reader is told, either explicitly or implicitly, to follow a human leader. One finds frequent recommendations to subscribe to the books and magazines pouring from the holiness presses. Such literature is said to provide a clearer understanding of sanctification and protection from erroneous views.[75] By listening to and reading the works of holiness preachers, such as Godbey's seven volume commentary on the New Testament, one would gain a better understanding of God's word. For this reason, such works should be kept close to the Bible.[76]

Why is it that at times the reader is told to follow only Christ and at other times to follow a human authority? Far from contradictory, the difference has to do with a somewhat informal but very important evaluative procedure that took place. Those who passed the test were approved and recommended, those who failed were to be avoided. Perhaps the highest compliment that could be paid to an author was that he or she was "a reliable expositor of the Holy Scriptures."[77]

72. Steele, *Milestone Papers*, 155.

73. Godbey, *Commentary*, 2:294.

74. Ibid., 3:234.

75. Carradine, *Sanctified Life*, 114–15; Robinson, *Pitcher of Cream*, 156; Knapp, *Christ Crowned Within*, 195; Knapp, *Out of Egypt*, 142; Knapp, *Double Cure*, 81; Godbey, *Spiritual Gifts and Graces*, 45; Rose, *Theology of Christian Experience*, 148.

76. Godbey, *Commentary*, 7:533; Godbey, *Work of the Holy Spirit*, 71; Godbey, *Bible*, 44; Godbey, *Illumination*, 31.

77. This phrase was used to describe Godbey by Winfred R. Cox, one of his publishers. Cf. Godbey, "Divine Healing," 2.

The most important factor in the evaluation was a clear, personal testimony to the experience of entire sanctification in terms acceptable to the movement. As well, this experience must be accompanied by a burning passion to promote the doctrine of holiness. Godbey described this combination as "the Holy Ghost and fire."[78] Finally, the approved author should interpret the Bible along approximately the same lines as the rest of the movement. As evidenced by the diversity of eschatological viewpoints, for example, variability in biblical interpretation was far more tolerable than variability in the experience and explanation of entire sanctification.[79]

Conclusion

The Holiness movement clearly continued to interpret the Bible using the characteristic elements of the populist hermeneutic. They were critical of formal education, considering it to be at times useless and often dangerous. Bible schools were started to provide what was useful: a study of the Bible and practical ministry training. Far more important for pastor and parishioner was the Holy Spirit, who could provide the understanding and fire unavailable elsewhere.

Holiness leaders considered the Bible to be plain and able to be interpreted using common sense. So plain was the Bible that even the interpretation of difficult and contradictory passages did not require scholarly assistance. The people and events of the Bible were taken as patterns for emulation or avoidance with the New Testament period the model for the movement.

Holiness leaders distrusted human authority, such as creeds. These inventions were too burdened with preconceptions to permit uninhibited freedom to read God's word. However, the movement permitted itself a certified, Spirit-led group of authorities to guide them. Those baptized by the fire of full salvation, with a red-hot testimony, and teaching the Bible "properly" were essential to maintain a vital experience of heart purity and a clear understanding of God's word. These authorities served, under the

---

78. Godbey, *Commentary*, 3:270. Elsewhere Godbey permits the use of "all other books which explain the Bible *in harmony with the Holy Ghost*" (ibid., 2:334; emphasis mine).

79. If one still had a question about the trustworthiness of an author, a glance at the book's binding could put the mind to rest. The vast majority of primary sources consulted for this study were published by Knapp or his Revivalist publishing organization.

leading of the Holy Spirit, as trusted friends who would help read the compass of the populist hermeneutic. Such navigational aids for the interpretation of the Bible were crucial for guiding the movement through the rough waters of the late nineteenth and early twentieth centuries.

6

Four Pillars of Holiness Interpretation

THE PRESUPPOSITIONS THAT PEOPLE bring to the Bible, consciously or unconsciously, serve as the foundation and framework for their biblical interpretation. The Holiness movement, like every other movement, used certain presuppositions in their biblical interpretation. Many of these, such as the Christ-centeredness of the Bible, have been common to Christianity through the centuries. Others, while found elsewhere, either serve as important supports for holiness interpretation or take on a unique dimension in sanctified hands. This chapter examines four important presuppositions that shaped the biblical interpretation of the American Holiness movement: the immanence of God, the Spirit-centeredness or pneumatocentricity of the Bible, the unity of the Bible, and the assumption that the Bible may be interpreted in a more-than-literal manner.

God Is Immanent

The understanding that God is active in history and in the lives of his people is at least as old as the earliest experiences of Israel. While Genesis portrays God as active at particular times, with particular people, in striking ways, Exodus displays God's power at work in Israel's history.[1]

Wesley shared this conviction. In his sermon, "On Divine Providence," he observes, "And it is nothing strange that He who is omnipresent, who 'filleth heaven and earth,' who is in every place, should see what is in every

---

1. Urban, *Short History*, 14–15.

place, where he is intimately present."[2] Such an understanding of God as personal and intimate was required for Wesley to give experience so large a place in his theological methodology.

Wesley's heirs in the Holiness movement, sharing his respect for experience, also considered God's immanence to be very important. Like Wesley, they did not restrict God to operating only in the private, present, and personal sphere, but evidenced a healthy respect for the transcendence of God.[3] Their emphasis, however, is on divine immanence, that God has been and remains present and active, making himself known, revealing his will, guiding his people, and relating to each one individually.

American society was becoming more secularized during this period with the religious explanation for things carrying less weight than it had previously. Some retired God from active duty, while others relegated him to the status of First Cause. Watson marveled at the secularization and resultant skepticism of his day.

> Strange to say that the rapid increase of the knowledge of nature, and inventions, and arts, and sciences in modern years, has brought a flood of materialistic skepticism, and instead of "looking through nature up to nature's God," men look downward and see no God at all, and never think of reverting to God any more than if He did not exist.[4]

Many in the church reacted by emphasizing the immanence of God. Some followed the path marked out by Schleiermacher or pantheism,[5] others, such as the Holiness movement, pursued a more conservative course, giving greater weight to the Bible.

As had the church for centuries, holiness folk saw God as active throughout history on behalf of his people providing them with a Redeemer and the sanctifying Spirit. He had superintended the writing and preservation of the Bible for the church's edification. He was involved with the affairs of world history, providentially masterminding details on behalf of his people. The movement's eye for divine providence can be illustrated by Godbey's comments on the Roman Empire, Alexander the Great, and the

---

2. Wesley, "On Divine Providence," 315. Cf. Burtner and Chiles, *John Wesley's Theology*, 58.

3. Such respect for God's transcendence can be observed, among other ways, in their treatment of the Bible as one unified and divine work, a pillar, to be considered shortly.

4. Watson, *Our Own God*, 188.

5. Aulen, *Faith of the Christian Church*, 55–58.

A Holiness Hermeneutic

Greek and Hebrew languages. Rome was established by God, "in His wonderful providence," as "the whole world in one vast consolidated empire, as a grand preparation for the universal propagation of the gospel, which would have been an impossibility without the protection of the universal government."[6]

Alexander conquered the world, although only a "boy of one and twenty, with no money and a handful of men," because "God was in it." The reason God gave Alexander the world was so that the Greeks could tutor the world in their language. This tongue, the "culmination of that climacteric Greek learning in which they excelled all nations," was prepared by God to be "His chosen vehicle, in which to preach the gospel to every nation." As he had done with the Hebrew language, God removed Greek from common usage after it had served its purpose to avoid corruption. "Therefore we have the inspired archives of the Hebrew and Greek kept in their pristine purity, locked up in these dead languages, whither we can all go and find the unadulterated truth as it is in Jesus, and transmit it to the world. Oh, the wonders of the divine administration!"[7]

More characteristic of their understanding of divine immanence was their conviction that God is actively involved in the present with his people. He is at work in the affairs of the world. Watson averred,

> He watches every movement of your inner being, and has His hand this very moment on every thing in creation, and He is incessantly adjusting causes to effects, and the inner spirit to the outer circumstances, and things near to things hundreds of thousands of miles away. Nothing can be too small for His loving notice and superintendence.[8]

God chose the earth from all the planets of the solar system and Canaan from all the countries of the world because each was centrally located. If you think that happened by chance, Watson said, "you have never yet got hold of the great thought of God's creation or His plan in all His ways."[9]

God is not only at work in such monumental ways but is nearby to communicate with us and make himself known. He confirms by "inward revelations of the Comforter" that we are God's children and entirely sanctified. He speaks to us through his word. He converses with us "face to

---

6. Godbey, *Commentary*, 5:12.
7. Ibid., 134–35.
8. Watson, *Our Own God*, 226.
9. Watson, *God's First Words*, 49.

face in spiritual communion." Set aside all incredulity, said Steele, for if one creature can reveal himself or herself to a fellow creature, certainly the Creator can reveal himself to his creation.[10]

At times, God comes very near to his people to guide them in decisions they should make. The majority of the authors surveyed gave some attention to God's guidance and how to know it; Knapp devoted an entire book to the subject.[11]

Most described a triple dimension to God's leadership: Bible, Spirit, and Providence. Godbey believed God speaks to our mind using the word, to our human spirit using the divine Spirit, and to our bodies using providence.[12] Watson even found a trinitarian basis for this triple leadership. Providence is God's way of guiding, the written word is Christ's, and the "peculiar sphere of the Spirit's guidance is direct conviction and illumination upon the heart and spiritual senses."[13]

When these three are in agreement, one can proceed with confidence. "We are perfectly safe. These three unitedly will always give you all the light you need."[14] However, one must follow all three. Deception can follow from heeding only the Spirit, without the other two. "Dead formality" comes from only listening to the word, without the Spirit and Providence. "If you follow Providence alone, regardless of the Word and Spirit, you will apostatize into rationalistic infidelity and make your bed in hell."[15] Godbey considered these three in complete agreement as "infallible" guidance.[16]

This presupposition passed into the Holiness movement through Methodism from Wesley. His stress on experience required a God who was actively involved with his people. By placing even greater emphasis on experience than had Wesley, the Holiness movement depended heavily on this presupposition. Of the four assumptions considered in this chapter, the immanence of God should probably be identified as the most foundational, the one on which the other three are based.

---

10. Steele, *Milestone Papers*, 154.
11. Knapp, *Impressions*.
12. Godbey, *Commentary*, 5:130.
13. Watson, *White Robes*, 158.
14. Godbey, *Holiness or Hell*, 76–77.
15. Godbey, *Commentary*, 5:130.
16. Ibid., 1:204.

A Holiness Hermeneutic

The Bible Is Pneumatocentric

The presupposition most characteristic of the Holiness movement is that the Bible is primarily concerned with the person and work of the Holy Spirit. The church has long recognized the importance of the Holy Spirit for biblical interpretation, citing 1 Corinthians 2 and other passages.[17]

The Holiness movement's emphasis on the Spirit was not meant to disparage the work of the other two members of the Trinity; God and Christ were essential and foundational to their message. There is the unmistakable acknowledgment that the Spirit would have no ministry had not the Father sent the Son and the Son sent the Holy Spirit. The whole Bible, said Godbey, is the biography of Christ, "the Old Testament that of Christ excarnate, and the New Testament that of Christ incarnate."[18] His life and death are central to the Christian's hope; he stands as the central pillar of the church.[19] In the Old Testament, Jesus appears in the figure of Jehovah, and is in fact the culmination of that corpus.[20]

Found in holiness exegesis is an emphasis on the Spirit that surpasses without intending to replace an emphasis on the rest of the Trinity. These writers continued to see in Scripture the "scarlet thread" of redemption but took as their mission the task of pointing out another thread running through the word. "It is the white one of the promise of the Pentecostal outpouring of the Holy Ghost. Of all the promises of the Bible, God exalts this as 'The Promise' of all the ages."[21]

Why did the Holiness movement place such an emphasis on the Holy Spirit? The logical place to begin to answer this question is with John Wesley. Whether one sees Wesley as Christocentric or Pneumatocentric in his doctrine of Christian perfection, he clearly emphasized the Spirit by his stress on Christian experience. The American Holiness movement's pneumatocentricity drew its nourishment from the well Wesley had uncovered a century and a half earlier.

The dispensational framework of John Fletcher also influenced the spirit-centeredness of the Holiness movement. All of our authors utilized his structure in their interpretations of the Bible. Fletcher saw history

---

17. Williams, *Receiving the Bible*, 15.
18. Godbey, *Commentary*, 2:120.
19. Ibid., 3:19, 21.
20. Ibid., 4:296; 6:133; Watson, *God's First Words*, 180.
21. Knapp, *Lightning Bolts*, 13, 140.

divided into three periods: the dispensation of God the Father, during the giving of the Law and prophecies; the dispensation of the Son, from John the Baptist to Christ's ascension; and the dispensation of the Spirit, from Pentecost to the second coming of Christ.[22]

Throughout the nineteenth century, holiness came to be thought of increasingly in relation to Pentecost. Influential in this regard was Phoebe Palmer who after 1857 began using pentecostal terms for entire sanctification. Catalysts for her shift were the teaching of Fletcher, William Arthur's *The Tongue of Fire*, published in 1855, and Palmer's own study of Acts 2 in preparation for her book, *The Promise of the Father*.[23]

Since this was regarded as the Age of the Spirit, Pentecost became the paradigmatic experience in the life of the believer. Christians living in this age were crowned with a privileged perspective and abundant authority, and awaited a glorious future at its conclusion. Godbey placed the Holiness movement at the center of this glorious future when he spoke of the "dismal night of sin" relieved "by the glorious millennial day, whose auspicious dawn methinks I see in the present Holiness movement, gilding every land with the fair-fingered Aurora of the coming kingdom."[24]

The spirit-centeredness of the Holiness movement in the late nineteenth and early twentieth centuries served several purposes. It provided a sense of power to a movement which by this time was moving more and more to the margins of society. It also permitted the movement to explain its teachings using biblical imagery. Whether or not referring to entire sanctification as a "personal Pentecost" was biblically accurate, it certainly helped to make it understandable to the sympathetic listener. Most important, such spirit-centered language and imagery fit well the highly experiential nature of the movement.

While all the movement shared a commitment to the pneumatocentricity of the Bible, some variety existed in the specifics of how this was carried out. There were those who emphasized the person and work of the Spirit in a general sense while others put the emphasis on one particular work, that of entire sanctification. The best representative of those emphasizing the Spirit's work and person was Steele. If doctrine is the skeleton of religion, then the scriptural doctrine of the Holy Spirit is "the backbone of

---

22. Cf. Dayton, *Theological Roots*, 51–54; Knight, "John Fletcher's Influence," 13–33; Watson's summary of Fletcher's dispensations can be found in *Love Abounding*, 51.

23. Dayton, *Theological Roots*, 87–88.

24. Godbey, *Commentary*, 3:191.

A Holiness Hermeneutic

that skeleton."[25] The vertebrae of this backbone, the work of the Holy Spirit, is multiform. Regeneration cannot occur, no matter how eloquent the preaching, unless the Spirit "purges the film from blind eyes."[26] The Spirit's work included the "double inspiration" of the Bible, both of the original authors and of the modern interpreter, the latter being thereby granted "an astonishing insight into the Holy Scriptures."[27]

Steele considered one work of the Holy Spirit to deserve special notice due to its importance for Wesley, its perceived neglect in the Methodism of Steele's day, and especially, because of its importance in the life of the believer. This work is the Spirit's witness to our hearts that we are sons and daughters of God that enables us to say, "Abba, Father." It was this assurance of the Spirit that had warmed Wesley's heart at Aldersgate, confirming for him that "Christ had taken away my sins, even mine." Steele described this assurance as "the immediate contact of the Holy Spirit with the human soul, affording a certainty beyond a doubt of pardon and adoption into the family of God" for all believers.[28]

Steele was not only concerned to rekindle this truth but to emphasize that such assurance came through the inner witness of the Holy Spirit, not through the Bible alone. The believer is to trust the promises of Scripture as they "are designed to awaken faith in the penitent soul by showing that God is able and willing to save now." However, as Steele pointed out, "no one of them contains the record of your personal pardon."[29] The Bible was never intended to provide this assurance and never claims this role. It does contain "the marks of the new birth, the fruit of the Spirit" which "constitute an inferential testimony confirming the direct witness of the Spirit." Yet it must not be put in place of the Spirit, for to do so results in danger for the convert who then lacks the "satisfactory certification of sonship to God which He in His goodness has provided." To do so also dishonors the Spirit.[30] Steele counseled seekers to "trust the written word of God till you have the spoken word of the Spirit in your heart."[31]

---

25. Steele, *Gospel of the Comforter*, 224.
26. Ibid., 20–21.
27. Ibid., 140; *Half-Hours with Saint Paul*, 17, 77; Steele, *Love Enthroned*, 261.
28. Steele, *Jesus Exultant*, 162–63.
29. Steele, *Half-Hours with Saint Paul*, 315.
30. Steele, *Gospel of the Comforter*, 237.
31. Steele, *Half-Hours with Saint Paul*, 315.

Four Pillars of Holiness Interpretation

Another work of the Holy Spirit was Christian perfection, considered by Steele to be the "key-note" of our Christianity. He pointed out the importance of this doctrine in many ways, the most interesting being its significance in 1 John. Steele thought this book to be probably the last of the New Testament books to be written. The apostle John wrote as if he knew he were penning the "last statement of Christian truth in epistolary form." As the last book, "it may very properly be regarded as the interpreter of the whole series," that is, the Bible. How significant, noted Steele, that in this final book by which the entire Bible can be better understood we find Christian perfection taught more clearly than anywhere else.[32]

However, as important as this doctrine is to Steele, he emphasizes it much less than other holiness writers. In his commentary on Leviticus and Numbers, where the sacrificial system and the Holiness Code could be seen as fertile ground for typologizing, he makes virtually no mention of entire sanctification, even in a typological sense. In fact, although he believed sanctification to be very important, it was the atonement, not simply sanctification, that was the "central Christian doctrine."[33] Steele specifically warned against entire sanctification being "isolated from its connection with the whole system, and magnified out of due proportion by being exclusively dwelt upon. Such treatment of a most vital truth creates error."[34]

Leon Hynson, in his analysis of biblical interpretation in the American Holiness movement, recognized what he called the "Holiness Hermeneutic." Believing that entire sanctification (as they understood it) was the central truth of scripture, they permitted this doctrine to shape and guide their interpretation of the Bible.[35]

The origins of the holiness hermeneutic may be found in a combination of factors. First, as we have seen, the Holiness movement treated the person and work of the Holy Spirit as central to the Bible. As sanctification came to be more controversial within Methodism later in the century, the force of the conflict drove the parties to extremes, erasing Wesley's more balanced presentation. The resultant stress in the movement on the crisis moment of sanctification prompted many interpreters to move from the Spirit's work in general to this particular aspect of the Spirit's work. The holiness hermeneutic was perpetuated in part because the movement lacked

---

32. Steele, *Saint John's Epistles*, xxi, xxviii.
33. Ibid., xxiii.
34. Steele, *Love Enthroned*, 414–15.
35. Hynson, "Wesleyan Quadrilateral," 19–33.

the capacity to check its own interpretation. While Wesley's quadrilateral maintained balance, the holiness bilateral could not. It continued as well because holiness interpreters found that it helped them to better understand the Bible.

To speak of the holiness hermeneutic does not imply that entire sanctification was the only doctrine that concerned the movement. While it was this truth that received the greatest emphasis, the Holiness movement also taught divine healing, the ministry of women, the second coming of Christ and, for the most part, premillennialism, and was considered God's vehicle for doing so.[36]

The holiness hermeneutic is evident in many ways in the biblical interpretation of the movement. It led to more-than-literal interpretation, a topic to which we will return later in this chapter. The entire book of Song of Solomon is interpreted allegorically, not only as a human love song, but as *The Divine Love Song*, proclaiming the beauty of entire sanctification. For example, Watson quotes Song of Solomon 7:9 from the King James Version, "And the roof of thy mouth like the best wine for my beloved, that goeth down sweetly, causing the lips of those that are asleep to speak," and then comments, "And hence purified souls will often pray in their sleep, or sing songs in their sleep, or preach sermons in their sleep, and sometimes awaken themselves uttering sweet worship, which is the effect of the best wine of the kingdom which goeth down sweetly, causing the lips of those that are asleep to speak."[37]

Robinson considered the life of Lazarus (John 11–12) to be a type of Christian experience as understood by the Holiness movement. His sickness, death, shrouding, burial and putrification refer to a person who is born with a carnal heart, is dead in sin, bound by Satan, buried in hopelessness, and stinking with corruption. Lazarus' resurrection, liberation from the graveclothes, feasting with Jesus, and living testimony symbolizes the new birth, entire sanctification, the joyous life of holiness, and our task as soul-winners. The persecution of Lazarus by the high priest is just like what happens to the sanctified person. "Just as sure as you get filled with the Holy

---

36. Premillennial eschatology represents the majority of the Holiness movement, especially after the turn of the century. Several writers devoted attention to the matter of prophecy, Knapp even charting the return of Jesus (*Lightning Bolts*, 135). Steele was staunchly postmillennial and Carradine may have been; Smith may have been amillennial. Cf. Steele, *Substitute*; Carradine, *Revival Sermons*, 101; Rose, *Theology of Christian Experience*, 260.

37. Watson, *Divine Love Song*, 102.

Four Pillars of Holiness Interpretation

Ghost and go to feasting with your Lord your testimonies will stir up the carnal mind in the man that has not got a clean heart, and he will become jealous of you, and the fight will be on, O Christian soldier."[38]

The holiness hermeneutic not only led to a more-than-literal reading of the Bible, it also read its particular understanding of sanctification back into both the Old and New Testaments. Carradine considered "that you cannot read the Bible without perceiving that there is a 'higher life' constantly recognized and brought forward in its pages. It is held up as an attainment; we are expected to come unto it; we are commanded to possess it, and are presented with characters who enjoyed and lived in this life."[39]

He found holiness taught in the two references to snow in Ps 51:7 and Isa 1:18. Because he took Isaiah's phrase, "as white as snow" to refer to regeneration, "whiter than snow" must be the psalmist's reference to sanctification.[40] Ezekiel spoke of sanctification in 36:25, "Then will I sprinkle clean water upon you, and ye shall be *clean*: from *all* your filthiness, and from all your idols, will I cleanse you." This refers to holiness, said Carradine, because "it is a promise made to *God's people*, and that the blessing is one of *purity*, and *not pardon*" (emphasis his).[41]

Godbey also saw the Bible including the Old Testament as a book on holiness and unashamedly interpreted with the holiness hermeneutic, or as he put it, "from the standpoint of purity." In *Christian Perfection*, he claimed to have "proved every New Testament writer to be a perfectionist" and to be able to do the same with the Old Testament, since "the Bible is perfectionism. Theologians may howl and Satan may rage, but the Bible is a book on perfectionism."[42]

We have already met Watson as the man who found holiness in parts of the Old Testament where others never thought to look. Such was his discovery when he turned his attention to the "sundry laws and customs which God prescribed to his Jewish people." One has very clear insight into these if it is remembered "that God was not only dealing with the outward well-being of that people, but he had in his mind as well the ulterior and spiritual benefit of his people in all subsequent ages."[43]

---

38. Robinson, *Story of Lazarus*, 9–11.
39. Carradine, *Sanctification*, 106. Cf. Carradine, *Second Blessing*.
40. Ibid., 93.
41. Ibid., 112.
42. Godbey, *Christian Perfection*, 108–9.
43. Watson, *Coals of Fire*, 39.

Steele maintained, "Of course entire sanctification except in a ceremonial sense was not enjoyed by the Old Testament saints,"[44] but his fellow holiness authors thought otherwise. Watson taught that the religious experience of Jacob as detailed in Genesis 28 to 33 reflected "the New Testament teachings of adoption, consecration, and the baptism of power." More specifically, he asserted that Jacob was sanctified at Peniel.[45] The list of Old Testament figures who experienced sanctification is long and illustrious, including Isaiah, whose sanctification occurred during his vision in the temple (Isaiah 6).[46]

When they applied the holiness hermeneutic to the New Testament, the holiness authors were unanimous in anchoring their doctrine of entire sanctification in the didactic sections. While some may have spent a great deal of time interpreting narrative passages, they only did so because they felt they could prove the doctrine from the Epistles. In their interpretation of the Gospel narratives they found Jesus a perfect model of holiness and the disciples in need of it. After Pentecost, the apostles demonstrate the sanctified life.

One of the clearest manifestations of the holiness hermeneutic is found in Knapp's treatment of the Book of Revelation. He purposed in writing on Revelation, "not so much to deal with its 'times and seasons' as to magnify the great central truth, 'holiness triumphant,' which gleams from every chapter. In reading it from this standpoint, we believe that its meaning can best be mastered."[47]

With this presupposition, Knapp identified the woman portrayed in Revelation 12 as "the true holiness movement from its beginning to its final triumph," and the woman in chapter 17 as "the anti-holiness movement from its incipiency to its end." The silence in heaven recorded in Revelation 8 as the seventh seal was about to be opened reflects the "intense interest in heaven . . . over the outcome of holiness on earth."[48]

Considering the novelty of this approach it is not surprising that holiness interpreters felt the need to justify the holiness hermeneutic. An important component of their defense was the claim that entire sanctification

---

44. Steele, *Gospel of the Comforter*, 38.

45. Watson, *Coals of Fire*, 113.

46. Ibid., 7–28. Carradine, *Sanctification*, 110–11. Godbey, *Visions*, 10. Knapp, *Out of Egypt*, 62.

47. Knapp, *Holiness Triumphant*, 6.

48. Ibid., 6, 127, 186.

represents the central theme of the Bible and the "crowning experience of the Christian life."[49] "Holiness," wrote Godbey, "is the theme of the Bible, set forth specifically six hundred times, and inferentially in thousands of instances."[50] It is, as we noted earlier, the white thread running through the Scriptures.

The central importance of entire sanctification for the Holiness movement is evident in two more implicit, but nevertheless important, ways. In this survey of the literature, those who most commonly appeared as enemies of the author and his readers were those who opposed entire sanctification as the movement understood it. This included those who eliminated the need for any sanctification, such as the "Zinzendorfians" (who taught that inbred sin is removed at conversion). It also included those who believed in holiness but with different connotations, such as those who emphasized a gradual process over a crisis experience, those who taught suppression rather than eradication of the sin nature, and those who believed Spirit-baptism brought power or tongues rather than purity.[51]

The centrality of holiness was also implied in the purposes for which the authors wrote. While they offered several, their chief purpose was to foster the experience of entire sanctification within their readers. Often this will be clearly expressed, such as this statement from Godbey, "Of course, the great end in view is to lead the reader into the experience of Christian perfection, and establish him there."[52] Even when it is not so stated, it is common to find appeals to the reader to "tarry right here, until you have your Pentecost!"[53]

Their belief in the centrality of holiness in the Bible is explicitly stated in many places and is implied in who they considered the enemy and in why they wrote. Armed with this conviction, the outcome of finding holiness taught throughout the scriptures was assured.

These interpreters also defended the holiness hermeneutic as the perspective by which the Bible was best understood. Such a reading made sense of the central biblical theme of holiness, both divine and human.

49. Carradine, *Sanctification*, 202.

50. Godbey, *Commentary*, 1:297.

51. Carradine, *Old Man*, 153–56; Carradine, *Golden Sheaves*, 55; Carradine, *Sanctified Life*, 261; Knapp, *Lightning Bolts*, 66; Robinson, *Honey*, 202; Robinson, *Story of Lazarus*, 95–103; Watson, *White Robes*, 99; Watson, *Coals of Fire*, 86; Watson, *Love Abounding*, 208.

52. Godbey, *Christian Perfection*, 3–4.

53. Smith, *From Glory to Glory*, 88.

A Holiness Hermeneutic

"The Bible is called the Holy Bible, it came from a Holy God, shows the way to obtain a holy heart, live a holy life, and finally reach a holy heaven."[54] The holiness hermeneutic did justice to the omnipotence of God. "Look at it, reader; if God can take a perfect giant of sin and make him a babe in Christ in a moment, can he not take a babe in Christ and make him a perfect man in Christ Jesus in a moment?"[55]

This presupposition fully accounted for the New Testament commands to become holy, such as, "Be ye therefore perfect" (Matthew 5:48). It explained why the New Testament authors use the aorist tense of the Greek language when they speak of sanctification, a tense which "always denotes an instantaneous action, forever annihilating the gradualistic theology of sanctification out of the Bible."[56]

To read the Bible using the hermeneutic of holiness also accounted for the "Dual Symmetry of the Bible." One of the distinctive features of the doctrine of entire sanctification and one of the more controversial was that it was a second crisis experience of grace subsequent to regeneration, a "double cure" for the disease of sin. Taking this understanding to their study of the Bible, they were struck by how much there occurred in pairs. "It is wonderful," wrote Watson, "how, all through the Bible, divine truth is double-barreled."[57] There are two testaments, Old and New, two natures of Christ, two elements--blood and water--that flowed from Christ's side, two touches on the eyes of the blind man; the list is almost endless. In fact, confessed Godbey, "If I were to notice everything in the Bible setting forth this glorious double salvation, it would take me the balance of my life."[58]

Carradine was so certain of this double nature of the Bible that he used it to argue against those who taught a third work of grace, saying "it mars what we call the dual symmetry of the Bible."[59] Watson noticed that not only does the Bible possess a propensity to pairing but the second element is usually the "uppermost and the best and the most significant, as the first and second Adam, the first and second birth, the first and second bird sent from the ark," and so forth.[60] With the double work of grace as their

---

54. Carradine, *Old Man*, 188.
55. Carradine, *Sanctification*, 75.
56. Godbey, *Commentary*, 2:282; Godbey, *Holiness or Hell*, 144.
57. Watson, *Love Abounding*, 19.
58. Godbey, *Holiness or Hell*, 139–40.
59. Carradine, *Sanctified Life*, 261.
60. Watson, *God's First Words*, 220.

interpretative key, the Bible was unlocked and a double blessing of insight, hitherto unseen, poured out.

Still another component of their defense of the holiness hermeneutic was the argument that only those who employed it could really understand the Bible. After all, if entire sanctification truly opened the Bible as never before, without this grace the Bible remained closed. Many passages of scripture will be "all dry or gross hieroglyphics to believers who have not yet entered the sanctified bridehood of the Lamb."[61] Because the unsanctified are "without the indwelling Expositor," the "Bible is a sealed book until revealed by the Holy Ghost."[62] Watson, while explaining Isaiah's sanctification in the temple, wrote, "It is likely that persons who have not experienced the witness to heart purity, may disagree with these statements; but those who have received the full baptism of the Spirit, will confirm their truthfulness."[63]

Reliance on the Holy Spirit for biblical interpretation has been a practice of the church since its beginnings. What set the Holiness movement apart as unique among modern Christian movements was their understanding of the Spirit and his role. This was now the Dispensation of the Spirit, when Pentecost became the defining moment and entire sanctification the defining experience. The Spirit continually indwelt the sanctified believer, bringing purity and a deeper insight into the Bible than could otherwise be obtained. To deny the centrality of holiness was to miss the true message of the Bible and to demonstrate the absence of the Holy Spirit in one's life.

The Bible Is One Unified Work

For centuries the church has recognized the composite nature of the Bible. It was acknowledged early that it had been written by many different authors over many centuries and that there was much in the Old Testament that differed from the New. More important to the church than its composite nature, however, has been the unity of the Bible. It was seen as God's message to humanity, anticipating the coming of the Savior in the Old Testament, recognizing and celebrating that coming in the New.

---

61. Watson, *Steps to the Throne*, 100.
62. Godbey, *Commentary*, 6:192.
63. Watson, *Coals of Fire*, 9.

A Holiness Hermeneutic

With the rise of historical criticism came greater attention to the human elements of the Bible, including authorship, dating, and sources. Most Christians, up through the period under consideration, continued to read the Bible as God's word to humanity, while the scholarly world came increasingly to read it as humanity's word about God.

The American Holiness movement accepted that the Bible was unified; divided into two Testaments and written by many over long periods of time it was nevertheless a single word from God. It was God who spoke it through the human writers and it bears all the marks of a single mind with a common overarching theme and sub-themes. To interpret the Bible without recognizing this unity was to eliminate the possibility of understanding. For the most part such unity was assumed although at least one of these writers felt it necessary to defend this unity, employing it for apologetic purposes.

One of the more comprehensive ways used by this movement and others to demonstrate the Bible's unity was to divide it into dispensations. Such an approach reveals the Bible's overarching structure into which can be placed its events, characters, and themes; the structure demonstrates that the Bible proceeds from a single divine author. John Fletcher referred to three dispensations, corresponding to God, Jesus and the Holy Spirit. The ages of God and Jesus are past and we are now living in the dispensation of the Spirit.

Fletcher's framework was adopted by most holiness authors although some modified it. At one point, in his enthusiasm for the "dual symmetry" of the Bible, Carradine criticized the tripartite nature of Fletcher's system, opting instead for the notion of two covenants. Later, however, we find him again using Fletcher's categories.[64] Godbey frequently spoke of dispensations but not always with a consistent meaning. While he referred at times to Fletcher's three ages, he also spoke of the present as the sixth dispensation, that of the Holy Ghost. The Edenic, Antediluvian, Patriarchal, Mosaic, and Messianic ages have come and gone; the kingdom age would begin at the return of Christ.[65]

At various times Watson spoke of Fletcher's three dispensations, at other times to a different three (antediluvian, prophetic, and Christian), and at still other times, he referred to four. These were the Age of Conscience, which extended from Adam to the Flood, the Age of Law or of Moses or

---

64. Carradine, *Second Blessing*, 87; Carradine, *Better Way*, 55.
65. Godbey, *Commentary*, 3:189–91.

Four Pillars of Holiness Interpretation

the Jewish Age, the Gospel or Christian Age, in which we presently live, and the Kingdom Age, which will begin with Christ's second coming.[66] Each of these ages has been patterned after the first age, "proving in all things God's first words supply the key to all successive words."[67] The total of these ages, if a thousand years is counted as one day, will be six days, the final millennial age completing the week and containing "all the features of God's true Sabbath."[68] With each age there has been an increase in the activity of the Holy Spirit and each age has ended with tragedy, demonstrating humanity's failure apart from the grace of God.[69]

It was important, said Watson, to interpret the Bible with these dispensations in mind. "If each portion of Scripture could be rightly placed in relationship to time and dispensation, it would give people great light in understanding the different ages and dispensations of revealed truth." Without such an understanding, people attempt "to make the Scriptures fit into a period for which they are not intended," with "awkward" results.[70]

The use of dispensations by the Holiness movement—whether three, four, or seven—demonstrated the movement's conviction that the Bible was one unified revelation from God. Their use also provided the movement with a system by which to interpret the Bible. What did not agree with the holiness hermeneutic could be explained away by reference to its being from a different age.[71]

Their use of dispensations also sheds light on the close relationship that developed later in the twentieth century between dispensationalism of the Scofield variety and the Holiness movement. This enigma, called "one of the strangest theological anachronisms of our time" by H. Ray Dunning, can be better understood by recognizing the long-standing tradition of the Holiness movement, extending back at least as far as Fletcher, of reading the Bible according to some type of dispensational framework.[72]

---

66. Watson, *God's First Words*, 73, 83, 105, 128; Watson, *God's Eagles*, 219, 247–55.

67. Watson, *God's First Words*, 74.

68. Watson, *God's Eagles*, 254.

69. Ibid., 252–54. Although his system differed in many respects, Scofield also observed that each dispensation ended in the failure of humanity (Weber, "Dispensationalism").

70. Watson, *God's Eagles*, 189, 192.

71. Marsden makes this point about Dispensationalism in *Fundamentalism*, 54.

72. Theological incompatibilities still remain between the two movements, as Dunning shows in "Biblical Interpretation," 47–51.

The use of dispensations was not the only way the Holiness movement demonstrated their conviction that the Bible is unified. This can also be seen in their frequently repeated, almost instinctive practice of interpreting scripture by scripture. In the hands of the holiness interpreters, this legitimate exegetical method was carried to questionable lengths. Robinson and others applied the meaning of one metaphor to another passage.[73] Comparing scripture with scripture left Watson "assured that each of the twelve apostles in a special way represented some great cardinal doctrine." While we cannot be sure which apostle represented which doctrine, he speculated, after having "put all the words of Scripture together concerning this subject," that Paul may stand for faith, Peter for holiness, John for love, James for good works, and so forth.[74]

The assumption of unity is also demonstrated in their harmonizing of one passage with another for the purpose of clarity. In his commentary on Leviticus, Steele harmonizes the reference to the high priest entering the most holy place three times (16:12–15), with Hebrews 9:7 which speaks of him entering only once, by interpreting the latter as meaning one day every year.[75] On a broader scale, Godbey harmonized the four gospels according to the order of events (of which he felt confident). In this way, he claimed to eliminate repetitious expositions that can be "irksome" and "monotonous."[76]

Watson, after identifying four distinct outpourings of the Holy Spirit in Acts, harmonizes these with the four gospels. Both the first outpouring and the first gospel were directed to Jews. The second outpouring was on Samaritans, the group "principally addressed by Mark." Luke's Gospel and the third outpouring came to converted Romans while the Gospel of John was written for converted Greeks in Ephesus, the same group on whom the fourth outpouring came. Realizing that his readers would be amazed at such a correlation, Watson summarizes, "The Bible was not written by haphazard, nor by chance. There is a marvelous arrangement everywhere."[77]

Scriptural unity was also demonstrated by the successive reading and exposition of biblical passages. This took the form of the Bible reading, or the stringing together of "chains" of scripture. These passages, coming from

73. Robinson, *Honey*, 111.
74. Watson, *God's Eagles*, 240–41.
75. Steele, *Leviticus and Numbers*, 122.
76. Godbey, *Commentary*, 6:6.
77. Watson, *Love Abounding*, 52–53.

different books, different authors, different types of literature, and different testaments, were read together by virtue of their sharing a common theme. Watson explained the practice this way: "One of the beautiful ways of studying the things of God, is to select a single truth or attribute of God or His government, and trace it from its first revelation in Scripture or providence through all the Bible, and see how it expands and brightens with ever increasing beauty and strength to the close of revelation."[78] Elsewhere he counseled similarly, "A very good way to find out the mind of the Holy Spirit on any one thing, is to trace out, in the Scriptures, what He has said on the subject."[79]

For these authors, the subject they wanted to explore usually had something to do with holiness. After all, this was for them the summit of scriptural truth, the common theme around which the unity of the Bible revolved. Robinson noted a divinely ordained similarity, exalting holiness, between the first two and the last two chapters of the Bible. In Genesis one and two we find happy, holy people living in a garden they are then forced to flee because of sin. In Revelation 21 and 22 again people have returned to live in paradise, forever forgiven, happy and holy.[80]

A corollary to the unity of the Bible and in fact an extension of it is the assumption that revelation is progressive. As Watson said, truth "expands and brightens with ever increasing beauty and strength to the close of revelation." Such an assumption made possible the interpretation of the Old Testament by the New. It enabled Watson to consider that the closing parts of the Bible stated explicitly what was illustrated in the Old Testament, what he called "panoramic theology."[81] Because he assumed revelation was progressive, Steele regarded 1 John––thought by him to be the last New Testament book written—as the key to interpret the entire Bible.[82] He referred to progressive revelation as "the great key to the meaning of so many dark passages of Scripture."[83] There was even some feeling within the Holiness movement that God was continuing to reveal his truth, primarily to "those who are entirely devoted to God," the holiness movement.[84]

78. Watson, *Our Own God*, 191.
79. Ibid., 227.
80. Robinson, *Pitcher of Cream*, 57–58.
81. Watson, *Coals of Fire*, 112.
82. Steele, *Saint John's Epistles*, xxi.
83. Steele, *Gospel of the Comforter*, 136.
84. Watson, *Steps to the Throne*, 7–8.

A Holiness Hermeneutic

The unity of the Bible was under heavy fire even as these authors wrote, prompting George Watson to argue for this unity. However, based on the superficiality of his arguments he seems to have been more concerned to confirm the convinced in their convictions, than to convince the critics.

We have already noted many illustrations of Watson's commitment to the unity of the Bible. Two additional examples will suffice before identifying the goals Watson sought to accomplish by his appeal. Watson was convinced that "The Bible is composed of thousands of miniature Bibles." In these a person can find "certain blocks of truth" and "a miniature gospel." God so arranged his word that "if some poor fellow should only succeed in getting hold of one of these blocks, he would have enough to convert and sanctify and glorify him."[85]

The book of Genesis, for Watson, played a very important role in the Bible, and his comments on the book demonstrate how important the unity of the Bible was to him. It was in Genesis that God revealed his first words to humanity, "and these first words are the pattern and sample of all other words contained in the Bible." Watson continued, "I discovered some years ago that every doctrine that is taught in the Scripture is first mentioned or referred to in the book of Genesis, and that this wonderful book is the seed bed of every growth in the entire scope of divine revelation."[86]

If a person wants to understand the Bible, said Watson, Genesis is the "key to all Scripture" and "to unlock the great outlines of salvation in Jesus Christ."[87] Here the sanctified believer, led by the illuminating torch of the Holy Spirit, can find light and truth. This is why the critics have aimed their weapons of destructive criticism on Genesis. While they may not realize it, they are acting as minions of Satan, who knows that to discredit the first book of the Bible is to destroy all the Scriptures.[88]

Two of Watson's purposes in defending the unity of the Bible are evident in the preceding paragraph. First, he sought to provide a key to the interpretation of the Bible. Second, he sought to enlighten his readers about the purpose and motive of the critics who were attacking Genesis.

More than this, in defending the unity of the Bible Watson sought to defend the inspiration of the Bible then under heavy fire. By demonstrating its "marvelous arrangement" he would show, at least to a sympathetic eye,

---

85. Watson, *Love Abounding*, 73.
86. Watson, *God's First Words*, 8–9.
87. Ibid., 28, 78.
88. Ibid., 28.

that this book must be from God. That this is Watson's goal is clear when, after recounting another example of such arrangement, he wrote, "It would be absolutely absurd to say or to suppose that all these things could happen by chance in the Bible. No; they are all divinely inspired."[89] By defending its inspiration with this emphasis on the unity of the Bible, Watson sought to counter the trend in scholarship away from the divine origin of Scripture. He presented a Bible so intricately woven, it could only have been produced at God's hands. This message would have been welcome news to his holiness audience who may have been troubled by the salvos leveled at their precious word of God.

The Bible May Be Interpreted in a More-Than-Literal Manner

The phrase, "more-than-literal" includes such symbolic interpretations as typology and allegory. According to Raymond Brown, such a reading depends on the presupposition that the Bible is inspired by God who knew when the Scriptures were written how the words of the human author would apply beyond their immediate context, though the human author was unaware.[90]

In his magisterial treatment of medieval exegesis, Henri de Lubac distinguished between two types of more-than-literal interpretation. One approach identified four senses of Scripture popularized in the medieval verse:

> The letter teaches events,
> Allegory what you should believe,
> Morality teaches what you should do,
> Anagogy what mark you should be aiming for.[91]

Those who preferred the fourfold approach, according to de Lubac, focused on the person of Christ, seeking "first and foremost 'the spiritual mysteries of Christ.'" They are "above all men of doctrine."[92]

---

89. Ibid., 93.

90. Brown, "Hermeneutics," 610. Brown treats "more-than-literal" interpretation somewhat more broadly than we are doing under this heading.

91. De Lubac, *Medieval Exegesis*, 1.

92. Ibid., 261.

De Lubac's second approach identified only two senses of Scripture, the literal and the spiritual, or the letter and the spirit. "The letter is good and necessary, because it leads to the spirit."[93] "The spiritual understanding comes to remove the veil that covers the letter or the veil that is the letter, in order to extricate the spirit from it. Or else, in opposite terms, it comes to cover up the poverty of the letter with a royal mantle that transfigures it."[94]

While the first approach—describing four meanings for each passage—focuses on the person of Christ, the second is "more attentive to the interior principle of the spiritual understanding, which is the Holy Spirit."[95] While the first is more doctrinally oriented, the second is more focused on spiritual experience. About the second approach he says, "In Scripture they seek, in a direct way, 'an understanding of the spiritual life.'"[96]

The American Holiness movement clearly falls into de Lubac's second category. They consistently described their interpretive approach as involving a literal and a spiritual meaning.[97] Whether they called it typology or allegory, they were referring to the discovery of this "spiritual" meaning. De Lubac's conclusion about the goal and emphasis of this type of approach fits the Holiness movement as well. They were more concerned for spiritual experience than right doctrine. Even while exalting Christ to his rightful place, they saw themselves celebrating the work of the Holy Spirit in entire sanctification.

While all the authors studied employed more-than-literal interpretation, not all used it to the same degree. Steele, for example, employed

---

93. Ibid., 226.

94. Ibid., 226.

95. Ibid., 261.

96. Ibid., 261. He emphasizes that "what is explicit with the one group is found implicitly in the other group, and vice versa. The first have no intention of exhausting the spiritual life by cutting it off from its source any more than the second intend to blaspheme this source by denying or neglecting its spiritual fecundity. They are both well aware that Christ cannot be recognized except through the Spirit, and that this Spirit is always the Spirit of Christ" (ibid., 261).

97. At least once W. B. Godbey referred to three levels: the first, the "superficial, ceremonial and materialistic . . . is entirely without salvation; the second[, the] modified spiritual, . . . embraces initial salvation," and third, the "literal spiritual, . . . embraces . . . full salvation" (Godbey, *Sanctification*, 53). Otherwise, Godbey, like the other writers studied, treated Scripture as having two senses, the literal and the spiritual. See his conclusion that "nearly all of the heresies originate either from spiritualizing the literal Scriptures or literalizing the spiritual" (Godbey, *Commentary*, 3:187).

Four Pillars of Holiness Interpretation

typology infrequently and was critical of the symbolical interpretation he found among the Plymouth Brethren.

Other holiness authors relied heavily on these methods; in fact, more-than-literal interpretation became something highly valued. Watson was extolled by his publisher for this ability. Robinson and others made special appeals to God to show them something new in the Bible.[98] Their emphasis on symbolical interpretation is unique within American Protestantism of this period. The question must be raised: Why did holiness interpreters employ more-than-literal interpretation so heavily?

One must begin by recognizing the influence of Pietism which considered that certain historical and narrative passages were normative for the individual Christian, making it possible to employ narrative passages for subjective purposes.[99] We have also noted how the holiness interpreters considered themselves Spirit-enabled for their task. "Now for the first time," remarked Carradine, "the real depth of certain Bible expressions are understood and the heart fairly revels in them."[100] The assurance that one has the Holy Spirit who is willing and able to provide new interpretations gave these writers the confidence needed to produce the more-than-literal interpretations which emerged.

The fact that these new discoveries were hidden in symbols did not appear to trouble our authors. In fact, what was hidden and mysterious was regarded as having special importance. Those things "imbedded and hidden away in the Bible for the recognition and future use of all generations" are the "deep truths." One must look under the surface to find the blessed facts placed there by God.[101]

They were not the first to be faced with the enigma of hidden but important. The early Christians experienced the disequilibrium of discovering that their profound and inescapable experience of Christ was not explicitly manifested in their Bible (our Old Testament). Luke's portrayal of the disciples on the road to Emmaus conveys this dilemma, but also its solution: the disciples were bewildered by the turn of events surrounding the resurrection until Jesus, "beginning at Moses and all the Prophets" showed them what their Bible said about him (Luke 24:25–27).

---

98. Robinson, *Chickens*, 75.
99. Welch, *Protestant Thought*, 1:28
100. Carradine, *Revival Sermons*, 90.
101. Carradine, *Second Blessing*, 27; Carradine, *Revival Sermons*, 45.

A Holiness Hermeneutic

Immediately the early church became convinced that their whole Bible spoke of Jesus and set about to reveal him in its pages. De Lubac describes these early believers as "entirely enthralled by their admiration for the unique, unsurpassable Newness, utterly special and transfiguring everything it touched, that in their eyes constituted the 'New Testament.'"[102]

> The Lord Jesus was the unique and incomparable summit: "the mountain of mountains, not one of the mountains." In him, Scripture in its entirety had "once and for all" received its fulfillment. Moses and Aaron had lived. Following the true Joshua, Christians had entered into the promised land of the Gospel. Now they could work hard, in the cheerful boldness of their faith, to relate in detail the great allegory of Scripture. They were well aware that in this endless task they were not in any way extending or completing the total allegorization that had been made once and for all by Christ.[103]

No one would suggest that the experience of the Christ-event can be equated to the experience of entire sanctification, certainly no one within the Holiness movement. They would agree that the latter is entirely derivative of the former; one could not speak of holiness unless one spoke first of Christ.

But one could speak of holiness. At least for those who experienced entire sanctification, its reality was inescapable and so was the need to find it in the Bible. Compelled by their spiritual experience and assuming holiness to be central to the Bible they found holiness where others had missed it.

One wonders how much of the Holiness movement's appreciation for the hidden had to do with the fact that they were hidden—set aside from the mainstream of society and from the majority of the church. Robinson drew a connection between the hiddenness of truth and the pious minority when he referred to the unpopularity of the holiness message. Those on the unpopular side should take heart, for "the majority has always been wrong and the minority has always been right on the moral questions of the day."[104]

It would appear that the further the Holiness movement moved from the mainstream of society, the more subjective their arguments became. This should not be surprising for without a critical audience to hold

---

102. De Lubac, *Medieval Exegesis*, 233.
103. Ibid., 234.
104. Robinson, *Honey*, 187.

Four Pillars of Holiness Interpretation

interpretations accountable, the movement had only to convince itself of the truth of its claims and the validity of its often subjective methods.

Generally, the holiness preacher and audience were not as highly educated as their cousins in the Keswick movement. This difference, while not the only factor, certainly contributed to the fact that interpretation of the Bible by the American Holiness movement was far more subjective than that from Keswick.[105] The correlation between the lack of formal education and subjective interpretation may help to explain why Daniel Steele, the only professional educator among those studied, rejected subjective interpretation. This flourishes, he explained, among those whose minds "are easily captivated by types which are purely fanciful, the cunning inventions of men."[106]

Without seminary, homiletical training for the preacher was limited to what was read and what was heard on Sunday and at revival meetings. Such "training" would tend to foster more of the same type of subjective interpretation. Exegetical method counted for less than emotion and fervor. The preacher succeeded, not when the argument was won, but when the fire fell.

By deemphasizing reason and church tradition, the Holiness movement neglected moorings that would have protected them from the abuses that are common to more-than-literal interpretation. Instead, they emphasized experience, which had no difficulty finding itself in the symbols and narratives of the Bible.

It is striking that this subjective approach to scripture became so widespread during a time when scholarship was promoting a scientific, highly objective approach. In the face of scholarly objectivity we find sanctified subjectivity. While the critics down-play the divine authorship of the Bible, holiness authors are relying on the presence of the Holy Spirit to inspire new interpretations of it. While the focus of the scholarly attack is the Old Testament, holiness exegetes are finding this a gold mine of spiritual experience.

It seems unlikely, given their criticisms and warnings, that our interpreters are totally out of touch with the implications of scholarship. More likely their approach was a conscious and categorical affirmation of exactly

---

105. Cf. the treatment of Isaiah 6 by Smith, "Vision of God," 57–65, and that of Watson, *Coals of Fire*, 7–28. Cf. also Pierson, "Sin of Habitual Unbelief," 41–50, with that of Godbey, "Out of Egypt into Canaan," 80–92.

106. Steele, *Substitute*, 76.

A Holiness Hermeneutic

what the critics denied. Such a strategy was designed to reassure their hearers that in spite of the wild winds of controversy blowing around it the Bible can still be believed.

Interpreting symbolically does not mean that the historical context is ignored. Most of these writers acknowledged the literal sense of the passage as present and important. Smith criticized those who considered Revelation 1–3 a prediction of the chronological sequence of the church through the ages when it was in fact a picture of the church as it existed in the time of the John the Revelator.[107]

Even Watson, who interpreted more-than-literally so often, recognized the importance of the historical context. In the opening pages of his allegorical treatment of the Song of Solomon, he admits, "This Song was written by Solomon on the human side as a memorial of his courtship and marriage with Pharaoh's daughter, the beautiful brunette of Egypt."[108] It was this concern for the historical elements of Scripture that called forth cautions against "over-spiritualizing." By this they meant "taking everything figuratively, until there is nothing historical and real; it is all mystical. There is no real devil, no real Christ, no real cross."[109]

This concern for the historical context was demonstrated in another more subtle way. Considering the actual events of the Bible as important, many of these authors made the expensive and difficult journey to the Holy Land, Palestine. Some recorded the events of their journeys as well as the new insight they had gained into the Bible.[110]

The symbolic interpretations that occurred were not intended to ignore the historical context but to supplement or surpass it. Events such as Elijah's encounter on Mount Carmel, the crossing of the Red Sea, Gideon's raid on the Mideonites, were treated as historical events, and one could profit by studying them as such. Much more profit could be obtained, however, from looking beyond the historical meaning to find what deeper meanings were symbolized there, to find the "literal spiritual" meaning, as Godbey put it.[111] The quote from Watson above recognized the historical

---

107. Smith, *Things of the Spirit*, 96.

108. Watson, *Divine Love Song*, 5.

109. Watson, *Love Abounding*, 389.

110. Among those who made this trip were Carradine, *A Journey to Palestine*; Godbey, *Footprints of Jesus*; and Robinson, *My Travels*.

111. Godbey, *Sanctification*, 53.

meaning of Song of Solomon. The remainder of that paragraph demonstrates how the symbolic surpasses the historical:

> In addition to this fact [i.e. the historical meaning of Song of Solomon], it is so inspired by the Holy Spirit as to be perfectly true of the mutual love between Christ and his Bridehood Saints. The most universal law in God's works is to engraft the supernatural upon the natural, and the divine upon the human, . . . Thus we are to read this Song in the double light of earth and heaven, of the human and the divine.[112]

Carradine referred to this double meaning as near and remote, narrow and wider, "like seeing the blue, wavy outline of a distant range of mountains just appearing over a nearer line of hills."[113]

Generally speaking, these authors, when they interpret "more-than-literally," think of their work as typology. Typology involves discovering the deeper meaning possessed by a person, place or event in Scripture, put there by the divine author to foreshadow something future. The type is the thing (person, place, or event) latent with deeper meaning, the antitype is that which is foreshadowed.

Each of these writers employed typology to a greater or lesser degree. At times they simply followed the lines laid down by the New Testament writers, including the treatment of Adam, David, Melchizedek, and the paschal lamb as types of Christ.

More frequently they found types in the Old Testament to which the New Testament did not refer. The antitype may be a New Testament figure, usually Christ, or a New Testament doctrine, most often entire sanctification. Common to many of these authors was the typologizing of the Tabernacle and sacrificial system. Close attention was paid to the arrangement of the furniture, the activity of the priests, the order and substance of the sacrifices, and many other elements which tell us about Christian experience. It was not uncommon for types to be drawn from the Mosaic legislation. The prohibition against the garment mixed with wool and linen and the process of cleansing the leper were understood to teach entire sanctification.[114]

The patriarchs and events from their lives were treated as types which teach holiness. To Watson, every great biblical character "is a whole world

---

112. Watson, *Divine Love Song*, 5–6.
113. Carradine, *Sanctification*, 133.
114. Godbey, *Commentary*, 1:231; Carradine, *Sanctification*, 98.

A Holiness Hermeneutic

in itself of significance and typology."[115] Abraham, Jacob, and others are models for us to follow, each experiencing both conversion and sanctification.[116] Jacob's marriage's typified holiness in that "The Leah of conversion must precede the Rachel love-union of full salvation." The expulsion of inbred sin by sanctification is symbolized in the story of Ishmael and Isaac.[117]

The search for typology was not limited to the Old Testament. Many types were found in the New Testament with antitypes usually discovered in the life of the believer. The second cleansing of the temple by Jesus, the two sisters of Lazarus, the double touch on the eyes of the blind man, all these and more teach entire sanctification.[118]

One of the characteristics of typology as used by these authors was that the antitype was often found in the believer's experience. Godbey had this in mind when he wrote, "The entire Old Testament symbolizes the New Testament experiences wrought in the heart by the Holy Ghost."[119] For example, the dove released by Noah was taken by Watson to typify not only the work of the Holy Spirit in the three dispensations of human history, but also the Spirit's work with the individual.[120] The offering of Isaac typified the offering of Jesus, but also the offering of the believer in consecration.[121] Even when it is not presented so clearly, the implication of such typologizing is that the antitype is open-ended and includes all who enter into entire sanctification.

Another characteristic of the use of typology by the holiness interpreters is that it often became allegory, whatever they might have called it. Such was the case, for example, when they treated entire stories or scenes. Treated allegorically were the account of Noah and the Flood, Abraham's offering of Isaac, the life of Joseph, the Song of Solomon, the Prodigal Son, the healing of the man born blind, the life of Lazarus and other events.[122]

---

115. Watson, *God's First Words*, 100.

116. Abraham's sanctification is recounted in Carradine, *Second Blessing*, 94–108, while that of Jacob is told in many places, including Watson, *Love Abounding*, 112–37.

117. Knapp, *Double Cure*, 22–23. Many more examples could be cited from the chapter in this book entitled "Typified in the Old Testament."

118. Carradine, *Sanctification*, 90, 95–96; Knapp, *Double Cure*, 31–32.

119. Godbey, *Commentary*, 4:512.

120. Watson, *Love Abounding*, 333.

121. Ibid., 184.

122. Watson treats Noah and Isaac in *Love Abounding*, 329–46 and 178–98. Joseph's life is dealt with in *Pot of Oil*, 89–105, and Song of Solomon in *Divine Love Song*. Robinson allegorizes the story of the prodigal son in *Honey*, 259–62, the man born blind in

Four Pillars of Holiness Interpretation

The most important allegory used by the holiness interpreters was the account of Israel's journey from Egypt to Canaan. This referred to a person's journey from sin to entire sanctification[123] and received its fullest treatment in Knapp's *Out of Egypt into Canaan*. To plot the journey using Knapp's chapter headings: A person begins "In Egypt; or, Spiritual Bondage" where emancipation from sin can only occur by the shedding of blood and a divine work like the crossing of "The Red Sea; or, Spiritual Deliverance." Unfortunately, such a crossing may leave the new believer languishing unnecessarily in "The Sinai Wilderness; or, Spiritual Twilight," hampered by inbred sin. "Kadesh Barnea: or, the Believer's Waterloo" results from the unwillingness to claim the promise of full salvation, and is followed by the "Desert Wilderness Experience; or, Wretched Religion." Finally, the delay is ended by "Entering Canaan" through a second body of water, this time the Jordan River. Now the believer dwells in "Canaan; or, Spiritual Sunshine," conquering enemies and enjoying the fruit of the land. Like Israel, believers can break God's covenant and be forced to vacate the promised land, going "Out of Canaan into Babylon." But thanks to the promise of restoration and through consecration and trust, one can come "Back from Babylon," and return to Beulah land. Here one remains in the "Antechamber of Heaven" until the believer passes "Out of Canaan into Heaven."[124]

By going beyond the types used in the New Testament, holiness interpreters stepped outside what are considered the legitimate boundaries for typology. This did not stop these authors, but may have been why they felt it necessary to defend their more-than-literal interpretations.

In self-defense they pointed to the great benefit gained through biblical symbolism and the methods needed to unlock its meaning. Watson considered symbolism—"concrete truth embodied in living form and

---

47–53, and Lazarus in *Story of Lazarus*.

123. Hebrews 4:10–11 was thought to be another New Testament example (cf. Godbey, *Commentary*, 2:46–57), referring to entire sanctification in mentioning the "sabbath-rest" that remains for God's people. Even if this is what the author of Hebrews meant—an interpretation not widely shared—the Holiness movement certainly extended the typology far beyond that writer's stated intent. There is nothing of the allegorical meaning in Steele's commentary on Joshua. Instead, he confines himself largely to the historical and critical questions. See *Book of Joshua*.

124. Knapp, *Out of Egypt*. The Holiness movement was certainly not the first to use the Exodus as a metaphor for the spiritual life. Evidence for doing so can be found in the book of Hebrews, and elsewhere. They are certainly the only modern movement in church history to make such extensive application of this biblical event to entire sanctification.

color"—to be "the most impressive form in which truth can be stated."[125] It keeps Satan and evil men from clearly understanding the truth, thus preventing them from causing greater harm. It "inflames the soul with ardor for the pursuit and possession of that which is just before it half revealed and half concealed."[126]

More-than-literal interpretation was also defended as implicit in the progressive nature of biblical revelation, a conviction we noted earlier as integral to the thought of these writers. To grant that the Old Testament reveals by object lesson what the New Testament reveals clearly in doctrine was to legitimize such typologizing and allegorizing.[127]

A very important rationale for the use of more-than-literal interpretation was that it was used by the writers of the New Testament. Carradine turned to this defense prior to a typological interpretation of circumcision. "Some people protest against spiritualizing any Scripture. We refer these objectors to the author and book of Hebrews."[128] The example of the Apostles and Jesus was all the permission these interpreters needed for their practice.

The use of more-than-literal interpretation of the Bible arose from the movement's commitment to the centrality of sanctification. The syllogism ran like this: Since holiness is central, it should appear throughout the Bible. Holiness does not appear clearly stated in the Old Testament, as found in the New Testament. Therefore, holiness must be stated symbolically in the Old Testament, requiring appropriate methods to unlock it.

Even while defending its use, these interpreters recognized the necessity for certain rules to govern more-than-literal interpretation. One rule was to proceed with caution. "The typology of the scapegoat is a subject beset with difficulties," said Steele. "No light is reflected upon it from the New Testament, for none of its writers allude to it. It becomes us to walk carefully on ground on which apostles have not ventured."[129] To caution must be added humility, reverence, and patience. Good interpretation was not likely to arise from a bad interpreter, one who was arrogant, immoral, irreverent, unholy and hurried.[130]

125. Watson, *Love Abounding*, 258.
126. Carradine, *Second Blessing*, 27–28.
127. Watson, *Coals of Fire*, 112.
128. Carradine, *Second Blessing*, 261.
129. Steele, *Leviticus and Numbers*, 123.
130. Godbey, *Commentary*, 5:72; Carradine, *Sanctified Life*, 117.

Four Pillars of Holiness Interpretation

These authors insisted that more-than-literal interpretation must proceed only when the context is taken into account. Steele insisted, "as a canon of interpretation, that a homogeneous passage of God's Word must be expounded homogeneously; that is, it must be entirely literal or entirely symbolic."[131]

While Steele obeyed his own rules, not all of his fellow holiness interpreters did so. One reason they did not was that they saw a second context with which the interpretation must agree, the context of the whole Bible. To interpret consistently with this context meant one's interpretation had to agree with what was plainly taught elsewhere.[132] To interpret in the context of the whole Bible meant the interpretation must fit the biblical message generally. Most importantly, it must agree with the central truth of the Bible, holiness. Any interpretation that contradicted their understanding of the Bible in general, or holiness teaching in particular, was judged incorrect or worse.

How is it that these authors could so obviously ignore the immediate context and still commend contextual interpretation? The answer is found in the relative values of the two contexts. They considered it more important that an interpretation agree with the central teaching of the Bible than that it agree with its immediate context. Here again the holiness hermeneutic guided interpretation, acting as a canon to discern truth from falsehood.

Holiness interpreters had several guidelines to determine the meaning of a type that was not first used by a New Testament author. First, there should be some similarity between the type and anti-type. Robinson could be certain that the man born blind represents the unregenerate sinner because they are both blind and without light, the first physically and the second spiritually.[133] Moses' rod was a type of the word of God for although lifeless in the hand of Moses, it became a living thing when he threw it down in obedience to God.[134]

Similarities could be found between the name or number of the type and the nature of the antitype. "We can always find a revelation of Divine truth in studying the different names that God gives to persons, places or things in the Scriptures," writes Watson.[135] For example, "Laban is a very

---

131. Steele, *Substitute*, 204–5.
132. Smith, *Daily Holiness*, 172.
133. Robinson, *Honey*, 47.
134. Watson, *Coals of Fire*, 145.
135. Watson, *God's Eagles*, 209.

accurate type of the mere letter of the written law. The word Laban signifies "whiteness," and the mere letter of law, whether ceremonial or moral, is holy, just and good, yet in itself utterly void of all mercy or love."[136] Special attention to proper names, places, and numbers has long been a feature of more-than-literal interpretation.

Godbey demonstrates the important role of numbers in determining the meaning of a type when he explained that "seven is the sanctified number always representing Christ," four stands for humanity, and three for divinity. Just as four plus three equals seven, so Christ was the combination of the human and divine nature.[137]

The meaning of a type could also be discovered by determining what that type meant elsewhere, since most felt that the meaning of a type was generally consistent throughout the Bible. Watson went further insisting, "The metaphors of the Holy Scripture are always consistent, the same metaphor running through the Old and New Testaments."[138] After all, he reasoned, "The thoughts of God are the same in all ages; and, if He saw the baptism of the Spirit when in the flesh, under the emblem of the rivers flowing out of the soul, then that is the same emblem under which He saw it at the creation of the world."[139] This type of reasoning left Watson with some awkward moments, such as explaining why the raven, who always typified Satan, would have brought food to Elijah. "Some may argue against this, that the raven which fed Elijah was a minister of good; but the raven is a bird of prey, and, in the East, a great thief as well, often snatching meat from market-places and homes for its young, and God had a sovereign right to cause this bird to drop the meat it had taken at the feet of Elijah."[140]

One of the most important tests to determine whether a type has been properly interpreted was whether or not it "harmonizes with the experience" of a Christian.[141] Carradine was certain that manna typified salvation since both are bread from heaven, are sweet to the soul, and may seem to disappear in the heat and struggle of the day. "If this is not a true picture of the regenerated life, then have we failed to see, hear, and feel correctly."[142]

136. Watson, *Coals of Fire*, 120.
137. Godbey, *Commentary*, 1:14.
138. Watson, *Love Abounding*, 330.
139. Watson, *Coals of Fire*, 57.
140. Watson, *Love Abounding*, 330–31.
141. Carradine, *Second Blessing*, 33.
142. Ibid., 29.

At times experience may shape rather than test the interpretation, such as when Carradine interpreted the parable of the virgins (Matthew 25:1–13). These women did not represent the church, he said. In fact, "the sanctified Church which never slept is represented not by the virgins, but by the invisible and unmentioned Bride of the parable, who, the reader may be sure, never closed her eyes. The idea of a bride sleeping when the bridegroom is on the way to her to have the nuptials celebrated"![143] As we noted earlier, experience, an indispensable aid in biblical interpretation, is not easily kept in its proper place; without necessary safeguards, it may take control.

Conclusion

These four presuppositions do not represent the totality of holiness exposition. Much could be said about presuppositions the Holiness movement shared in common with the church. The intention of examining these four has been to provide a clearer picture of what was important and distinctive about holiness exegesis.

They interpreted the Bible believing that God was immanent in this book and in their lives. An important emphasis in the thought of Wesley, this also represented a reaction to the secularization of society. God was treated as active in history, in the affairs of the world, and in communicating with his people to make himself known. God's immanence was evident in the guidance he provided for his people, generally perceived to occur through the triple leadership of the word, the Spirit, and Providence.

The Holiness movement viewed the Bible as pneumatocentric, a perspective that included, but surpassed Christocentricity. Such a Spirit-centeredness was traceable to Wesley's emphasis on spiritual experience as well as to the dispensationalism of Fletcher, with its stress on Pentecost as the defining spiritual experience. Some emphasized the person and work of the Holy Spirit, Daniel Steele serving as the best illustration. Others had a more narrow focus, putting their emphasis only on one particular aspect of the Spirit's work, that of entire sanctification. The latter emphasis has come to be known as the holiness hermeneutic, reading the Bible as a book of holiness concealed in the Old Testament, brightly revealed and illustrated in the New. The holiness hermeneutic was defended as doing justice to the central teaching of the Bible, entire sanctification. With this key, scriptural

---

143. Ibid., 239.

treasures were unlocked and meaning abounded. Without this key, the Bible remained a sealed book.

With much of the rest of the church, but against the current of scholarship, the movement viewed the Bible as a unified product of the divine mind. Most read it through Fletcher's dispensational framework or some variation of it. Much of the time this unity was simply assumed, whether by the practice of interpreting scripture by scripture, harmonizing variant passages, reading thematically, or tracing the common theme. Revelation was viewed as progressive, growing brighter with time. Watson made a point to argue this unity in order to demonstrate the Bible's inspiration and to counter its critics.

Finally, the Bible may be interpreted in a more-than-literal manner. This arose from the movement's pietistic roots, from its emphasis on the Spirit as the interpreter's inspirer, from the movement's marginal status, and from a conscious effort to counter criticism. The more-than-literal approach considered the historical context but sought to surpass it. Typology was the method of choice, relying on those types found in the New Testament, and many others beside. At times, the typology extended into allegory.

Feeling the need to defend their approach, a rationale was presented which included the benefits of symbolism, the fact that God revealed his truth progressively, the New Testament's allowance of such symbolic interpretation, and the centrality of holiness to the Bible. The movement also developed several rules for interpreting in this fashion. Caution, humility and reverence were essential. Biblical passages should be interpreted in line with their contexts, both immediate and biblical, the latter being the more important of the two. The meaning of the type could be determined by the similarities between type and antitype, from the meanings for that type found elsewhere, and from one's own experience.

7

Summary Observations on Holiness Interpretation

THE AMERICAN HOLINESS MOVEMENT of the late nineteenth and early twentieth centuries was a movement in retreat. In many ways, they could still point to successes: the National Camp Meetings, numerical and organizational growth,[1] and a passion for the disinherited. Though never intellectually oriented, the Holiness movement retreated almost entirely from the scholastic and scientific challenges. Its tendency to withdraw from established denominations represented a retreat from the struggles of modernity that Methodism and others were facing. The movement's single-issue theology—entire sanctification—represented a retreat from the theological issues being addressed. Its ministry among those in the lower socio-economic strata represented a continued retreat from the influential and powerful of society. Even when those from the lower strata began the climb to middle class, the Holiness movement continued to identify itself as outcast, retreating still further from the mainstream of thought.

The influence of the Protestant church in late-nineteenth-century America was also retreating.[2] H. L. Mencken defined Christendom in 1924 as "that part of the world in which, if any man stands up in public and sol-

---

1. Ahlstrom, *Religious History*, 920 refers to the numerical growth of the Holiness movement. For example, from 1926 to 1936, the Church of the Nazarene grew from 63,558 to 136,227.

2. Handy refers to the church's loss of morale and enthusiasm, and to an intellectual atmosphere less than congenial to religion following the First World War in *Christian America*, 174–76.

A Holiness Hermeneutic

emnly swears that he is a Christian, all his auditors will laugh."[3] By the last quarter of the 1800s, society was shaking free from the traditional restraints it had known and fast becoming a secular society. The rapid growth of the cities not only brought challenges to the church's ministry but weakened the church's power and influence. The intellectual and scientific revolution, especially as it concerned the Bible, left the church with a whole new set of questions to be answered but without confidence in an authoritative word from God from which to answer them. The church continued to be an important institution in this secularized society, but was seen by more and more as irrelevant or worse. The church was becoming marginalized as a shaper of public opinion.

As the Holiness movement was retreating to the margins of the ecclesiastical world while the ecclesiastical world was retreating to the margins of society, the movement was left doubly isolated. Its isolation prompted it to turn inward. It spoke to itself rather than its world because the world was not listening. It spoke to itself about its world and the message was discouraging. Among other concerns, the movement was troubled by challenges to the inspiration, unity, and message of the Bible. The Holiness movement addressed these concerns to itself, but indirectly. What society was calling into question, holiness interpretation emphasized and paraded. It made an effort to impact its society by living a holy life, but its candle was barely visible from the margins.

In spite of its reluctance to deal directly with the issues being faced by society, the Holiness movement made an honest effort to maintain what it felt were important teachings of the church. The cost of retreat was isolation, but isolation did achieve their desired goal: preservation.

Because the Holiness movement was isolated, its biblical interpretation lacked accountability. With its only audience being itself, there was no one to question presuppositions and methodology. The results included rampant typologizing, a singular concern for entire sanctification, and at times, a Bible held hostage to experience.

Isolation did permit holiness biblical interpretation to perpetuate the populist hermeneutic free from the troubling questions that prompted many to abandon their compass. These were common people who wanted to hear a word from God. The populist hermeneutic, with its emphasis on the individual conscience and common sense, gave them permission to do so even without educational advantages and scholarly sophistication. So

---

3. H. L. Mencken, quoted in Marsden, *Fundamentalism*, 3.

Summary Observations on Holiness Interpretation

content were they with the populist hermeneutic, that they wanted no part of the critical study of the Bible.

Enough questions about the availability of truth dogged their minds that they found it necessary to bring along a friend to read the compass. The most important quality this friend needed to possess was the experience of entire sanctification. This experience would purge out all that obscured sound vision, such as pride. It would also endow that friend with the company of the true and original interpreter of the Bible, the Holy Spirit. The Spirit held the key to unlocking God's word so that its treasures could be discovered. In other words, the movement did not bring along one friend, it brought two—one human and one divine.

The populist hermeneutic, at least early in the nineteenth century, had a radical, anti-establishment theme. Leland, Dow, and others spoke against the authoritative elite in power. By the end of the century, the anti-establishment message and methods of the populist hermeneutic had largely lost their potency. The potential still existed for an interpreter to read the Bible with radical consequences, but such prophetic voices were few and far between. The Holiness movement attempted to be prophetic and radical, but for some reason—perhaps it was their emotionalism and extremely strict standards of behavior and dress—they came across as almost comical. The radical connotations of a Spirit-filled, holy life were lost on a society too far from the isolation of the margins.

Another movement trying to conserve orthodoxy in these difficult days was fundamentalism. While they shared many things in common, holiness biblical interpretation differed from fundamentalist interpretation in at least two ways. First, the Holiness movement was more open to subjective sources (e.g. dreams) and outcomes (e.g. typology) than fundamentalism. Second, holiness interpretation emphasized that the authority of the Bible is confirmed by the work of the Spirit more than by anything else. Fundamentalism saw that confirmation coming primarily from inerrancy. Both of these differences are the result, to one degree or another, of the Methodist heritage that the Holiness movement enjoyed. Subjectivity was the consequence of Wesley's emphases on the Spirit and on human ability and experience. To speak of the Spirit as the guarantor of biblical authority was also a Wesleyan theme.

While the Holiness movement inherited much from Wesley, they were not always careful stewards of what they received. They failed to maintain the balance of his Wesleyan quadrilateral, neglecting tradition and reason.

Essentially they considered tradition to extend back only a century or two and to include only those who taught holiness as they did. As a result, the movement lost its connections to the rich heritage of the past lying outside this slender line of piety. It lost appreciation for the eclectic theology that made Wesley's thought so rich and irenic. Their tendency was in the opposite direction, focusing so narrowly on holiness as they understood it and guarding themselves from any suspicious doctrines, they became impoverished and at times polemic.

Reason, another of Wesley's essential tests of interpretation, was also neglected. They minimized formal education, considering it neutral at best, harmful at worst. A high premium was placed on uniformity, especially when it came to explaining the doctrine of entire sanctification. The outcome was the avoidance of the constructive criticism that could have helped to preserve its audience.

Wesley's quadrilateral was intended to function as a system of checks and balances. By underemphasizing one aspect, another would become too influential. With the neglect of tradition and reason the Holiness movement unleashed experience. Experience, especially that of entire sanctification, was permitted to exercise tremendous freedom, even to the point of shaping interpretation. The preponderance of more-than-literal interpretation is one result of this imbalance. Had the movement continued to emphasize tradition and reason along with experience their interpretation would have been less subjective and more balanced.

One of the most important characteristics of the biblical interpretation of this movement was the holiness hermeneutic. This emphasis on entire sanctification as the central theme of the Bible arose, in part, out of the conflict over the nature of sanctification. Had the movement possessed the internal workings to govern its own interpretation or an audience to hold it accountable it might have maintained a more balanced presentation of the Spirit's work. From this imbalance came many subjective interpretations defended as inspired by the Spirit. The overemphasis on holiness led to the neglect of certain important doctrines. For example, justification was sometimes seen as being only the precursor to a second blessing. Doctrines important to Wesley and early Methodists, such as the assurance of salvation, failed to receive the attention they deserved.

The holiness hermeneutic made the experience of sanctification—narrowly defined and encumbered with specific requirements to prove its genuineness—to be the outcome they desired most from their audience.

Summary Observations on Holiness Interpretation

It had to be a crisis experience coming soon after conversion and should be accompanied by emotional manifestations. The sanctified should carry out certain behaviors such as testifying and attending a holiness meeting or holiness church. Certain behaviors should be avoided, such as smoking, drinking, sabbath-breaking, immodesty, and lodge membership. By focusing attention on sanctification in narrowly defined terms with specific requirements, other experiences and more important requirements were often neglected.

Through the holiness hermeneutic, they placed such great emphasis on entire sanctification as a second crisis experience that it became a wedge to drive apart the Holiness movement and Methodism. The conflict over the nature of sanctification fostered the holiness hermeneutic; the holiness hermeneutic made the conflict worse. Whether or not the holiness hermeneutic led to divisiveness even within the Holiness movement, as Hynson argues,[4] those divisions which did occur probably had more to do with the factors mentioned in chapter three regarding the put-outers and come-outers.

With the use of Spirit-imagery as promoted by John Fletcher, the teaching of sanctification took on a pentecostal look. By the conclusion of the nineteenth century it was exceptional to find sanctification spoken of in any terms but pentecostal. Pentecostal imagery made it easier to understand holiness as central, thereby nurturing the holiness hermeneutic. Emphasizing the event of Pentecost opened the door to a wider use of narrative passages to teach doctrine. Since it is much harder to produce *the* objective meaning of a Bible story, subjectivity was given permission to enter, one result being that narrative passages became the source for types and allegories.

Understanding sanctification in pentecostal terms helped to shape that experience into a crisis event accompanied by physical manifestations. It made the early church the paradigmatic Holiness movement, providing a pattern for living and ministering as well as a source of identity for the modern-day apostles.

The pneumatocentric understanding of holiness also provided the Holiness movement with something positive: the reassertion of the importance of vital Christianity. The Holiness movement maintained the view that the Bible alone was not the word of God, but only the Bible as enlivened by the Holy Spirit. This same Spirit was to come and dwell within the

---

4. Hynson, "Wesleyan Quadrilateral," 29.

heart of the believer and make it possible to understand Scripture. The sin nature was treated as foreign to be removed by the purifying flame of Spirit baptism. Being a Christian was understood as something more than eternal life since holiness meant life in the "Antechamber of Heaven." While the movement may be faulted at several points they did emphasize a vital faith in a personal God.

The Holiness movement was the soil from which modern Pentecostalism sprang. This is evident in a myriad of ways, not least of which being the amount of time the Holiness movement spent distancing itself from its younger cousin. Pentecostal biblical interpretation is similar to what we have observed within the Holiness movement. It rests on the activity of the Holy Spirit to illuminate the interpreter of the Bible to most fully comprehend the text's significance.[5] It is informed by experience, both the normative experience of Scripture, and the experience of the believer today.[6] It depends heavily on narrative passages of the Bible, particularly those found in Acts.

Pentecostal biblical interpretation continued the populist hermeneutic as found in the Holiness movement. The new movement, also drawn from society's margins, depended more on the Spirit's guidance than on formal education. Creeds and other human teachings were distrusted.

Given the similarities, perhaps the Holiness movement of today can benefit from the counsel that Arrington offers to the Pentecostal interpreter.[7] First, employ the panoply of critical tools that are available, but always with an awareness of the Bible's divine origin and the present availability of the Spirit's illumination. Second, be certain that biblical interpretation is carried out with all the elements of Wesley's quadrilateral in place. To do so is to admit that we not only interpret the Bible, we must allow the Bible to interpret us. Third, proper biblical interpretation for the Holiness movement must surpass earlier self-imposed limitations and take its place, with its distinctive theology, within the broader evangelical context.

Just as there is benefit in exploring how holiness biblical interpretation compares to Pentecostalism, there is also something to be gained by comparing the treatment of the Bible by the Holiness movement against another standard, that of biblical criticism.

---

5. Arrington, "Hermeneutics," 382.
6. Ibid., 383.
7. Ibid., 387–88.

8

Reflections on the Intersection of Critical Biblical Studies with the American Holiness Movement

Ships in the Night

THE FOREGOING CHAPTERS HAVE made it exceedingly plain that the turn-of-the-century American Holiness movement did not intersect with higher criticism. It did react to the biblical critics. Steele discriminated between "constructive" higher criticism and "destructive" criticism, the former seeking divine truth while the latter sought naturalistic interpretations. Others in the movement were even less tolerant of critical methods and conclusions. Watson and Godbey found nothing positive to say about them.

However, reaction to higher criticism is not intersection. No attempt was made at dialogue between the movement and the biblical critics. Except for Steele's commentaries on Leviticus, Numbers, and Joshua, the holiness writings betray no attempt to directly address critical issues for their holiness audience.

One reason why this intersection never occurred was that the Holiness movement tended to avoid formal education. Without this training, they lacked familiarity with the issues and the tools to discuss them. From their anti-intellectualism they gained a passion for practicality and a suspicion of abstruse theological reasoning.

A second reason is that some of the presuppositions dear to the Holiness movement and fundamental to their interpretive methods appeared to be directly opposed to the presuppositions of higher criticism. Perceived challenges to the divine authorship of the Bible and to the miraculous elements contained therein were seen to threaten the very heart of the gospel.[1] Such would have reinforced the sense of irreconcilable differences.

Nonetheless, some Holiness opposition may have been due to a misunderstanding of higher criticism fostered by the polemic atmosphere of the early twentieth century. Intersection was difficult because the two camps were essentially talking about two different books. The Holiness movement while recognizing the historical and human element of the Bible regarded it primarily as a divine book. The higher critics may have affirmed the Bible's message, but they chose to treat it primarily as a human book. While emphasizing matters such as authorship, dating, and sources, the critics were frequently inattentive to theological issues.

This traversing did not occur, thirdly, because the two groups were busily addressing themselves to different audiences for different purposes. While the critics educated academia about the "scientific" approach to the Bible, the holiness writers explained sanctification to largely uneducated laypersons. The critics sought to create modern, informed Bible readers while the movement set about making holy hearers.

As noted in the preceding chapter, the Holiness movement became increasingly isolated from the general society in the first two decades of this century. The tolerant references to biblical criticism found in Steele's commentaries arose from an earlier day and a more centrist position within Methodism. Watson's harsh denunciations were sounded after the Holiness movement had moved further to the margins. Isolation brought temporary relief from the nagging questions raised by the critics. This relief faded as the storm of controversy over the Bible grew worse, driving the Holiness movement to the shelter of fundamentalism.[2] Once in this shelter, the possibility of any positive or productive intersection of the Holiness movement with higher criticism grew virtually impossible.

---

1. De Vries, "Biblical Criticism," 416.

2. Bassett offers a case study from the Church of the Nazarene to demonstrate "Fundamentalist Leavening," 65–91.

Reflections on the Intersection of Critical Biblical Studies

Engagement

A Changing Holiness Movement

Today intersection between the Holiness movement and biblical criticism is well underway. As with evangelicalism as a whole, the Holiness movement has become conversant with the methods and results of biblical criticism.[3] The intersection began with holiness biblical students attending graduate school in the middle decades of the twentieth century and then into the classroom. Today these professors and their successors expose students in the movement's colleges and seminaries to the latest findings of critical scholarship. Exegetes from the holiness tradition are producing works that discuss critical questions openly and honestly.[4]

At least one scholar of the Holiness movement believes that among Evangelicals the Holiness movement is well-situated for engaging with biblical criticism. Dayton argues that the movement "has an inherent affinity to historical process and movement," unlike movements such as fundamentalism with its "more rationally articulated forms of theology and its ahistorical and biblicist patterns of thinking."[5]

The intersection between biblical criticism and the Holiness movement is occurring at this time for several reasons. Since the beginning of the last century, the Holiness movement has been traveling the path of refinement and respectability. It played an active role in the creation of the National Association of Evangelicals in the early 1940s, begun to provide a "centrist" position between the Federal Council of Churches and the fundamentalist American Council of Christian Churches.[6] In order to provide a forum for

---

3. Important for the acceptance of biblical criticism among many evangelicals, including the Holiness movement, has been Ladd's *The New Testament and Criticism*. An excellent treatment of the juncture of evangelicalism and biblical criticism can be found in Noll, *Between Faith and Criticism*. Cf. McCown, "Toward a Wesleyan Hermeneutic," 9. McCown received his ThD at Union Theological Seminary in Virginia.

4. Examples include Schenck, *Cosmology and Eschatology*; Wall, *Why the Church?*; Varughese, *New Beacon Bible Commentary*.

5. Dayton, "Use of Scripture," 133. He offers as evidence the different reactions to the ministry of women in the fundamentalist and Wesleyan movements. Unlike the former, the Holiness movement has been a pioneer of this practice in part because it viewed the Bible as the channel of a new source of life-changing power more than as "a norm and pattern for all time" (ibid., 133).

6. Cizik, "National Association of Evangelicals." Stephen Paine, then-president of Houghton College of the Wesleyan Methodist Church, was one of the founders of the NAE.

scholarly exchange among scholars from a Wesleyan-Arminian perspective, the Wesleyan Theological Society was organized in 1965. Many scholars from the holiness tradition actively participate in the annual meeting of the Society of Biblical Literature, the bell-weather of biblical scholarship.

Increasingly the educational institutions of the Holiness movement have moved away from a Bible college model to a liberal arts curriculum and university model.[7] Their biblical studies faculty have obtained doctorates in graduate schools which emphasize biblical criticism. More and more holiness denominations now require the Master of Divinity degree for ordination.

The Holiness movement's shift from isolation to respectability has meant greater exposure to biblical criticism for its graduate students, for pastors in seminary, and for students in the movement's colleges. This shift also signals the increased importance of education for its own sake, rather than as a way to produce Christian workers. This new purpose for education makes it possible for the Holiness movement to see biblical criticism as serving a valuable purpose, rather than being irrelevant or even demonic.

Concurrent with this rise in respectability has come a self-examination of the holiness message. Among other changes, this introspection has prompted a redefining of holiness away from an emphasis on a second crisis experience and toward an emphasis on the state of perfect love.[8] This new emphasis requires no strained biblical exegesis.

Such self-examination has also caused many within the movement to question its relationship to fundamentalism. More particularly, the question has been raised whether a doctrine of inerrancy in matters of science and history has any place in the history and message of the Holiness movement. Some believe this doctrine has always been a part of the movement's heritage but was not clearly expressed until the early decades of this century. To others, inerrancy is foreign to the apologetic of the movement, the Bible's inspiration being guaranteed by the witness of the Spirit.[9]

---

7. Messiah College, now one of the leading Christian liberal arts colleges in the country, was founded in 1909 by the Brethren in Christ Church, a denomination in the holiness tradition, like the Messiah Bible School and Missionary Training Home. A similar path has been followed by other Bible colleges, including Southern Wesleyan University, Taylor University, and others.

8. For a good example of this newer treatment, see Wynkoop, *A Theology of Love*.

9. The case for the latter is presented in Bassett, "Theological Identity," 72–108; and Dayton, "Use of Scripture," 121–36. Turner seems to be arguing for the former in "John Wesley" 156–78.

The wild storm over the Bible in the early decades of this century forced the Holiness movement to move closer to its nearest neighbor, fundamentalism. At this time, some in the holiness denominations either made explicit their implicit doctrine of inerrancy, or adopted this incompatible doctrine as a badge of trustworthiness, depending on one's position in the debate. Meanwhile others, while sharing the same umbrella as the inerrantist fundamentalists, never surrendered their distinctive Wesleyan doctrine of Scripture.

While the debate continues, several observations can be made. First, it is clear that Wesley and his followers in the Holiness movement had a very high view of the Bible, regarding it as God's inspired word and as the final judge of life and doctrine. Second, Wesley considered this inspiration to rest primarily on the work of the Holy Spirit, as the inspirer of the original author, the authenticator of Scripture's authority to the church, and the inspirer of the modern interpreter.[10] Third, while Wesley did not believe there were "mistakes" in the Bible, he did recognize the possibility of errors.[11] Fourth, recognizing the centrality of the Spirit's role in assuring biblical inspiration did not prevent these interpreters from offering other reasons for inspiration, including the fulfillment of prophecy and the effect of Jesus' teaching on the world. Among these writers, however, such reasons show virtually no sign of taking precedence over the work of the Spirit as the guarantor of inspiration.

It would appear, then, that the Wesleyan doctrine of scripture is a modified inerrancy which does not consist in scientific exactitude.[12] The Bible is authoritative because it has shown itself to reliably communicate through the Holy Spirit how one comes to faith in Christ. It is not inerrancy but the Bible's unsullied "work record" which helps the church realize its character as the authoritative word of God.[13]

Perhaps it would be better for the sake of clarity not to refer to inerrancy at all but to speak of the Holy Spirit enabling its authors to perfectly represent God's redemptive plan.[14] From this perspective, the holiness

---

10. Shelton, "Nature, Character, and Origin," 19.

11. McCown, "Toward a Wesleyan Hermeneutic," 8. Apparently, Wesley considered mistakes to abrogate the divine inspiration of the Bible, while an error did not have so serious an effect.

12. Bassett, "Theological Identity," 94–95.

13. Shelton, "Nature, Character, and Origin," 24.

14. Cannon, "General Introduction," 18.

interpreter finds a greater freedom to work within biblical criticism than would the person whose notion of inerrancy resembled the earlier fundamentalists or their successors.

A Changing Biblical Criticism

The intersection between biblical criticism and the Holiness movement occurred not only because the Holiness movement changed but also because biblical criticism has changed. Critical study, while affirming the most important findings of the earlier era, has moved in directions which make it easier for conservative groups like the Holiness movement to embrace biblical criticism.

One such shift involves an increased openness to what is known as theological interpretation.[15] This turn—in many respects a return to earlier interpretive assumptions—is characterized, first and foremost, by allowing theology a seat at the table of biblical interpretation.

For years the goal of biblical criticism was strict objectivity. Give theology a voice and any objective reading flies out the window.[16] Today many scholars admit we cannot properly understand the Bible without theology. The Bible's main subject matter is God who cannot be adequately studied only on the historical, literary, or sociological level. What is more, the main purpose of biblical authors was to write what we consider theology. Since they wrote for theological purposes, we will not understand what they have written unless we seek those theological purposes. It is only fair, says Kevin Vanhoozer, that we should "read the texts as they wish to be read, and as they should be read in order to do them justice."[17]

Third, our theology provides the reason we continue to study the Bible. Vanhoozer rightly affirms, "Only the assumption that these texts say something of unique importance can ultimately justify the depth of the exegete's engagement."[18] Fourth, interpretation was always theological even when we thought it was objective since we all come to the text with presuppositions theological in nature. We do not—we cannot approach the text

---

15. The annual meeting of the Society of Biblical Literature now includes a section on this sub-discipline of biblical scholarship. For an example of theological interpretation in the hands of a scholar operating within the holiness tradition, see Green, *Seized by Truth*.

16. Cf. Bultmann, "Is Exegesis without Presuppositions Possible?"

17. Vanhoozer, *Theological Interpretation*, 23.

18. Ibid., 21.

with strict objectivity. All our modernist assertions and good intentions have only demonstrated that objectivity is a mirage. Rather, one must be aware of one's presuppositions, including one's theological presuppositions, while not allowing them to distort the meaning of the text.

The nineteenth-century Holiness movement clearly allowed theology a seat at the table. One of the most important elements of holiness interpretation was the conviction that holiness was the central doctrine of the Bible. This hermeneutic of holiness was permitted to guide and shape their interpretation enabling them to find holiness wherever they looked for it. Those who disagreed with this reading were dismissed as unenlightened and devoid of the experience of entire sanctification which makes the white cord of holiness unmistakably evident. For this reason, some might contend the holiness hermeneutic was not just seated at the table, but occupied all the chairs. Such influence notwithstanding, holiness is clearly an important theme of Scripture. The movement made mistakes but seeing holiness as a dominant theme of Scripture was not one of them.

If as many mainstream biblical critics have argued the central theme of the whole Bible is salvation,[19] then the holiness of God and the incumbency of that holiness on God's people is also of great importance.[20] If holiness is defined, with Wesley, as perfect love for God and neighbor then the importance of holiness to the biblical message is even clearer.[21]

Among the most explicit theological presuppositions shared by both theological interpretation and the Holiness movement is the nature of the Bible as a single unified revelation from God containing common themes which, like threads in a fabric, make the garment a single piece. Among these themes the doctrine of salvation occupies a place of prominence. The Holiness movement emphasized a particular aspect of salvation, namely entire sanctification. They felt this emphasis was appropriate because this was where salvation had been pointing all along.

---

19. Richardson, "Salvation, Savior," 168. Cf. von Rad, *Old Testament Theology*, 357–58.

20. Recent efforts among the Holiness movement to locate holiness in the Old Testament are based on more solid footing than that provided by narrative passages. Cf. Thompson, "Old Testament Bases of the Wesleyan Message," 38–47 who identifies holiness as a relationship defined by the person and covenant of God. In this he acknowledges similarities with Eichrodt, *Theology of the Old Testament*, 276–77; Thompson could also have cited von Rad, *Old Testament Theology*, 1:182–83. Vriezen devotes no little attention to the importance of the holiness of God and the communion of that holy God with humankind (*An Outline of Old Testament Theology*, 163).

21. Wesley, *A Plain Account*, 18.

A Holiness Hermeneutic

Among biblical scholars today, many would find this assumption of biblical unity incompatible with the critical method since, for some, to be scientific eliminates the legitimacy of assuming divine origin and thus unity for the Bible. Biblical criticism, they contend, should interpret the Bible only as a human book.

For other biblical critics, even those who would not identify themselves as evangelical or practitioners of theological interpretation, the search for unity in the Bible remains a legitimate enterprise. One highly respected scholar of an earlier generation, John Bright, considered the unity of the Bible to be fundamental. While acknowledging the Bible's diversity, he censured the atomizing effect of criticism which focuses only on such diversity.[22]

For the Holiness movement, the Bible's unity proved it to be a divinely inspired book. The two issues were so closely related that to deny the first would be to deny the second. They sensed that without a divine word offering the possibility of full salvation a movement such as theirs which believes God has called his people to holiness and desires to graciously produce it within them lacks any reason to exist.

Mainstream biblical scholarship has not only accommodated those who affirm the Bible's unity, it has also made room for those who believe the Bible obtains that unity from divine origin.[23] No less an icon of biblical criticism than Gerhard von Rad contended that God is speaking to humankind through the Bible. He defended "the belief that the same God who revealed himself in Christ has also left his footprints in the history of the Old Testament covenant people—that we have to do with *one* divine discourse, here to the fathers through the prophets, there to us through Christ (Heb. 1:1) [emphasis his]."[24]

One sees this as well in the revival of biblical theology, described by Betz as "a scholarly presentation of the witness to faith, and of the theological views, of the biblical writers, in the context of the covenanted people." This approach relies on exegesis to disclose the text, history to reveal the context of the text, and systematization to express the faith elements of the

---

22. Bright, *Kingdom of God*, 9–10. For other examples, see Wright, *God Who Acts*; Wright and Fuller, *Book of the Acts of God*, note especially 42–43; Rowley, *Unity of the Bible*, 16–17.

23. See Krentz, *Historical-Critical Method*, 70.

24. Von Rad, "Typological Interpretation," 36.

text in a unified manner.[25] Such a presentation arose from dissatisfaction with a historical-critical method which failed to deal with the elements of faith within the Bible.[26]

Even while mainstream biblical scholarship tends to place less emphasis on the unity of the Bible and greater emphasis on the internal tension that exists between one biblical author and another, for some this is only a recognition that within unity there exists variety.[27] It remains clear that biblical criticism is not intrinsically opposed to the notion of the Bible as one unified, divine revelation.

For this reason, the Holiness movement need not abandon this presupposition so important to its interpretation and existence. It may find it necessary to make adjustments to its methodology in order to take full advantage of critical scholarship. While it has become more cognizant of the human aspects of the Bible, more attention must be given to acknowledging the Bible's diversity and development. This requires tools such as form and redaction criticism and calls for greater caution when interpreting scripture by scripture.[28]

A second characteristic of theological interpretation is that it functions as the project of an entire community rather than one individual. During the modernist era, the question of who has the right to interpret the Bible has increasingly been answered: the Bible scholar. This explains the plethora of commentaries and study Bibles produced in the last century.

---

25. Betz, "Biblical Theology," 432.

26. Prior to the recent rise of theological interpretation, biblical theology was one way for holiness scholars to employ biblical criticism while remaining in a faith context. Biblical theology has been sharply criticized for, among other things, forcing the Bible into a system rather than letting it speak for itself in all its diversity. By concentrating on biblical theology, the Holiness movement falls under this criticism as well. For more on the nature and difficulties of the biblical theology movement, see Stendahl, "Biblical Theology," 418–32; Barr, "Biblical Theology," 104–10; Childs, *Biblical Theology in Crisis*.

27. Barr, "Biblical Theology," 108–9. Attempts to portray the unity of the Bible have continued. Claus Westermann proposed that the theology of the Old Testament revolved around the central notion of blessing in *Blessing in the Bible and the Life of the Church*. In *Elusive Presence*, Terrien argued that the center of biblical faith is the reality of the presence of God.

28. Just as the movement has been attracted to biblical theology, it has warmed to the canonical approach to Scripture, agreeing with Childs that it is in the text where we find the redemptive history (Childs, *Introduction to the Old Testament*, 76). This approach has been criticized for minimizing the development of the text. Cf. Barr, "Biblical Theology," 110–11; Birch, "Biblical Hermeneutics," 3–12.

A Holiness Hermeneutic

Theological interpretation reminds us that God can speak through any believer, even someone without formal education. New Testament scholar and product of the Holiness movement, Ken Schenck, describes the Bible as a sacrament. God uses its words as He does the water of baptism, to communicate a greater, gracious work. God may use knowledge of the original meaning to accomplish this work, or He may do so apart from such knowledge. God meets us where we are in Scripture, says Schenck, as he does in the ordinary bread and wine of communion. Reading a passage in its literary and historic context is not required in order to hear from God.[29]

Theological interpretation releases the Bible from the exclusive domain of the Bible scholar and welcomes the involvement of all the theological disciplines. It recognizes that some of the questions can only be answered by those who know how the text has been understood in the past and who have considered how it can be applied in the present.

Make no mistake, theological interpretation welcomes the contributions of modern biblical criticism. One must know all one can about the historical and literary contexts, but with this caution: "What God is doing at this [canonical] level *depends* on the human discourse, but it cannot be *reduced* to human discourse (emphasis original)."[30] We must embrace the best of the inductive method, learning to look closely at what the text actually says. We must, Vanhoozer counsels, "employ critical methods, but not uncritically. Critical tools have a ministerial, not magisterial, function in biblical interpretation."[31]

The community of interpreters must also include those from non-Western settings. Philip Jenkins has documented how global Christianity is shifting from its powerbase in the Western hemisphere to the Southern, and with that shift has come a very different way of reading Scripture. Jenkins contends these new voices of Christianity must be listened to.[32]

The community of interpreters includes scholars and ordinary lay people, those from the West and from the non-Western world. It also includes the dead as well as the living. Theological interpretation allows those of yesterday's church a voice in deciding what a text might mean today. As we have seen, tradition was a valued partner in Wesley's theological work,

---

29. Schenck, *Jesus is Lord*, 11.
30. Vanhoozer, "Imprisoned or Free?", 69–70.
31. Vanhoozer, *Theological Interpretation*, 22.
32. Jenkins, *Next Christendom*, 257.

finding there a Christianity that was both intellectually rigorous and spiritually alive.[33]

The community of interpreters embraced by the Holiness movement was much more narrow than that sought by today's practitioners of theological interpretation. Other than Steele, none of our subjects had much tolerance for biblical criticism. Nor was this a movement marked by theological or ethnic diversity. As we have seen, they cared little for tradition, unless that tradition represented the slender line of piety.

For holiness interpreters to fully engage in theological interpretation they must, in the words of Rob Wall, "allow for countervailing accents that are well supported by the 'plain sense' of canonical Scripture, as well as by other non-Wesleyan interpretive traditions."[34] "To presume the simultaneity between every faith tradition of the whole," writes Wall, "without also adequately discerning the importance of each in turn, undermines the integral nature of the 'one holy, catholic, and apostolic church,' thereby distorting its full witness to God."[35]

To make greater use of tradition means repudiating any lingering associations with isolationism and fundamentalism. It will also require greater attention to the movement's ecclesiology. For theological interpretation to involve *Reading Scripture with the Church*[36] requires a right understanding of the church.

While the understanding of community employed by Holiness movement was circumscribed in several ways, it was robust in its attention to the role of experience in biblical interpretation. Modernist demands for strict objectivity put the reader's experience off-limits while the Reformed perspective dismisses experience as a rival to *Sola Scriptura*. To recognize the importance of experience in biblical interpretation allows one to accept the truth that God is able to speak to all people through Scripture, even to those lacking formal education.

A third characteristic of theological interpretation is its embrace of polyvalence or a more-than-literal approach to Scripture. In his groundbreaking essay celebrating "The Superiority of Pre–Critical Exegesis," Steinmetz argued that biblical language remains open to many meanings,

---

33. Thorsen, *Wesleyan Quadrilateral*, 168.
34. Wall, "Toward a Wesleyan Hermeneutic," 55.
35. Ibid., 55.
36. Adam et al., *Reading Scripture with the Church*.

any one of which has validity, whether or not it was in the mind of the human author.[37]

Polyvalence contradicts a cardinal rule of biblical scholarship: seek only the meaning the original author intended. To claim that the biblical texts had any meaning other than the literal sense was and is, for many biblical critics, an error of the grossest sort. This rejection of the more-than-literal sense is due in part to the abuses suffered by the text at the hands of allegorists through the centuries. Modern scholars, such as Friedrich Baumgärtel, oppose typology for forcing New Testament meanings onto the Old Testament text.[38] Milton described the danger more poetically. "Whatsoever time or the heedless hand of blind chance hath drawn from of old to this present in her huge Dragnet, whether Fish or Seaweed, Shells or Shrubbs, unpicked, unchosen, those are of the Fathers."[39]

Even prior to the recent rise of theological interpretation, well-respected biblical critics such as Eichrodt and von Rad have used and defended more-than-literal exegesis. The latter refers to typology as leaving behind the "historical self-understanding of the Old Testament texts in question" and proceeding on to that of which the Old Testament witness is unaware, that which was in preparation. It concerns itself only with "the witness to the divine event" and not "historical or biographical details."[40]

Raymond E. Brown devotes a significant portion of his article on Hermeneutics in the *Jerome Biblical Commentary* to the legitimate role of more-than-literal interpretation.[41] There he observes that while most critical scholars have rejected the allegorical approach of the past, many remain open to a more-than-literal approach, one rooted in modern historical

37. Steinmetz, "Superiority of Pre-Critical Exegesis," 31.

38. Smart, in *Interpretation of Scripture*, thus summarizes Baumgaertel's views (120) in his chapter on "Typology, Allegory, and Analogy" (93–133). Smart prefers "correspondences" to "typology" since the former term adequately recognizes the "striking analogy" that appears to exist between the Testaments, while avoiding and encouraging the excesses of earlier days (123). Particularly odious to Smart is the eisegesis that characterized the early church fathers and Reformers (123). Smart asserts that the Old Testament should be permitted to speak for itself, without need of correction from the New (119). Cf. Baumgaertel's criticisms, as noted in Eichrodt, "Typological Exegesis," 236.

39. Found in *Of Prelatical Episcopacy*, which is quoted in Farrar, *History of Interpretation*, and in Adam, "Poaching on Zion," 26n18.

40. Von Rad, "Typological Interpretation," 36–37. Von Rad warns against employing typology with "historical, cultural, or archaeological details," since this is where it "runs wild and becomes an overly subtle exhibition of cleverness" (37).

41. Brown, "Hermeneutics," 605–23.

criticism.[42] Given the critical scholarly inclusion of typology there appear to be no irreconcilable differences between contemporary holiness exegesis and biblical criticism on this matter.[43]

Theological interpretation, while not dismissing the human author's intent and while valuing its discovery through the best of biblical scholarship, recognizes that God is not limited to this meaning. As Vanhoozer writes, "Reason, together with its many critical children—source, form, tradition, redaction criticism, and so on—is qualified to interpret the Bible as a historical and human text. But to read the Bible as the word of God is to make a leap into the realm of 'grace' that either opposes, crowns, or outflanks reason"[44] Exegesis does not go far enough nor is it sufficient to hear the voice of God.[45]

To speak of Scripture as polyvalent makes people nervous. Unless the meaning is anchored, we are told, people will drag it wherever they like and make Scripture say whatever they want. Without denying that such abuse is possible, practitioners of theological interpretation not only validate this approach but offer safeguards to ensure legitimate results.

For validation, practitioners of theological interpretation point to the New Testament where this approach is encouraged and illustrated. Second, they observe that this approach follows naturally from an understanding of the Bible as divinely inspired, which gives the Bible a limitless fecundity of potential insights.[46] As Augustine put it, "what more liberal and more fruitful provision could God have made in regard to the Sacred Scriptures than that the same words might be understood in several senses, all of which are sanctioned by the concurring testimony of other passages equally divine."[47] In the words of Aquinas, "Since the literal sense is that which the author in-

---

42. Ibid., 614. In his comments on more-than-literal interpretation, Brown refers to "sensus plenior," the meaning which God intended as evidenced by a study of a biblical passage in light of later revelation (616).

43. If one defines more-than-literal interpretation broadly, then one could argue it is employed by the new hermeneutic of James M. Robinson, Ernst Fuchs, Gerhard Ebeling, Hans-Georg Gadamer and others. Others interpreting more-than-literally include the literary critics who employ structuralism, where reality is thought to lie well beneath the surface of the text in the deep structures. Cf. Robertson, "Literature," 547–51. The interpretive methods of the holiness exegetes have not ventured far in either of these directions.

44. Vanhoozer, *Theological Interpretation*, 19.

45. Magrassi, *Praying the Bible*, 13.

46. Williams, *Receiving the Bible*, 169.

47. Augustine, *On Christian Doctrine*, 3.27.38.

A Holiness Hermeneutic

tends, and since the author of Holy Scripture is God, Who by one act comprehends everything all at once in God's understanding, it is not unfitting, as Augustine says, if many meanings are present even in the literal sense of a passage of Scripture."[48]

Third, polyvalence is what one would expect given the need for the Bible to speak to all people everywhere at all times. God intended the Bible to communicate with several audiences and so took them into account when it was inspired.[49] Without polyvalence, argues Fowl, "it will become difficult if not impossible for Scripture to function as the lenses through which we order and comprehend things, including God." Unless we allow for multiple meanings, the Bible "will lack the capacity to address the ever-changing complexity of our world and of our lives."[50]

The best practitioners of more-than-literal interpretation, both past and present, recognize the need to employ safeguards. One must read according to the "rules," the two most important being the rule of faith and the rule of love.

No true interpretation will differ from apostolic doctrine, what has been believed by all Christians, throughout Christendom, from the beginning of Christianity.[51] St. Ignatius warned the Christians at Tralles to

> Keep yourselves from heretics. You will be able to do this if you are not puffed up with pride, and (so) separated from (our) God, Jesus Christ, and from the bishop, and from the precepts of the Apostles. He that is within the altar is pure, he that is without is not pure; that is, he who does anything apart from the bishop, and presbytery, and deacons, such a man is not pure in his conscience.[52]

Later in the same letter he counseled his readers to

> Stop your ears, therefore, when any one speaks to you at variance with Jesus Christ, who was descended from David, and was also of Mary; who was truly born, and did eat and drink. He was truly persecuted under Pontius Pilate; He was truly crucified, and [truly] died, in the sight of beings in heaven, and on earth, and under the earth. He was also truly raised from the dead, His Father quickening Him, even as after the same manner His Father will so

---

48. As cited in Fowl, "Multivoiced Literal Sense," 41.
49. Williams, *Receiving the Bible*, 206–7.
50. Fowl, "Multivoiced Literal Sense," 47.
51. Cf. Vincent of Lerins, "Commonitary."
52. Ignatius, "Epistle to the Trallians," 69.

raise up us who believe in Him by Christ Jesus apart from whom we do not possess the true life.[53]

Irenaeus says of heretics that by preaching their own doctrine, they are "depraving" the rule of faith.[54] This is that truth which it is easy to get from the church, "since the apostles, like a rich man [depositing his money] in a bank, lodged in her hands most copiously all things pertaining to the truth: so that every man, whosoever will, can draw from her the water of life."[55] "True knowledge," he writes,

> is [that which consists in] the doctrine of the apostles, and the ancient constitution of the Church throughout all the world, and the distinctive manifestation of the body of Christ according to the successions of the bishops, by which they have handed down that Church which exists in every place, and has come even unto us, being guarded and preserved, without any forging of Scriptures, by a very complete system of doctrine, and neither receiving addition nor [suffering] curtailment [in the truths which she believes]; and [it consists in] reading [the word of God] without falsification, and a lawful and diligent exposition in harmony with the Scriptures, both without danger and without blasphemy; and [above all, it consists in] the pre-eminent gift of love, which is more precious than knowledge, more glorious than prophecy, and which excels all the other gifts [of God].[56]

Irenaeus offered an analogy of how the rule of faith was meant to operate within the church. A mosaic is just a collection of small stones, tesserae, until one assembles these stones into the intended picture. To know how to arrange the tesserae required a key, in Greek, a *hypothesis*. The Rule of Faith serves as this key, permitting one to properly arrange the various parts of Scripture into the picture God intended us to see.[57]

More recently, the Rule of Faith has been defined as "a basic summary of the biblical story centered on identifying God to be triune."[58] It

---

53. Ibid., 69–70.
54. Irenaeus, "Against Heresies," 415.
55. Ibid., 416–17.
56. Ibid., 508.
57. Ibid., 326.
58. Treier, *Introducing Theological Interpretation*, 57.

represents "the sum content of apostolic teaching,"[59] essentially what we find in the Nicene or Apostles Creed.

To read according to the Rule of Faith implies interpreting Scripture by Scripture. Since the God who wrote the entire Bible is entirely consistent, what He wrote in one passage will illuminate, not contradict, what He wrote in another. This allows the entire canon to provide a third context—beyond the historical and literary—to be kept in mind when interpreting.

Augustine proposed another Rule by which we must read the Bible, the Rule of Love. "Whoever, then, thinks that he understands the Holy Scriptures, or any part of them, but puts such an interpretation upon them as does not tend to build up this twofold love of God and our neighbor, does not yet understand them as he ought."[60]

That person who "takes another meaning out of Scripture than the writer intended, goes astray, but not through any falsehood in Scripture." Augustine compares this scenario to a lost traveler. If he is misled by an understanding which builds up love, "he goes astray in much the same way as a man who by mistake quits the high road, but yet reaches through the fields the same place to which the road leads." Augustine adds that such an interpreter needs to be corrected by showing how much better it is to take the right path.[61]

One of the most important presuppositions of the Holiness movement at the turn of the century was that the Bible can be interpreted in a more-than-literal manner. As we have seen, the polyvalence of Scripture was an important source for discovering the truth of holiness.

As the Holiness movement has moved more into mainstream evangelicalism it has distanced itself from earlier extremes in more-than-literal interpretation. Holiness biblical scholars have been putting great distance between themselves and the earlier typologizing. John E. Hartley allows for the legitimacy of the typological approach within clear parameters as a way of considering how diverse passages of Scripture might connect.[62] His exegesis is closely tied to the Old Testament's historical context and the New Testament's use of Old Testament passages. One senses that the

---

59. Greene-McCreight, "Rule of Faith," 703, as cited in Treier, *Introducing Theological Interpretation*, 58.

60. Augustine, *On Christian Doctrine*, 1.36.40.

61. Ibid., 1.36.41.

62. Hartley, "Use of Typology," 197. Hartley earned his PhD from Brandeis University and taught Old Testament at Azusa Pacific University, a school with roots in the Holiness movement.

excesses of earlier holiness typologizing lie behind Hartley's warning that one must only use typology to explain rather than determine doctrine, and always with a caution that allows the texts to speak for themselves.[63]

The Holiness movement could have done better at employing the safeguard of the Rule of Faith. Certainly, their use of polyvalence did not take the movement outside the realm of theological orthodoxy, at least as evidenced in the authors studied. Their isolation—both cultural and theological—led to an overly narrow understanding of sanctification which failed to do justice to the broader testimony offered by Scripture and tradition. Without a robust Rule of Faith, the Rule of Experience exercised too much control.

One could make a stronger case that the movement employed the Rule of Love. Perfect love for God and neighbor, as Wesley defined entire sanctification, was the movement's stated goal. Those who possessed this spiritual endowment were best prepared to properly hear from God's Spirit through the Scriptures. The Holiness movement sought to integrate the Bible into practical living rather than turn to a systematized, doctrinal approach.[64] Bassett observes that such a commitment to "sanctidoxy" over orthodoxy has produced a movement more inclined to merge than divide,[65] continuing Wesley's spirit of irenicity.

A fourth characteristic of theological interpretation is its recognition of the essential work of the Holy Spirit. The Spirit witnesses to the true nature of Scripture as inspired. It is the Spirit, wrote Steele, who makes the believer "perfectly assured of the Divine origin of truths already accredited as inspired."[66]

The Spirit not only assures us of Scripture's inspiration, He also allows us to understand what God is saying to us through the Bible. Summarizing de Lubac, Williams explains that the Holy Spirit inspired the human author to compose the literal meaning, but took a far greater role in the spiritual meaning. The latter contains a perspective on the history of God's redemptive plan unavailable to the author, but fully known by God's Spirit.[67]

Origen believed anyone who grasps Scripture's hidden meanings must have the Spirit's help. As he wrote in his commentary on John, "And now let us ask God to assist us through Jesus Christ by the Holy Spirit, so that

---

63. Ibid., 218.
64. Shelton, "Nature, Character, and Origin," 19.
65. Bassett, "Theological Identity," 95. Cf. Dayton, "Holiness Witness," 92–106.
66. Steele, *Jesus Exultant*, 290.
67. Williams, *Receiving the Bible*, 143.

we may be able to unfold the mystical sense which is treasured up in the words before us."[68] Theological interpretation recognizes that exegesis and the inductive method are fine, but we need the Spirit of God to hear the voice of God.

The essential role of the Spirit of God in understanding the Bible provides another similarity between the Holiness movement and theological interpretation. Holiness interpreters credited the Spirit as the source of their insights. "Unschooled men, 'filled with the Spirit,' have led thousands into the spiritual Canaan, while doctors of divinity without it have proved 'blind leaders of the blind.'"[69]

The Holy Spirit serves a third role as it relates to Scripture, that of guiding the church how best to employ the "keys of the Kingdom." The Puritan divine, John Robinson, believed "God has more light yet to break forth from his holy word." It is hard to consider the history of the church without concluding he was right. While not adding any new revelation to the closed canon, God's Spirit has allowed the church to understand more from those 66 books than was immediately apparent.

The abolition of slavery is an excellent case in point. Nineteenth-century American Christians fought over whether or not slavery was immoral, each side using Scripture. Most agree that the pro-slavery side had the stronger argument, or at least a longer list of proof-texts. But today, no question remains. The church and the rest of society have settled the matter, determining that slavery is immoral and should be resisted at all costs.[70] God has shed more light from his holy word.

The Spirit is operative in at least a fourth way as it concerns Scripture for it is the Spirit who transforms the reader through the Bible, enabling her or him to better understand God's word. Theological interpretation believes the Holy Spirit has spoken and continues to speak through the Bible so we can hear God's word and be transformed. According to Vanhoozer, the early church fathers understood that "biblical interpretation both requires and results in spiritual formation."[71]

The most important virtue is humility. "Biblical interpretation is ultimately a spiritual affair that demands a certain 'mortification' of the

---

68. Origen, "Commentary on John," 305.
69. Knapp, *Out of Egypt*, 100.
70. Cf. Lennox, "One in Christ."
71. Vanhoozer, "Imprisoned or Free?", 72.

reader."[72] Another needed virtue is joy. Here Vanhoozer quotes Barth: "This readiness and willingness to make one's own the responsibility for understanding the Word of God is freedom under the Word."[73] "It is our privilege," says Vanhoozer, "to be glad servants and joyful performers of the biblical text. There is no more contradiction between interpretive freedom and obedience to the Word than there is between Jesus's freedom and obedience to his Father."[74] Augustine makes the connection even closer when he calls for the interpreter to be personally oriented toward holiness.[75]

Theological interpretation makes room for the experience of the reader, not only because experiences shape our interpretation of the text, but also because experiences shape our souls; transformed souls are both the goal of interpretation and a means toward achieving that goal. The Spirit works to restore the divine image in us, and as we experience this transformation, we become better able to understand God's word.

One may criticize the Holiness movement for too narrowly defining what transformation looked like and how it transpired, but they rightly recognized that a major goal of the Bible was the transformation of its readers and that spiritual transformation produces better readers. "The most cultivated intellect refusing to bow to God's commands inevitably misses that knowledge which the humble and God-fearing slave easily receives, because his nature is open God-ward." An obedient will "puts eye-salve upon men's eyes and they clearly see," wrote Steele.[76]

The Holiness movement and theological interpreters not only identify the need for the Spirit to transform the reader of the Bible they even emphasize many of the same virtues. As we saw earlier Vanhoozer highlighted humility and joy, qualities essential to the experience celebrated by Holiness movement as entire sanctification. Augustine not only called interpreters to be personally oriented toward holiness,[77] he celebrated the centrality of love in a proper understanding of the Bible.[78] Love for God and neighbor stood at the core of the movement's understanding of holiness.

---

72. Ibid., 92. Cf. Godbey, *Commentary*, 5:72; Carradine, *Sanctified Life*, 117.

73. Barth, *Church Dogmatics*, 1.2.696, as cited in Vanhoozer, "Imprisoned or Free?", 93.

74. Vanhoozer, "Imprisoned or Free?", 93.

75. Watson, "Authors, Readers, Hermeneutic," 122.

76. Steele, *Jesus Exultant*, 244, 281.

77. Watson, "Authors, Readers, Hermeneutic," 122.

78. Augustine, *On Christian Teaching*, 1.36.40–41.

Theological interpretation and the Holiness movement make room for the experience of the reader not only because experiences shape our interpretation of the text but also because experiences shape our souls. The Spirit works to restore the divine image in us, and as we experience this transformation, we become better able to understand God's word. Even more, we step into the story of redemption, not as impartial, scientific observers of the Bible, but as participants.

Conclusion

Daniel Steele was a well-respected academic, fully conversant with the critical scholarship of his day.[79] But this scholar also spoke clearly of the work of the Holy Spirit as the One who both inspires Scripture and explains it. "The Holy Spirit, . . . imparts life to the penitent believer and the power of spiritual perception . . . . Says Augustine, 'He who teaches hearts has His chair in heaven.'"[80] Steele articulately defended entire sanctification from the Bible and his own experience. Those who are sanctified, he wrote, gain "astonishing insight" into the words of Scripture.

> Gospel truth ceases to be vague and shadowy. It becomes real. A mysterious power unvails [sic] its meaning, and applies it to the soul. There is a voice within which attests the objective truth. An invisible interpreter attends the reading of the sacred page, and "we discover wonders in God's law." These new beauties, unfolding evermore, so commend themselves to our hearts—they yield us so much strength and comfort—that we are never again troubled with doubts of the inspiration of the Bible . . . The higher life takes root in the deeper knowledge of God's word. It lives by every word which proceedeth out of the mouth of God. Its possessor becomes a *homo unius libri*, a man of one book.[81]

"Experience outweighs theory," wrote Steele, "faith makes philosophy kick the beam," an old expression referring to a set of scales. When one pan is much lighter than the other, the lighter pan flies up and "kicks the beam."

Steele represents a very good model of theological interpretation operating in the Holiness movement. He allowed theology to inform his

---

79. As evidenced by his commentaries on Leviticus and Joshua in the *Whedon's Commentary* series from Methodist publishers, Hunt & Eaton.
80. Steele, *Saint John's Epistles*, 56.
81. Steele, *Love Enthroned*, 261–62.

interpretation of the Bible and remained strongly committed to the collective voice of the church. He recognized the value of experience and left ample room for the work of the Holy Spirit to illuminate and transform. While employing the best of biblical scholarship, Steele allowed for polyvalence. He gave serious attention to the literary meaning of the text but always for the purpose of identifying what it revealed of God's Truth. Steele approached the text as one fully committed to the doctrine and experience of entire sanctification—with a holiness hermeneutic—without distorting the biblical passage. Looking backward at the holiness interpreters of the late nineteenth century, especially as exemplified by Daniel Steele, we recognize a path forward, one in keeping with the holiness heritage and with that of the church universal.

Bibliography

Adam, A. K. M. "Poaching on Zion." In *Reading Scripture with the Church: Toward a Hermeneutic for Theological Interpretation*, edited by A. K. M. Adam, et al., 17–34. Grand Rapids: Baker, 2006.

Adam, A. K. M., et al. *Reading Scripture with the Church*. Grand Rapids: Baker, 2006.

Ahlstrom, Sydney E. *A Religious History of the American People*. New Haven: Yale University Press, 1972.

Alexander, James W. "On the Use and Abuse of Systematic Theology." *Biblical Repertory and Princeton Review* 4 (1832) 171–90

Arrington, F. L. "Hermeneutics, Historical Perspectives on Pentecostal and Charismatic." In *Dictionary of Pentecostal and Charismatic Movements*, edited by Stanley M. Burgess and Gary B. McGee, 376–89. Grand Rapids: Regency Reference Library, 1988.

Augustine, Saint. *On Christian Doctrine*. http://faculty.georgetown.edu/jod/augustine/ddc3.html.

Aulen, Gustaf. *The Faith of the Christian Church*. Translated by Eric H. Wahlstrom and G. Everett Arden. Philadelphia: Muhlenberg, 1948.

Austin, Benjamin, Jr. *Constitutional Republicanism in Opposition to Fallacious Federalism*. Boston: Adams & Rhoades, 1803.

Baird, Robert. *Religion in the United States of America*. London: Duncan & Malcolm, 1844.

Barr, James. "Biblical Theology." In *The Interpreters Dictionary of the Bible, Supplementary Volume*, edited by Keith Crim, 104–11. Nashville: Abingdon, 1976.

Bassett, Paul Merritt. "The Fundamentalist Leavening of the Holiness Movement, 1914–1940." *Wesleyan Theological Journal* 13 (1978) 65–91.

———. "The Theological Identity of the North American Holiness Movement: Its Understanding of the Nature and Role of the Bible." In *The Variety of American Evangelicalism*, edited by Donald W. Dayton and Robert K. Johnston, 72–108. Downers Grove, IL: InterVarsity, 1991.

Beecher, Lyman. *An Address to the Charitable Society for the Education of Indigent Pious Young Men for the Ministry of the Gospel*. New Haven: n.p., 1814.

———. "The Faith Once Delivered to the Saints." In *The American Evangelicals, 1800–1900: An Anthology*, edited by William G. McLoughlin, 70–85. Gloucester, MA: Peter Smith, 1976.

Benson, Joseph. *The Holy Bible, with Notes, all the Marginal Readings, Parallel Texts, and Summaries of each Book & Chapter*. 5 vols. London: Blanshard, 1810–1815.

Bibliography

Bercovitch, Sacvan. "Introduction." In *Typology and Early American Literature*, edited by Sacvan Bercovitch, 3–8. Amherst: University of Massachusetts, 1972.

Berger, Peter. "Toward a Critique of Modernity." In *Religion and the Sociology of Knowledge: Modernization and Pluralism in Christian Thought and Structure*, edited by Barbara Hargrove, 335–49. Studies in Religion and Society 8. Lewiston, NY: Mellen, 1984.

Betz, Otto. "Biblical Theology, History of." In *The Interpreter's Dictionary of the Bible*, edited by George Arthur Buttrick, 1:432–37. Nashville: Abingdon, 1962.

Birch, Bruce C. "Biblical Hermeneutics in Recent Discussion: Old Testament." In *A Guide to Contemporary Hermeneutics*, edited by Donald K. McKim, 3–12. Grand Rapids: Eerdmans, 1986.

Bodner, Keith. "Go Figure: Narrative Strategies for an Emerging Generation." In *Go Figure! Figuration in Biblical Interpretation*, edited by Stanley D. Walters, 9–24. Eugene, OR: Pickwick, 2008.

Booth, Catherine Mumford. *Female Ministry; or, Woman's Right to Preach the Gospel*. London: Morgan & Chase, 1859.

Brauer, Jerald C. *Protestantism in America*. Rev. ed. Philadelphia: Westminster, 1965.

———, ed. "Macarius the Egyptian." In *The Westminster Dictionary of Church History*, 517. Philadelphia: Westminster, 1971.

———, ed. "Pietism." In *The Westminster Dictionary of Church History*, 659–60. Philadelphia: Westminster, 1971.

Brereton, Virginia Lieson. *Training God's Army: the American Bible School, 1880–1940*. Bloomington: Indiana University Press, 1990.

Bresee, Phineas. "Baptism with the Holy Ghost." In *The Double Cure*, 326–36. Boston: Christian Witness, 1894.

Bright, John. *The Kingdom of God: The Biblical Concept and Its Meaning for the Church*. Nashville: Abingdon, 1953.

Brown, Dale. *Understanding Pietism*. Grand Rapids: Eerdmans, 1978.

Brown, Jerry Wayne. *The Rise of Biblical Criticism in America, 1800–1870: The New England Scholars*. Middletown, CT: Wesleyan University Press, 1969.

Brown, Raymond E. "Hermeneutics." In *The Jerome Biblical Commentary*, 605–23. Englewood Cliffs, NJ: Prentice-Hall, 1968.

Bultmann, Rudolf. "Is Exegesis without Presuppositions Possible?" In *New Testament and Mythology and Other Basic Writings*, edited and translated by Schubert M. Ogden, 145–53. Philadelphia: Fortress, 1984.

Burtner, Robert W. and Robert E. Chiles. *John Wesley's Theology: A Collection of His Works*. Nashville: Abingdon, (1954) 1982.

Byrne, Donald E., Jr. *No Foot of Land: Folklore of American Methodist Itinerants*. ATLA Monograph Series 6. Metuchen, NJ: Scarecrow and ATLA, 1975.

Calvin, John. *Institutes of the Christian Religion*. Volume 2. Philadelphia: Westminster, 1960.

Campbell, Thomas. "Declaration and Address of the Christian Association of Washington." Washington, PA: Brown and Sample, 1809.

Cannon, William R. "General Introduction." In *Asbury Bible Commentary*, edited by Eugene E. Carpenter and Wayne McCown, 15–18. Grand Rapids: Zondervan, 1992.

Carpenter, Joel A. "Fundamentalist Institutions and the Rise of Evangelical Protestantism, 1929–1942." *Church History* 49.1 (March 1980) 62–75.

Carradine, Beverly. *The Better Way*. Cincinnati: God's Revivalist, 1896.

———. *Golden Sheaves*. 4th ed. Chicago: Christian Witness, 1904.

Bibliography

———. *Heart Talks*. 3rd ed. Cincinnati: Knapp, 1899.
———. *A Journey to Palestine*. Chicago: Christian Witness, 1892.
———. *The Old Man*. Chicago: Christian Witness, 1896.
———. *Revival Sermons*. Dallas: Holiness Echoes, 1897.
———. *Sanctification*. Columbia, SC: Pickett, 1890.
———. *The Sanctified Life*. Cincinnati: Knapp, 1897.
———. *Second Blessing in Symbol*. 2nd ed. Louisville: Pickett, 1896.
Carter, Paul A. *The Spiritual Crisis of the Gilded Age*. Dekalb, IL: Northern Illinois University Press, 1971.
Cartwright, Peter. *Autobiography of Peter Cartwright, the Backwoods Preacher*. Edited by W. P. Strickland. New York: Carlton & Porter, 1856.
———. *Fifty Years as a Presiding Elder*. Edited by Walter S. Hooper. Cincinnati: Hitchcock & Walden, 1872.
Carwardine, Richard. *Transatlantic Revivalism*. Westport, CT: Greenwood, 1978.
Cherry, Conrad. "Symbols of Spiritual Truth: Jonathan Edwards as Biblical Interpreter." *Interpretation* 39 (1985) 263-71.
Childs, Brevard A. *Biblical Theology in Crisis*. Philadelphia: Westminster, 1970.
———. *Introduction to the Old Testament as Scripture*. Philadelphia: Fortress, 1979.
Chiles, Robert E. *Theological Transition in American Methodism: 1790-1935*. Lanham, MD: University Press of America, 1983.
Cizik, Richard C. "National Association of Evangelicals." In *Dictionary of Christianity in America*, edited by Daniel G. Reid, et al., 793-94. Downers Grove, IL: InterVarsity, 1990.
Clarke, Adam. *Christian Theology*. Edited by Samuel Dunn. New York: Lane & Tippett, 1846.
———. *The Holy Bible Containing the Old and New Testaments*. 3 vols. Nashville: Abingdon, 1977.
Cohen, Charles E. "Two Biblical Models of Conversion: An Example of Puritan Hermeneutics." *Church History* 58.2 (1989) 182-96.
Cooper, J. F. "Hutchinson, Ann Marbury (1591-1643)." In *Dictionary of Christianity in America*, edited by Daniel G. Reid, et al., 563. Downers Grove, IL: InterVarsity, 1990.
Dammerman, Bernhard. "Continental Versions from c. 1600 to the Present Day: German." In *Cambridge History of the Bible: The West from the Reformation to the Present Day*, edited by S. L. Greenslade, 3:339-47. Cambridge: Cambridge University Press, 1962.
Davis, Thomas M. "The Traditions of Puritan Typology." In *Typology and Early American Literature*, edited by Sacvan Bercovitch, 11-45. Amherst, MA: University of Massachusetts, 1972.
Dayton, Donald. "Asa Mahan and the Development of American Holiness Theology." *Wesleyan Theological Journal* 9 (1974) 60-69.
———. *Discovering an Evangelical Heritage*. Peabody, MA: Hendrickson, 1976.
———. "The Holiness Witness in the Ecumenical Church." *Wesleyan Theological Journal* 23.1-2 (1988) 92-106.
———. *Theological Roots of Pentecostalism*. Studies in Evangelicalism 5. Metuchen, NJ: Scarecrow, 1987.
———. "The Use of Scripture in the Wesleyan Tradition." In *The Use of the Bible in Theology: Evangelical Options*, edited by Robert K. Johnston, 121-36. Atlanta: John Knox, 1985.

Bibliography

Dayton, Lucille Sider, and Donald W. Dayton. "'Your Daughters Shall Prophesy': Feminism in the Holiness Movement." *Methodist History* 14.2 (1976) 67–92.

De Lubac, Henri. *Medieval Exegesis: The Four Senses of Scripture.* Vol. 1. Translated by Mark Sebanc. Grand Rapids: Eerdmans, 1998.

De Vries, Simon J. "Biblical Criticism, History of." In *The Interpreter's Dictionary of the Bible*, edited by George Arthur Buttrick, 1:413–18. Nashville: Abingdon, 1962.

Dieter, Melvin Easterday. *The Holiness Revival of the Nineteenth Century.* Studies in Evangelicalism 1. Metuchen, NJ: Scarecrow, 1980.

Dixon, James. *Personal Narrative of a Tour Through a Part of the United States and Canada; with Notices of the History and Institutions of Methodism in America.* New York: Lane & Scott, 1849.

Dunlap, E. Dale. "Tuesday Meetings, Camp Meetings, and Cabinet Meetings: A Perspective on the Holiness Movement in the Methodist Church in the United States in the Nineteenth Century." *Methodist History* 13.3 (1975) 85–106.

Dunning, H. Ray. "Biblical Interpretation and Wesleyan Theology." *Wesleyan Theological Journal* 9 (1974) 47–51.

Dwight, Timothy. *A Sermon Preached at the Opening of the Theological Institution at Andover.* Boston: Farrand, Mallory, 1808.

"Education in the Methodist Church." *Methodist Quarterly Review* 24 (October 1842) 530–40.

Eichrodt, Walther. "Is Typological Exegesis an Appropriate Method?" In *Essays on Old Testament Hermeneutics*, edited by Claus Westermann and translated by James Barr and James Luther Mays, 224–45. Richmond: John Knox, 1963.

———. *Theology of the Old Testament.* Vol. 1. Old Testament Library. Philadelphia: Westminster, 1961.

Farrar, Frederic. *History of Interpretation.* London: Macmillan, 1886.

Faupel, William. "Preface." In *Six Tracts by W. B. Godbey*, vii–xvii. New York: Garland, 1985.

Finney, Charles G. *Lectures on Revivals of Religion.* New York: Revell, 1868.

Fowl, Stephen E. "The Importance of a Multivoiced Literal Sense of Scripture." In *Reading Scripture with the Church: Toward a Hermeneutic for Theological Interpretation*, edited by A. K. M. Adam, et al., 35–50. Grand Rapids: Baker, 2006.

Francis, John W. *Old New York: or Reminiscences of the Past Sixty Years.* New York: Roe, 1858.

Frei, Hans W. *The Eclipse of Biblical Narrative.* New Haven: Yale University Press, 1974.

Garrett, John. *Roger Williams: Witness Beyond Christendom, 1603–1683.* New York: Macmillan, 1970.

Garrison, S. Olin, ed. *Forty Witnesses Covering the Whole Range of Christian Experience.* New York: Phillips & Hunt, 1888.

Godbey, W. B. *Autobiography of Rev. W. B. Godbey, A. M.* Cincinnati: God's Revivalist, 1909.

———. *The Bible.* Nashville: Pentecostal Mission, n.d.

———. *Bible Theology.* Cincinnati: God's Revivalist, 1911.

———. *Christian Perfection.* Louisville: Pentecostal, 1886.

———. "Church-Bride-Kingdom." In *Six Tracts by W. B. Godbey.* New York: Garland, 1985.

———. *Commentary on the New Testament.* 7 vols. Cincinnati: God's Revivalist, 1896–1900.

Bibliography

———. "Divine Healing." In *Six Tracts by W. B. Godbey*. New York: Garland, 1985.
———. *Footprints of Jesus in the Holy Land*. Cincinnati: God's Revivalist, 1900.
———. *Higher Criticism*. Cincinnati: God's Revivalist, 1909.
———. *Holiness or Hell*. Louisville: Pentecostal, 1899.
———. *Illumination*. Greensboro, NC: Apostolic Messenger, n.d.
———. "Out of Egypt Into Canaan." In *Six Pioneer Holiness Sermons*, 80–92. Dallas: Evangel, n.d.
———. *Sanctification*. N.p., 1884. https://archive.org/details/sanctificationoogodb.
———. *Six Tracts by W. B. Godbey*. New York: Garland, 1985.
———. "Spiritual Gifts and Graces." In *Six Tracts by W. B. Godbey*. New York: Garland, 1985.
———. *Translation of the New Testament from the Original Greek*. Cincinnati: Knapp, n.d.
———. *Visions*. Greensboro, NC: Apostolic Messenger, n.d.
———. *Woman Preacher*. Atlanta: Way of Life, 1891.
———. *Work of the Holy Spirit*. Louisville: Pickett, 1902.
Grant, Robert M., and David Tracy. *A Short History of the Interpretation of the Bible*. Rev. ed. Philadelphia: Fortress, 1984.
Green, Joel B. *Practicing Theological Interpretation: Engaging Biblical Texts for Faith and Formation*. Grand Rapids: Baker Academic, 2011.
———. *Seized by Truth: Reading the Bible as Scripture*. Nashville, Abingdon, 2007.
Greene-McCreight, Kathryn. "Rule of Faith." In *Dictionary for Theological Interpretation of the Bible*, edited by Kevin J. Vanhoozer, 703–4. Grand Rapids: Baker Academic, 2005.
Gwyn, Douglas. *Apocalypse of the Word: The Life and Message of George Fox: 1624–1691*. Richmond, IN: Friends United, 1986.
Hamilton, Barry W. *William Baxter Godbey: Itinerant Apostle of the Holiness Movement*. Studies in American Religion 72. Lewiston, NY: Mellen, 2000.
Hamilton, Victor P. *Handbook on the Pentateuch*. Grand Rapids: Baker, 1982.
Handy, Robert T. *A Christian America*. Rev. ed. New York: Oxford University Press, 1984.
———. *A History of the Churches in the United States and Canada*. New York: Oxford University Press, 1977.
Hardesty, Nancy, et al. "Women in the Holiness Movement in the Evangelical Tradition." In *Women of Spirit*, edited by Rosemary Ruether and Eleanor McLaughlin, 225–54. 1979. Reprint, Eugene, OR: Wipf & Stock, 1998.
Hartley, John E. "The Use of Typology Illustrated in a Study of Isaiah 9:1–7." In *Interpreting God's Word for Today: An Inquiry into Hermeneutics from a Biblical Theological Perspective*, edited by Wayne McCown and James Earl Massey, 195–220. Wesleyan Theological Perspectives 2. Anderson, IN: Warner, 1982.
Hatch, Nathan O. *The Democratization of American Christianity*. New Haven: Yale University Press, 1989.
———. "*Sola Scriptura* and *Novus Ordo Seclorum*." In *The Bible in America: Essays in Cultural History*, 59–78. New York: Oxford University Press, 1982.
Hensey, James A. *The Itinerancy: Its Power and Peril*. New York: Methodist Book Concern, 1918.
Hodges, George. *Faith and Social Service: Eight Lectures Delivered before the Lowell Institute*. New York: Whittaker, 1896.
Hofstadter, Richard. *Social Darwinism in American Thought*. Rev. ed. New York: Braziller, 1965.

Bibliography

Homer, Charlotte G. "Pentecostal Power." In *Praise and Worship*, 382. Kansas City, MO: Lillenas, n.d.

Houghton, Walter E. "Character of the Age." In *Backgrounds to Victorian Literature*, edited by Richard A. Levine, 15-40. San Francisco: Chandler, 1967.

Hudson, Winthrop. *Religion in America*. 4th ed. New York: Macmillan, 1987.

Hynson, Leon O. "The Wesleyan Quadrilateral in the American Holiness Tradition." *Wesleyan Theological Journal* 20.1 (1985) 19-33.

Ignatius. "Epistle to the Trallians." In *The Ante-Nicene Fathers: Translations of the Writings of the Fathers Down to A. D. 325*, edited by Alexander Roberts and James Donaldson, 1:66-72. Grand Rapids: Eerdmans, 1950.

Irenaeus. "Against Heresies." In *The Ante-Nicene Fathers: Translations of the Writings of the Fathers Down to A.D. 325*, edited by Alexander Roberts and James Donaldson, 1:315-567. Grand Rapids: Eerdmans, 1950.

Jenkins, Philip. *The Next Christendom: The Coming of Global Christianity*. Rev. ed. Oxford: Oxford University Press, 2007.

Jones, Charles E. *A Guide to the Study of the Holiness Movement*. Metuchen, NJ: Scarecrow, 1974.

———. *Perfectionist Persuasion: The Holiness Movement and American Methodism, 1867-1936*. ATLA Monograph Series 5. Metuchen, NJ: Scarecrow, 1974.

Kepler, T. S. "Sinaiticus." In *The Interpreter's Dictionary of the Bible*, edited by George A. Buttrick, et al., 4:378-79. Nashville: Abingdon, 1962.

Knapp, Martin Wells. *Christ Crowned Within*. Cincinnati: Revivalist, 1893.

———. *Double Cure*. Cincinnati: God's Revivalist, 1898.

———. *Holiness Triumphant, or, Pearls from Patmos*. Cincinnati: God's Revivalist, 1900.

———. *Impressions*. 5th ed. Cincinnati: Revivalist, 1892.

———. *Lightning Bolts from Pentecostal Skies*. Cincinnati: Revivalist, 1898.

———. *Out of Egypt, Into Canaan*. Cincinnati: Revivalist, 1898.

———. *Rescued, or, the River of Death*. Cincinnati: Knapp, 1901.

———. *Revival Kindlings*. 4th ed. Cincinnati: Revivalist, 1890.

———. *Revival Tornadoes, or, Life and Labors of Rev. J. H. Webber, Evangelist*. Boston: McDonald & Gill, 1889.

Knight, John A. "John Fletcher's Influence on the Development of Wesleyan Theology in America." *Wesleyan Theological Journal* 13.1 (1978) 13-33.

Knott, John R., Jr. *The Sword of the Spirit: Puritan Responses to the Bible*. Chicago: University of Chicago Press, 1980.

Krentz, Edgar. *The Historical-Critical Method*. Guides to Biblical Scholarship. Philadelphia: Fortress, 1975.

Ladd, George Eldon. *The New Testament and Criticism*. Grand Rapids: Eerdmans, 1967.

Langford, Thomas. *Practical Divinity*. Nashville: Abingdon, 1983.

Leland, John. *The Rights of Conscience Inalienable, and Therefore, Religious Opinions not Cognizable by Law; or, the High-flying Churchman, Stripped of His Legal Robe, Appears a Yaho*. New York: n.p., 1791.

Lennox, Stephen J. "'One in Christ': Galatians 3:28 and the Holiness Agenda." *Evangelical Quarterly* 84.3 (2012) 195-212.

Longfield, B. J. "Briggs, Charles Augustus (1841-1913)." In *Dictionary of Christianity in America*, edited by Daniel G. Reid, et al., 188. Downers Grove, IL: InterVarsity, 1990.

Lovelace, Richard. "Recovering Our Balance." *Charisma* (August 1987) 80.

Bibliography

Lowance, Mason I., Jr. "'Images or Shadows of Divine Things' in the Thought of Jonathan Edwards." In *Typology and Early American Literature*, edited by Sacvan Bercovitch, 209–44. Amherst: University of Massachusetts, 1972.

Luther, Martin. *Luther's Works*. Edited by Jaroslav Pelikan and Helmut Lehman. 55 vols. St. Louis: Concordia; Philadelphia: Fortress, 1958–86.

Magrassi, Mariano. *Praying the Bible: An Introduction to Lectio Divina*. Translated by Edward Hagman. Collegeville, MN: Liturgical, 1998.

Marsden, George. "Everyone One's Own Interpreter? The Bible, Science, and Authority in Mid-Nineteenth-Century America." In *The Bible in America: Essays in Cultural History*, 79–100. New York: Oxford University Press, 1982.

———. *Fundamentalism and American Culture: The Shaping of Twentieth-Century Evangelicalism, 1870–1925*. Oxford: Oxford University Press, 1980.

Mather, Cotton. *Magnalia Christi Americana*. Vol. 1. Hartford: Silas Andrus, 1855.

McCown, Wayne. "Toward a Wesleyan Hermeneutic." In *Interpreting God's Word for Today: An Inquiry into Hermeneutics from a Biblical Theological Perspective*, edited by Wayne McCown and James Earl Massey, 1–30. Wesleyan Theological Perspectives 2. Anderson, IN: Warner, 1982.

McDonald, William. "Introduction." In *Coals of Fire: Being Expositions of Scripture on the Doctrine, Experience, and Practice of Christian Holiness*, by George D. Watson, 3–4. Boston: McDonald, 1886.

McLoughlin, William G. "'Enthusiasm for Liberty': The Great Awakening as the Key to the Revolution." In *Preachers and Politicians: Two Essays on the Origins of the American Revolution*, edited by Jack P. Greene and William G. McLoughlin, 47–73. Worcester, MA: American Antiquarian Society, 1977.

———. "Introduction." In *The American Evangelicals, 1800–1900: An Anthology*, edited by William G. McLoughlin, 1–27. Gloucester, MA: Peter Smith, 1976.

———. "Introduction." In *Perfectionist Persuasion: The Holiness Movement and American Methodism, 1867–1936*, by Charles Edwin Jones, xvii–xix. ATLA Monograph Series 5. Metuchen, NJ: Scarecrow, 1974.

———. *Modern Revivalism: Charles Grandison Finney to Billy Graham*. New York: Ronald, 1959.

Mead, Sidney E. "The Rise of the Evangelical Conception of the Ministry in America (1607–1850)." In *The Ministry in Historical Perspectives*, edited by H. Richard Niebuhr and Daniel D. Williams, 207–49. New York: Harper, 1956.

Methodist Episcopal Church. *The Doctrines and Discipline of the Methodist Episcopal Church in America*. 10th ed. Philadelphia: Tuckniss, 1798.

Moody, Dwight L. *Secret Power*. N.p., 1881.

Nevin, John Williamson. "The Sect System." In *Catholic and Reformed: Selected Theological Writings of John Williamson Nevin*, edited by Charles Yrigoyen, Jr., and George H. Bricker, 128–73. Eugene, OR: Pickwick Publications, 1978.

Niebuhr, H. Richard, et al. *The Advancement of Theological Education*. New York: Harper, 1957.

Noll, Mark A. *Between Faith and Criticism: Evangelicals, Scholarship, and the Bible in America*. Society of Biblical Literature Confessional Perspectives. San Francisco: Harper, 1986.

———. "The Founding of Princeton Seminary." *Westminster Theological Journal* 42 (1979) 72–110.

BIBLIOGRAPHY

———. "The Image of the United States as a Biblical Nation, 1776–1865." In *The Bible in America: Essays in Cultural History*, 39–58. New York: Oxford University Press, 1982.

Origen. "Commentary on John." In *The Ante-Nicene Fathers: Translations of the Writings of the Fathers Down to A.D. 325*, edited by Allan Menzies, 10:297–408. Grand Rapids: Eerdmans, 1951.

Outler, Albert C. "'Biblical Primitivism' in Early American Methodism." In *The Wesleyan Theological Heritage*, edited by Thomas C. Oden and Leicester R. Longden, 145–57. Grand Rapids: Francis Asbury, 1991.

———, ed. "Introduction." In *John Wesley*, 3–33. Library of Protestant Thought. New York: Oxford University Press, 1964.

Perkins, George. "The New Nation and the House Divided." In *The American Tradition in Literature*, edited by Sculley Bradley, et al., 461–67. 5th ed. New York: Random House, 1981.

Peters, John L. *Christian Perfection and American Methodism*. Reprint ed. Grand Rapids: Francis Asbury, 1985.

Pierson, A. T. "The Sin of Habitual Unbelief." In *Keswick's Authentic Voice*, 41–50. Grand Rapids: Zondervan, 1959.

Pointer, Richard W. "Scottish Realism." In *Dictionary of Christianity in America*, edited by Daniel G. Reid, et al., 1061. Downers Grove, IL: InterVarsity, 1990.

Rad, Gerhard von. *Old Testament Theology*. 2 vols. Translated by D. M. G. Stalker. San Francisco: Harper & Row, 1962–65.

———. "Typological Interpretation of the Old Testament." In *Essays on Old Testament Hermeneutics*, edited by Claus Westermann, 17–39. Translated by John Bright and James Luther Mays. Richmond: John Knox, 1963.

Reinitz, Richard. "The Separatist Background of Roger Williams' Argument for Religious Toleration." In *Typology and Early American Literature*, edited by Sacvan Bercovitch, 107–37. Amherst: University of Massachusetts Press, 1972.

Review of *Personal Narrative of a Tour through a Part of the United States and Canada; with Notices of the History and Institutions of Methodism in America*, by James Dixon. *Methodist Quarterly Review* 31 (October 1849) 653–61.

Richardson, Alan. "Salvation, Savior." In *The Interpreters Dictionary of the Bible*, edited by George Arthur Buttrick, 4:168–81. Nashville: Abingdon, 1962.

Ringenberg, William C. "Bible Institutes and Colleges." In *Dictionary of Christianity in America*, edited by Daniel G. Reid et al., 141–43. Downers Grove, IL: InterVarsity, 1990.

Robertson, David. "Literature, the Bible as." In *The Interpreters Dictionary of the Bible, Supplementary Volume*, edited by Keith Crim, 547–51. Nashville: Abingdon, 1962.

Robinson, Reuben. *Chickens Come Home to Roost*. Kansas City, MO: Beacon Hill, 1958.

———. *Honey in the Rock*. Cincinnati: God's Revivalist, 1913.

———. *My Life's Story*. Kansas City, MO: Nazarene, 1928.

———. *My Travels in the Holy Land*. Louisville: Pentecostal, n.d.

———. *A Pitcher of Cream*. Louisville: Pentecostal, 1906.

———. *Story of Lazarus*. Louisville: Pentecostal, 1909.

———. *Sunshine and Smiles*. Greenville, TX: Texas Holiness Advocate, 1902.

Rose, Delbert. *A Theology of Christian Experience: Interpreting the Historic Wesleyan Message*. Minneapolis: Bethany Fellowship, 1965.

Rowley, H. H. *The Unity of the Bible*. Philadelphia: Westminster, 1953.

Bibliography

Runia, Klaas. "The Hermeneutics of the Reformers." *Calvin Theological Journal* 19 (1984) 121–52.

Rutman, Darrett B. *American Puritanism*. New York: Norton, 1977.

Sabine, George H, ed. *The Works of Gerrard Winstanley*. New York: Cornell University Press, 1965.

Sandeen, Ernest. *The Roots of Fundamentalism: British and American Millenarianism, 1800–1930*. Chicago: University of Chicago Press, 1970.

Schenck, Kenneth. *Cosmology and Eschatology in Hebrews: The Settings of the Sacrifice*. Society for New Testament Studies Monograph Series. Cambridge: Cambridge University Press, 2010.

———. *Jesus Is Lord: An Introduction to the New Testament*. 2nd ed. Marion, IN: Triangle, 2009.

Schlesinger, Arthur M. "A Critical Period in American Religion, 1875–1900." In *Religion in American History: Interpretive Essays*, edited by John M. Mulder and John F. Wilson, 302–17. Englewood Cliffs, NJ: Prentice, 1978.

Shelton, R. Larry. "Nature, Character, and Origin of Scripture." In *Asbury Bible Commentary*, edited by Eugene E. Carpenter and Wayne McCown, 19–37. Grand Rapids: Zondervan, 1992.

Smart, James D. *The Interpretation of Scripture*. Philadelphia: Westminster, 1961.

Smith, John. "The Vision of God." In *Keswick's Authentic Voice*, 57–65. Grand Rapids: Zondervan, 1959.

Smith, Joseph H. *Daily Holiness Text Book: Selections and Comments by Rev. John Thompson and Rev. E. I. D. Pepper. Autograph Album with Twelve Holiness Homilies by Joseph H. Smith*. Cincinnati: God's Bible School and Revivalist, 1922.

———. *From Glory to Glory, or, Degrees in Spiritual Life*. Philadelphia: Christian Standard, 1898.

———. *Pauline Perfection; Being a Series of Expository Messages Upon Various Aspects of Christian Perfection from the Pauline Epistles*. Salem, OH: Schmul, 1975.

———. *Things of the Spirit*. Chicago: Chicago Evangelistic Institute, 1940.

Smith, Timothy L. "The Doctrine of the Sanctifying Spirit: Charles G. Finney's Synthesis of Wesleyan and Covenant Theology." *Wesleyan Theological Journal* 13 (1978) 92–113.

———. "Foreword." In *The Beauty of Holiness*, by Charles Edward White, vii–xiv. Grand Rapids: Francis Asbury, 1986.

———. "The Holiness Crusade." In *History of American Methodism*, edited by Emory S. Bucke, 2:608–27. New York: Abingdon, 1964.

———. "How John Fletcher Became the Theologian of Wesleyan Perfectionism, 1770–1776." *Wesleyan Theological Journal* 15 (1980) 68–87.

———. *Revivalism and Social Reform in Mid-Nineteenth Century America*. New York: Abingdon, 1957.

Stanley, Susie C. "Wesleyan/Holiness Churches: Innocent Bystanders in the Fundamentalist/Modernist Controversy." In *Re-forming the Center: American Protestantism, 1900 to the Present*, edited by Douglas Jacobsen and William Vance Trollinger, 178–93. Grand Rapids: Eerdmans, 1998.

Steele, Daniel. *Book of Joshua*. Commentary on the Old Testament 3. New York: Nelson & Phillips, 1873.

———. *A Defense of Christian Perfection, or, A Criticism of Dr. James Mudge's "Growth in Holiness Toward Perfection."* New York: Hunt & Eaton, 1896.

———. *Gospel of the Comforter*. Rochester, PA: Schmul, 1897.

BIBLIOGRAPHY

———. *Half-Hours with Saint John's Epistles*. Boston: Christian Witness, 1901.
———. *Half-Hours with Saint Paul and Other Bible Readings*. Rochester, PA: Schmul, 1894.
———. *Jesus Exultant, or, Christ No Pessimist, and Other Essays*. Boston: Christian Witness, 1899.
———. *Leviticus and Numbers*. [Whedon's] Commentary on the Old Testament 2. New York: Eaton & Mains, 1891.
———. *Love Enthroned: Essays on Evangelical Perfection*. Rev. ed. New York: Methodist Book Concern, 1875.
———. *Milestone Papers: Doctrinal, Ethical and Experimental on Christian Progress*. Salem, OH: Schmul, 1878.
———. *A Substitute for Holiness, or, Antinomianism Revived, or, the Theology of the So-Called Plymouth Brethren Examined and Refuted*. 3rd ed. Chicago: Christian Witness, 1899.
Stein, Stephen J. "The Quest for the Spiritual Sense: The Biblical Hermeneutics of Jonathan Edwards." *Harvard Theological Review* 70 (1977) 99–113.
Steinmetz, David C. "The Superiority of Pre-Critical Exegesis." In *The Theological Interpretation of Scripture: Classic and Contemporary Readings*, edited by Stephen E. Fowl, 26–38. Malden, MA: Blackwell, 1997.
Stendahl, Krister. "Biblical Theology, Contemporary." In *The Interpreter's Dictionary of the Bible*, edited by George Arthur Buttrick, 1:418–32. Nashville: Abingdon, 1962.
Stoeffler, F. Ernest. "Pietism, the Wesleys, and Methodist Beginnings in America." In *Continental Pietism and Early American Christianity*, edited by F. Ernest Stoeffler, 184–221. Grand Rapids: Eerdmans, 1976.
Stout, Harry S. "Great Awakening." In *Dictionary of Christianity in America*, edited by Daniel G. Reid, et al., 494–96. Downers Grove, IL: InterVarsity, 1990.
———. "Puritanism." In *Dictionary of Christianity in America*, edited by Daniel G. Reid, et al., 964–66. Downers Grove, IL: InterVarsity, 1990.
———. "Word and Order in Colonial New England." In *The Bible in America: Essays in Cultural History*, edited by Nathan O. Hatch and Mark A. Noll, 19–38. New York: Oxford University Press, 1982.
Strong, Josiah. *Our Country: Its Possible Future and Its Present Crisis*. New York: American Home Missionary Society, 1885.
Stuart, Moses. *Elements of Interpretation, Translated from the Latin of J. A. Ernesti, and Accompanied by Notes and an Appendix Containing Extracts from Morus, Beck and Keil*. Andover, MA: Newman, 1827.
———. "Have the Sacred Writers Anywhere Asserted That the Sin or Righteousness of One is Imputed to Another?" *American Biblical Repository* VII (1836) 247.
Sykes, Norman. "The Religion of Protestants." In *Cambridge History of the Bible: The West from the Reformation to the Present Day*, edited by S. L. Greenslade, 3:175–98. Cambridge: Cambridge University Press, 1962.
Synan, Vinson. *The Holiness-Pentecostal Movement in the United States*. Grand Rapids: Eerdmans, 1971.
Taylor, Thomas T. "Gorton, Samuel (c. 1592–1677)." In *Dictionary of Christianity in America*, edited by Daniel G. Reid, et al., 488–89. Downers Grove, IL: InterVarsity, 1990.
Terrien, Samuel. *The Elusive Presence: Toward a New Biblical Theology*. 1978. Reprint, Eugene, OR: Wipf & Stock, 2000.

Bibliography

Terry, Milton S. *Biblical Hermeneutics: A Treatise on the Interpretation of the Old and New Testaments.* Grand Rapids: Zondervan, 1883.

Thompson, David L. "Old Testament Bases of the Wesleyan Message." *Wesleyan Theological Journal* 10 (1975) 38–47.

Thompson, W. Ralph. "An Appraisal of the Keswick and Wesleyan Contemporary Positions." *Wesleyan Theological Journal* 1.1 (1966) 11–20.

Thorsen, Donald A. D. *The Wesleyan Quadrilateral: Scripture, Tradition, Reason and Experience as a Model of Evangelical Theology.* Grand Rapids: Francis Asbury, 1990.

Treier, Daniel J. *Introducing Theological Interpretation of Scripture: Recovering a Christian Practice.* Grand Rapids: Baker, 2008.

Turner, George A. "John Wesley as an Interpreter of Scripture." In *Inspiration and Interpretation*, edited by John F. Walvoord, 156–78. Grand Rapids: Eerdmans, 1957.

Tyerman, Luke. *Wesley's Designated Successor: The Life, Letters and Literary Labors of the Rev. John William Fletcher.* London: Hodder & Stoughton, 1882.

Tyson, John R. "Terry, Milton Spenser (1846–1914)." In *Dictionary of Christianity in America*, edited by Daniel G. Reid, et al., 1165–66. Downers Grove, IL: InterVarsity, 1990.

Urban, Linwood. *A Short History of Christian Thought.* New York: Oxford University Press, 1986.

Vanhoozer, Kevin J. "Imprisoned or Free? Text, Status, and Theological Interpretation in the Master/Slave Discourse of Philemon." In *Reading Scripture with the Church: Toward a Hermeneutic for Theological Interpretation*, edited by A. K. M. Adam, et al., 51–93. Grand Rapids: Baker, 2006.

———, ed. *Theological Interpretation of the Old Testament: A Book-by-Book Survey.* Grand Rapids: Baker, 2008.

Varughese, Alex, et al., eds. *The New Beacon Bible Commentary Series.* 29 vols. Kansas City, MO: Nazarene, 2008–17.

Vincent of Lerins. "Commonitory: Chapter 2." http://www.newadvent.org/fathers/3506.htm.

Vriezen, Th. C. *An Outline of Old Testament Theology.* Translated by S. Neuijen. Oxford: Blackwell, 1962.

Wall, Robert W. "Toward a Wesleyan Hermeneutic of Scripture." *Wesleyan Theological Journal* 30.2 (1995) 50–67. http://wesley.nnu.edu/fileadmin/imported_site/wesleyjournal/1995-wtj-30-2.pdf.

———. *Why the Church? Reframing New Testament Theology.* Nashville: Abingdon, 2015.

Ward, Graham. "To Be a Reader: Bunyan's Struggle with the Language of Scripture in *Grace Abounding to the Chief of Sinners*." *Journal of Literature and Theology* 4.1 (1990) 29–49.

Watson, Eva. *Glimpses of the Life and Work of George Douglas Watson.* Cincinnati: God's Revivalist, 1929.

Watson, Francis. "Authors, Readers, Hermeneutics." In *Reading Scripture with the Church: Toward a Hermeneutic for Theological Interpretation*, edited by A. K. M. Adam, et al., 119–23. Grand Rapids: Baker, 2006

Watson, George D. *Coals of Fire: Being Expositions of Scripture on the Doctrine, Experience, and Practice of Christian Holiness.* Boston: McDonald, 1886.

———. *The Divine Love Song: An Exposition of the Song of Solomon.* Salem, OH: Schmul, n.d.

BIBLIOGRAPHY

———. *God's Eagles, or, Complete Testing of the Saints*. Cincinnati: God's Revivalist, n.d.

———. *God's First Words—Studies in Genesis: Historic, Prophetic and Experimental*. New York: Revell, 1919.

———. *Love Abounding and Other Expositions on the Spiritual Life*. Cincinnati: God's Revivalist, 1891.

———. *Our Own God, Psalm 67:6: Treating the Personalities, the Knowledge, and the Fellowship of God*. Cincinnati: Revivalist, 1904.

———. *A Pot of Oil, or, the Anointed Life as Applied to Prayer, the Mental Faculties, the Affections and Christian Service*. N.p., 1900.

———. *Steps to the Throne*. Dallas: Holiness Echoes, 1898.

———. *White Robes, or, Garments of Salvation*. Cincinnati: n.p., 1883.

Watson, Richard. *Biblical and Theological Dictionary: Explanatory of the History, Manners, and Customs of the Jews and Neighbouring Nations*. Rev. ed. New York: Lane & Sandford, 1843.

———. *An Exposition of the Gospels of St. Matthew and St. Mark, and of Some Other Detached Parts of Holy Scripture*. New York: Lane & Scott, 1852.

Weber, Timothy P. "Dispensationalism." In *Dictionary of Christianity in America*, edited by Daniel G. Reid, et al., 358. Downers Grove, IL: InterVarsity, 1990.

———. *Living in the Shadow of the Second Coming: American Premillennialism, 1875-1925*. Grand Rapids: Zondervan, 1983.

———. "The Two-Edged Sword: The Fundamentalist Use of the Bible." In *The Bible in America: Essays in Cultural History*, edited by Nathan O. Hatch and Mark A. Noll, 101-20. New York: Oxford University Press, 1982.

Welch, Claude. *Protestant Thought in the Nineteenth Century*. 2 vols. New Haven: Yale University Press, 1972-1985.

Wesley, John. *Explanatory Notes Upon the New Testament*. London: Epworth, 1948.

———. "Letter to Dr. Rutherforth, March 28, 1768." In *The Works of John Wesley*, 14:347-59. Peabody, MA: Hendrickson, 1984.

———. "Letter to Mr. Walter Churchey, of Brecon, February 21, 1771." In *The Works of John Wesley*, 12:432. Peabody, MA: Hendrickson, 1984.

———. "On Divine Providence," In *The Works of John Wesley*, 6:313-25. Peabody, MA: Hendrickson, 1984 (1872).

———. *A Plain Account of Christian Perfection*. Kansas City: Beacon Hill, 1966.

———. "Preface." In *The First Series of Sermons (1-39): A Life of John Wesley*, 49-54. Vol. 5 of *The Works of John Wesley*. Peabody, MA: Hendrickson, 1984.

Westermann, Claus. *Blessing in the Bible and the Life of the Church*. Translated by Keith R. Crim. Overtures to Biblical Theology. Philadelphia: Fortress, 1978.

Whedon, Daniel. "Preface." In *Commentary on the Gospels: Intended for Popular Use, Matthew-Mark*, 3. New York: Carlton & Lanahan, 1870.

White, Charles Edward. *The Beauty of Holiness*. Grand Rapids: Francis Asbury, 1986.

White, Conrad E. "Palmer, Phoebe Worrall (1807-1874)." In *Dictionary of Christianity in America*, edited by Daniel G. Reid, et al., 860-61. Downers Grove, IL: InterVarsity, 1990.

Williams, David M. *Receiving the Bible in Faith: Historical and Theological Exegesis*. Washington, DC: Catholic University Press, 2004.

Wright, G. Ernest. *God Who Acts: Biblical Theology as Recital*. Studies in Biblical Theology 8. Chicago: Allenson, 1952.

Bibliography

———. "The Study of the Old Testament." In *Protestant Thought in the Twentieth Century: Whence and Whither?*, edited by Arnold S. Nash, 15–44. New York: Macmillan, 1951.

Wright, G. Ernest, and Reginald H. Fuller. *The Book of the Acts of God: Contemporary Scholarship Interprets the Bible*. Garden City, NY: Anchor, 1957, 1960.

Wynkoop, Mildred Bangs. *A Theology of Love: The Dynamics of Wesleyanism*. Kansas City, MO: Beacon Hill, 1972.

Index

A

Acts, Book of, 53, 87, 90, 92, 105, 116, 138
Adam, 44, 114, 125
America, 1–2, 4–5, 9, 22–23, 25, 29, 31–32, 34, 38, 40, 45, 47–48, 51, 53, 66
  urbanization of, 2–4, 8, 38, 51, 57, 134
American Christianity, 1, 8, 13–14, 28, 32, 34, 37, 40, 51
Anglicanism, x, 17, 27, 43, 47
Asbury, Francis, 23, 25, 72
Augustine, 16, 70, 151–52, 154, 157–58
authority, 5–6, 8, 16, 18–20, 24–26, 28, 31, 33, 41, 62–64, 66–67, 81–82, 95, 97–98, 134–35

B

Bacon, Francis, 34, 41, 80
Baptists, 2, 9, 22, 37, 51
Bible, ix–xi, 8, 15, 59–65, 71–77, 81–83, 90–101, 103–9, 111–19, 121–24, 128–32, 134–38, 140, 145–48, 154–58
  authority of, 8, 26, 33, 38, 41, 62–64, 66, 81, 89, 95, 135, 143
  canon of, 129, 154, 156
  critical scholarship of, 4, 6, 8, 13, 34–35, 37–40, 46, 66–67, 81, 114, 118, 136, 138–42, 144–51, 158–59
  fundamentalist interpretation of, 40–41, 66, 135
  guide to interpretation of, 17, 25–26, 39, 72, 98, 145
  holiness interpretation, ix–x, 8–10, 12–13, 60–66, 72–74, 82–83, 96–100, 107–8, 116–18, 123–24, 129, 131–32, 134–36, 138–43, 145–47
    critical scholarship, 66–67, 81, 135, 138–42, 144, 149, 151, 159
    divine immanence, 101, 103, 131
    holiness hermeneutic, 97, 104, 106–13, 115, 126, 129, 131, 136–37, 145, 159
    inspiration, 64–65, 118–19, 132, 138, 140, 142
    more-than-literal, 13, 61–62, 83, 103, 107–9, 120–30, 132, 134–37, 149, 151, 154–55
    normativity, 91–93, 98
    perspicuity, 59, 88–90, 93, 98
    pneumatocentricity, 104–7, 113, 131, 135, 137
    role of exegesis, 74, 78, 116, 123, 141, 154
    role of experience, x, 64, 73–81, 83, 98, 103–4, 108, 123, 125, 131, 134, 136, 138, 155, 158
    role of Holy Spirit, 65, 81, 121
    role of reason, 68–70, 81, 90, 136
    role of tradition, 12, 70–73, 81, 93, 123, 135–36, 149, 151, 155
  inerrancy, infallibility of, 38–39, 41, 135, 142–44

Index

Bible (*continued*)
    inspiration of, 38–39, 62–66, 81, 114, 118–19, 123, 125, 132, 134, 138, 140, 142–43, 146, 155, 158
    interpretation of, 8–10, 15–18, 21, 23, 26–31, 33–35, 37–41, 82, 98, 100, 104, 144, 148–49, 152, 156
    literal interpretation of, 40, 120, 124, 129, 150–52, 155
    more-than-literal interpretation of, 18, 28–30, 83, 119–22, 149–52, 155
    narrative passages, 110, 121, 137–38, 145
    New Testament, 10–11, 23, 25, 71, 76, 79, 91–93, 96–98, 107, 109–10, 112, 125–30, 132, 148, 150–51
    Old Testament, 38, 78–79, 91, 104, 109–10, 113, 117, 121, 123, 125–26, 128, 131, 146, 150, 154
    perspicuity of, 16–18, 22, 35, 41, 88
    populist hermeneutic, 8, 13, 18–32, 34–37, 39–41, 49, 62, 82–83, 86, 88, 90, 93, 96–99, 134–35, 138
    presuppositions guiding interpretation of, 16, 29, 39, 62, 83, 100, 103, 119, 144–45
    role of exegesis, 16, 28, 144, 146, 151, 154, 156
    theological interpretation of, 144–58
    translations of, ix, 28–29, 66, 88, 96, 108
    unity of, 13, 61, 100, 113–14, 116–19, 132, 134, 146–47
    Wesleyan quadrilateral, 12, 32, 44, 62, 108, 135–36, 138
Bible as guide, 25, 77, 83, 86, 103
Bible colleges, institutes, schools, 11, 24, 69, 83, 86, 98, 142
Bible in America, 8, 15, 18, 31, 82
bishops, 39, 55, 58, 152–53

C

Calvin, John, Calvinism, 16–18, 22, 28–30, 36, 46, 54, 56, 82, 149
camp meetings, 48, 50, 54, 57, 59, 84

Carradine, Beverly, 10, 66, 69, 73–75, 79–80, 84, 109, 112, 114, 121, 125, 128, 130–31
Christ, 26, 28, 68–69, 76–77, 92, 94, 103–6, 108, 112, 114–15, 118–22, 124–25, 130, 146, 152–53
Christian Church, Disciples of Christ, 19, 22–23
Christian Perfection, 10, 44–47, 51–52, 104, 107, 109, 111
church, 1–3, 6, 8–9, 15–16, 22, 25–28, 53–60, 70–71, 94–95, 113, 124, 131–32, 134, 153, 156
    early, 16, 45, 70, 78, 81, 92–93, 122, 137, 149–50, 153, 156
Civil War, 1–3, 6, 8, 11, 18–19, 26, 31, 36–38, 54, 56, 82
Clarke, Adam, 25, 46, 49, 53
clergy, 17, 19–20, 22, 30–31, 37, 57, 82, 86
come-outers, put-outers, 59–60, 137
common people, 8, 17–24, 26, 31, 34–35, 40–41, 51, 70, 76, 90, 93, 134
common preaching, 20, 30, 32, 36
common sense, Common Sense Realism, 25, 31–32, 34–36, 38, 40–41, 48, 70, 81, 90–91, 98, 134
compass, 39–41, 99, 134–35
Congregationalism, 9, 26–27
conscience, 21, 25–27, 31, 36–38, 97, 114, 134, 152
consecration, 48, 50, 52, 79, 93, 110, 126–27
creeds, 18–19, 21, 35, 71, 92–96, 98, 138, 154
crisis, ix, 1, 31

D

Dayton, Donald W., 60, 141
democracy, 20, 31, 82
denominations, 2, 9, 11–12, 15, 20, 22, 32, 37–38, 43, 47, 50–52, 55–59, 67, 96, 133
dispensation, age, 40–41, 45, 87, 94, 105, 113–16, 126, 130–31
divine healing, 60, 76, 108, 126

Index

E

education, 19–20, 22, 24–26, 30–32, 64, 67, 72–75, 80–81, 83–86, 98, 123, 136, 138–40, 142, 148–49
emotions, 20, 25, 32, 36, 57, 123, 135
entire sanctification, 43–52, 54–55, 57–58, 60, 72–74, 77, 79–81, 95–98, 105, 107–13, 125–28, 130–31, 133–37, 145–46, 157–59
eschatology, 94, 98, 108
Europe, 15, 38, 48, 53
evangelicalism, Evangelical, 15, 51, 55, 141, 146
evangelism, 10–12, 30, 40, 46, 53–54, 56–57, 77
experience, 32–33, 41, 44–45, 47–49, 62, 72–81, 98, 101, 103, 105, 110–11, 120–23, 130–32, 134–38, 157–59

F

faith, 23, 28, 48, 50–52, 57–58, 68, 74, 77, 89, 93, 143, 146–47, 149, 152–55, 158
Finney, Charles G., 9, 19, 32, 46–47, 51–54
Fletcher, John, 45, 49, 72, 104–5, 114–15, 131–32, 137
fundamentalism, 13, 40–41, 57, 66, 135, 140–44, 149

G

Genesis, 5, 38, 79, 100, 110, 117–18
Germany, 34, 38, 56
God, immanence of, 13, 62, 75, 100–101, 103, 131
grace, 43–44, 48–49, 56, 65, 77, 95, 112–13, 115, 151
Great Britain, 17, 43, 48, 53–54, 56

H

heart, ix–x, 34, 36, 38, 64–65, 69, 75–77, 79–80, 89, 93, 103, 106, 108–9, 112–13, 158
heresy, 38–39, 95, 152–53

holiness churches, denominations, 13, 50, 52, 57, 59, 137, 142–43
holiness message, ix, 45, 47–52, 54–55, 57–60, 97–98, 108–11, 113–14, 116–17, 121–23, 128–29, 131–32, 136–39, 145–46, 157
Holiness movement, ix–xi, 8–11, 13, 52–64, 66–75, 78–83, 86–88, 90–93, 100–101, 103–5, 107–8, 113–17, 122–23, 133–49, 154–55
  leaders, 3, 8, 10–12, 53, 56, 58, 60, 97–98, 107, 123
  restorationism, 92–93
  source of Pentecostalism, 60, 138
  theology, 51, 58, 62, 64, 72, 91, 93, 97, 104–5, 107–8, 111, 113, 122
  view of education, 24, 64, 67, 72–75, 80–81, 83–86, 90, 98, 102, 123, 136, 138–42, 148–49
Holy Spirit, 40–41, 43–45, 63–66, 84–86, 88–94, 96–101, 103–7, 113–18, 120–21, 125–26, 131, 135–38, 143, 155–56, 158–59
  age of, 104, 114–16, 126
  baptism of, x, 41, 45, 60, 73, 79, 93, 110–11, 113, 130, 138
  guide to interpretation, 155–56, 158
  inspiration of, 32–33, 63–66, 68, 86, 88–90, 94, 96–99, 103–4, 106, 117–18, 120–21, 137–38, 143, 155–56, 158–59
  sanctifier, 49–50, 53, 64, 73, 91, 93, 101, 104–5, 107, 109, 113, 120, 126, 131, 137
  witness of, 27, 55, 93, 106, 121, 136
  work of, 17, 26, 40, 43, 45, 85, 126, 131, 136, 156
humility, pride, 18, 128, 132, 135, 152, 156–57
Hynson, Leon, 107, 137

I

individualism, 4, 32, 35–36, 70, 97
intellect, 38–39, 65, 67–70, 74, 89–90, 157

177

Index

interpreters, 16, 18, 33, 65, 96, 106–7, 111, 123, 128, 135, 138, 143–44, 148–49, 154, 157–58
Ireland, ix, 53
Irenaeus, 16, 153
Isaiah, 109–10, 113
Israel, ix, 79, 100, 127
itinerancy, 19, 23–24, 30, 32, 40, 56, 58

J

Jacob, 79, 110, 126
Jesus, 16, 18, 60, 89, 91, 93, 95, 102, 104, 108, 110, 114, 121–22, 126, 128
Jews, Jewish, Judaism, 38, 92–93, 109, 115–16
Judas Iscariot, 78, 89
justification, 16, 28, 136

K

Keswick movement, 56, 123
kingdom, 77, 93, 105, 108, 114–15, 146, 156
Knapp, Martin Wells, 11, 64, 71, 74–75, 77–78, 80, 83, 85–87, 94, 103, 110, 127

L

Lazarus, 108, 126
leadership, 11, 23–24, 26, 31–32, 41, 47, 50, 53, 55, 67, 92, 95–97, 103, 131
Lubac, Henri de, 119–20, 122, 155
Luther, Martin, 16–17, 71

M

Methodism, x–xi, 9–12, 22–25, 32–34, 37, 39, 43, 45–48, 50–55, 57–60, 71–73, 82, 96, 106–7, 135–37
ministry, 2, 6, 10–12, 19, 24, 26, 32, 43, 50, 53–54, 63, 83–87, 130, 133–34, 137
Moody, Dwight L., 3, 19, 40
Moses, 88, 114, 121–22, 125, 129

N

National Camp Meeting Association, 12, 47, 50, 54–56, 58–59, 133
Nazarene, Church of the, 11, 41, 57
New England, 12, 24, 26, 29, 46, 52
New York, 1, 10, 47, 52–54

O

Oberlin, 6, 47, 49
objectivity, 123, 144–45, 149
opposition, 5, 19, 27, 39, 50, 52, 71, 81, 92, 94
ordination, 20, 59, 87, 142
Outler, Albert, 72, 81

P

Palmer, Phoebe, 47–50, 52–55, 105
pastors, 10, 12, 57, 77, 84, 98, 142
Paul, 16, 53, 63, 65, 78, 91, 116
perfect love, 43–44, 51–52, 75, 87, 142, 145, 155
philosophy, 32, 34, 39, 67, 74, 89–90, 158
Pietism, ix, 17, 33–34, 44, 47, 51, 121, 132
piety, ix, 52, 72, 81, 136, 149
Pilgrim Holiness Church, 11, 57
prayer, 51–52, 78, 83, 92, 108
prophesy, 40, 53, 55, 64, 75, 87, 105, 114, 121, 135, 143, 146, 153
Protestantism, x, 3, 8–9, 17–18, 20–22, 26, 31, 35–36, 38, 53, 121, 133
Puritanism, 17, 27–30, 49, 83, 156

R

reason, 12, 32, 35–36, 44, 48, 61–62, 65, 68–70, 73, 81, 123, 135–36, 151
religion, x, 2, 4–7, 15, 18–19, 22, 31–32, 34, 38, 51, 54, 68, 101, 105
revelation, 16, 27–28, 35, 63–66, 76, 88, 102, 117, 128–29, 132, 156
Revelation, Book of, 78–79, 110, 117, 124
revivalism, x, 3, 19–20, 30, 32, 45, 48, 51, 54, 77, 123
Revolutionary War, 8, 18, 22, 26

Index

Robinson, Reuben, 11, 61, 67, 83, 85, 88–89, 91, 108, 116–17, 121–22, 129
Roman Catholicism, 19–20, 27, 71, 93–96
Romanticism, 30, 32, 36, 51

S

sacrificial system, 78, 107, 125
salvation, 18, 22, 40, 46, 60, 63, 77, 79, 91, 93, 98, 112, 126–27, 130, 145–46
Salvation Army, 3, 11, 56–57
sanctification, 44, 46, 58, 136
schism, 43, 55, 58, 93, 96
science, x, 4–6, 34, 39, 67, 69, 73, 101, 142
Scofield Reference Bible, 40–41, 115
sects, sectarianism, 14, 21, 37, 71, 95
secularization, 5, 101, 131
seminaries, graduate education, 19, 84, 123, 141–42
sin, 5, 24, 44, 46, 48, 64, 68, 73, 93, 96, 105–6, 108, 111–12, 117, 126–27
skepticism, 34, 40, 69, 101
slavery, abolition, 2, 10, 37, 51–52, 56, 73, 156
Smith, Joseph H., 12, 61, 67, 76, 84, 94, 124
society, 1–2, 4–5, 13–14, 23, 26, 28, 37–38, 51, 56, 80, 83, 122, 131, 133–35, 140
Sola Scriptura, 16–17, 35, 149
Solomon, Song of, 108, 124–26
Steele, Daniel, 10, 61, 63–70, 73–74, 88, 90, 93, 103, 105–7, 116–17, 128–29, 131, 139–40, 155, 157–59
Stuart, Moses, 35, 38
subjectivity, 25, 29, 33, 35–36, 83, 123, 135–37

T

Terry, Milton, 39–40
testimonies, 47–49, 73, 85, 98, 106, 108–9
theology, 10, 12, 19, 21–22, 31, 36, 44, 50, 53, 58–59, 62, 68–69, 133, 138–41, 144–45
Thorsen, Donald J., 70, 72
tradition, ix–xi, 5, 8–9, 12, 16, 19, 32–33, 44, 48, 62, 70–73, 81, 135–36, 148–49, 151
truth, 20–21, 26–27, 31–32, 34–36, 40, 63–66, 68–70, 74–75, 88–89, 93–97, 106–8, 117–18, 121–23, 127–29, 153

V

Vanhoozer, Kevin J., 144, 148, 151, 156–57
visions, 20, 75–76, 82–83, 96, 110, 135

W

Watson, George D., 11–12, 65, 67, 69, 75, 77–79, 88–89, 92–94, 101–3, 108–10, 112–13, 115–19, 124–27, 129–30, 139–40
Wesley, John, 9–10, 12, 32–33, 43–52, 62–68, 70–73, 80–81, 100–101, 103–4, 106–7, 131, 135–36, 143, 145, 155
Wesleyan, 10, 43, 81, 135, 142–43
Wesleyan Methodist Church, 11–12, 52
women, ix, 4, 19, 26–27, 32, 47, 49–50, 52–54, 56–57, 86–87, 108, 110, 131
worship, 57, 59, 79, 108

www.ingramcontent.com/pod-product-compliance
Lightning Source LLC
Chambersburg PA
CBHW051743230426
43670CB00012B/2143